From the beginnings of the East India Company in the seventeenth century down to 28 February 1948, when the 1st Battalion, the Somerset Light Infantry became the last British soldiers to leave Indian soil, Geoffrey Moorhouse charts the course of British rule in India. He does so with enthusiasm and even-handedness: the result is a highly individual and vivid portrayal of Britain's greatest imperial possession.

'This is the book on British India we have been waiting for – waiting without knowing it . . . Geoffrey Moorhouse has produced a triumph, the definitive and yet splendidly readable account of a time for which he feels – despite his very considerable dislike of the Imperial ideal – affection, some admiration and a great deal of sympathy . . . to anyone wanting either to learn of this extraordinary period of our two countries' past, or to remember the glory and grief of it all, then *India Britannica* is the best possible account to read'
Simon Winchester *Books and Bookmen*

'Daringly ambitious . . . diligence, research, compassion, criticism and – what is very rare in a serious work about India – wit'
James Cameron *The Spectator*

'A disturbing and totally enthralling story, expertly told'
Margaret Lane *Daily Telegraph*

'The romance of the British entanglement with India . . . a pageant of meanness and nobility, of humour and of tragedy, of the exotic and the eccentric'
Woodrow Wyatt *Sunday Times*

GEOFFREY MOORHOUSE

India Britannica

PALADIN
GRAFTON BOOKS
A Division of the Collins Publishing Group

LONDON GLASGOW
TORONTO SYDNEY AUCKLAND

Paladin
Grafton Books
A Division of the Collins Publishing Group
8 Grafton Street, London W1X 3LA

Published in Paladin Books 1984
Reprinted 1984, 1986

First published in Great Britain by
Harvill Press 1983

ISBN 0-586-08480-0

Reproduced, printed and bound in Great Britain by
Hazell Watson & Viney Limited,
Member of the BPCC Group,
Aylesbury, Bucks

Set in Baskerville

To Brigie

Rennell's Map 1784

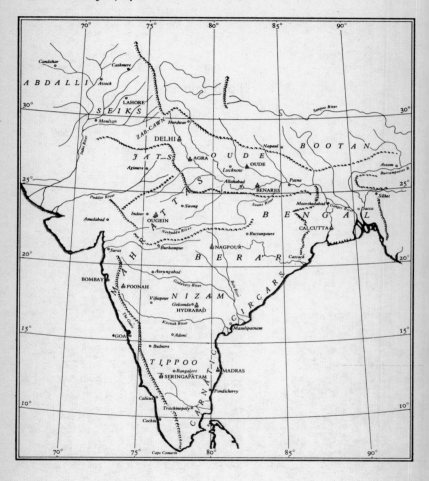

Indian Empire 1947

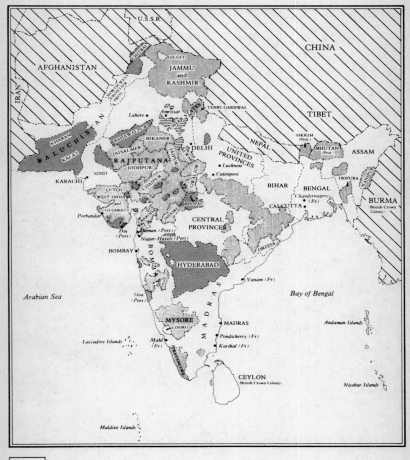

Contents

'As long as we rule India we are the greatest power in the world. If we lose it we shall drop straight away to a third-rate power.'

Lord Curzon, 1901

'The English are a sensitive people, and yet when they go to foreign countries there is a strange lack of awareness about them.'

Jawaharlal Nehru, 1946

PROLOGUE

AS THE SUN
BEGAN TO SET

When I was a small boy and Europe stood on the threshold of the
Second World War, references to the British Empire were almost
commonplace. I can dimly remember radio broadcasts made by
politicians and commentators mustered by the BBC, in which the
phrase was used so easily that the British Empire seemed practically
interchangeable with the British Isles. There was a comfortable
assumption behind those speeches and talks that if hostilities did
begin, then our side would not be confined to those of us who lived
between the Atlantic Ocean and the North Sea: whatever alliances
were formed by the foreigners – the French, the Dutch, the Czechs
and so on – our side would automatically include our cousins and our
Dominions beyond the seas. No elaboration of this tonic concept
was needed to fortify my juvenile patriotism, because maps and
geography had been one of my first interests and I was well aware of
the British Empire's extent, and therefore implicitly its power, even
if I was less than clear about its precise nature and origin. John
Bartholomew & Co's atlas had long been a great standby on rainy
days and its most striking feature was the vast amount of the earth's
surface which was coloured in pillar-box red, making the yellow
allotted to the Soviet Union and the green awarded to the United
States look paltry by comparison. I was as familiar with the ruddy
shapes where our cousins dwelt – Australia, Canada, New Zealand
and South Africa – as I was with the shadows on my bedroom wall,
and I could even name many of the less substantial red marks on
the pages of the atlas which constituted, I wrongly supposed, our
Dominions. These lesser marks ranged through several shades of
possessiveness, though I never did work out whether a Crown colony
took precedence over a territory, a dependency over a protectorate,
or where in the sequence a mandate should be inserted. By far the
most intriguing of them was the pendant mass of India, both because
the outline was distinctive and because it was so much bigger – about

the size of Europe – than any other country in that segment of Empire whose inhabitants were crucially referred to not as cousins but as natives. I suspect it also attracted me because a certain mystique of that remote land had already seized my imagination. I used to pore over the map of the sub-continent, reciting the place names in my head, trying to fit them into the flickering pattern of what little I knew. No-one had yet told me that its full style and title was the British Indian Empire, which was just as well, for it would have greatly confused my essentially unsubtle young mind.

At this distance I cannot begin to guess what first drew my attention to the idea rather than the bare geographical fact of India. Conceivably it was some domestic remark about Mr Gandhi, who had come to England in the year of my birth and, after discussing the possibility of India's freedom with the Government in London, had headed north to see what life was like in the Lancashire cotton towns, whose inhabitants had been for a hundred years arch economic rivals of his own people. I don't think any member of my family had personally witnessed what must have been a quaint progress round our part of the world, but they had all followed it closely in the local press and in the columns of George Lansbury's *Daily Herald*. It seemed to me, whenever the event was mentioned later, that they not only sympathized with the Indian leader but actually identified with his cause. If this was so, their response would have been muddled with several other reactions that Mr Gandhi would not have found in the least congenial. For while my family was irrevocably working class, convinced that there should be drastic alteration of a social and economic pattern which regularly produced high unemployment in our neighbourhood, they never for one moment questioned the existence, much less the basis of the British Empire. They fiercely condemned the exploitation of some British by other British, and their humanity would not deny a parallel between their own predicament and that of Mr Gandhi's people. But if anyone in 1939 had suggested that the Empire was about to decline rather abruptly and cease to exist before another generation had passed, I imagine it would have shaken them as desperately as an assurance that we might well lose the war. Indeed, they wouldn't have thought the one catastrophe possible except as a consequence of the other. Like many people who have been born and bred on the superior side of imperialism, whoever practises it, their fundamental decency was greatly outweighed by their ignorance and even more by a primitive need not to have the foundations of their world disturbed. My grandfather had been a young volunteer soldier in the Boer War and he still spoke of his time at Ladysmith and on Spion Kop with excitement and pride. He would have been shocked if someone had told him that he had been an imperialist aggressor, engaged in a morally indefensible act: to him it had been something between a duty to Queen and Country and a chance for adventure far from the dismal back streets of his home mill town.

The military side of British imperialism, seen in just those terms, most certainly coloured my second-hand impressions of India more vividly than anything else. Among my earliest reading was a comic which ran weekly episodes of a rollicking yarn set on the North West Frontier. Its hero was an Englishman whose status I have forgotten, and what captivated me most of all was the relationship he had with an Indian who was inseparable from all his daring deeds. A drawing accompanied each episode and in this the Indian was depicted as a stocky fellow who wore nothing but a pair of ragged breeches and carried, wherever he went, what might have been mistaken for a club but was, in fact, a very battered old cricket bat. The author of the serial caused him to call this object Clicky Ba, which gave me to understand that Indians didn't quite speak English as we did at home, but otherwise this native was admirable. He did use that beaten-up chunk of willow as a club, whenever he and the British hero of the piece got into a tight corner, which was at least once a week. His greatest pleasure, it was established, was to crack skulls with Clicky Ba, which he did when coming to the rescue of the hero or when fighting back to back with him against a mob of hostile tribesmen. This was the especial excellence of the Indian in the yarn; in spite of his curious pronunciation and the oddity of his looks, he was a man you'd be glad to have guarding your back. No doubt at all, even in my young mind, that the relationship between those two characters was master and servant ennobled into perfect comradeship, with each ready to die for the other – or for the Cause, whatever that might have been.

That serial influenced me in a peculiar way. I presumably read it when I was just beginning to attend elementary school, because I hadn't been there more than a week or two before my class was instructed to write a composition on any subject we chose, provided we worked in the sentence 'Then I saw the most beautiful thing I had ever seen'. We were supposed to submit our efforts after an hour or so's scribbling, but by then I was barely into my stride and obtained permission from a surprised teacher to finish the thing at home. Her surprise grew day by day for a week or more, but she was an astute and patient lady whose tolerance was eventually rewarded (though I don't suppose that's the word she would have used) when I presented a composition that occupied the best part of two exercise books. I had, of course, written an adventure story set on the North West Frontier and I believe the most beautiful thing I had ever seen was some exotic view in the Himalaya, casually thrown in to meet Miss Berry's requirements, but having nothing whatsoever to do with the epic I was burning to tell. This was about fighting for the British cause all right, but the narrator was called Akbar Khan and I was a sturdy Sikh in the service of the Raj (I didn't then appreciate the vital point that no Sikh would be a Khan, which is a Muslim name). I cannot for the life of me remember the ins and outs of my loyalty to the alien white man and I can only speculate upon the strange reasons which had me imitating an Indian rather than one of my own kind. And though I was obviously under the influence of what I'd read in the comic, I'm sure that what I offered would not have been described as a straight crib. There were, by then, a number of other sources that my imagination could draw upon.

I was exposed to one of these several times a week, at three choir practices and two Sunday services in our parish church. The building was pickled in its associations with my grandfather's old regiment, the Lancashire Fusiliers, who turned up *en masse* once a year to celebrate and lament the anniversary of their landing at Gallipoli in 1915. But every time you entered the church you were immediately confronted with memorials of regimental history, stirring and poignant reminders of the part the Fusiliers had played in the creation and defence of the British Empire. A choirboy couldn't look up from his chant book without noticing the flags that drooped in long rows from the clerestory down both sides of the nave. Some of them were so ancient that they had become transparently threadbare, hanging over the pews like huge and dusty cobwebs. But the majority still bore the detectable names of battle honours upon the faded buff or the red, white and blue of their cloth. And so, while most of my attention was dutifully fixed on Orlando Gibbons or Stanford in C, part of it would wander round that litany of outlandish words; Minden, Corunna, Sevastopol, Khartoum and the rest. As I could see, among those heavily embroidered honours there was also Lucknow, where the Fusiliers had fought to make and keep British India many generations before; which gave me another place to look up in my atlas.

At about the same time, we who collected cigarette cards began to accumulate a new set that John Player & Sons had just started to distribute. It came under the title of 'Military Uniforms of the British Empire Overseas' and included a palpitating variety of soldiers in ceremonial and working dress, which opened with the Cape Town Highlanders and ended with the Singapore Volunteer Corps. There were 50 cards in the set and the most numerous (29) as well as the most attractive were those representing forces in India and Burma. I spent hours looking at those pictures, which were masterpieces of the cartophilist's art, meticulously drawn and delicately tinted, with some of the Indian ceremonial uniforms quite dazzling in their use of deep scarlets and golds and blues. As a background to these figures, standing proud in their shiny long boots, plumed or turbaned, sashed or frogged, the artist had sketched something of the locality from which each regiment came or where it had seen action on the sub-continent. A dapper little Gurkha strode across a mountainside, a risaldar of The Poona Horse stood with gloved hand on sword in front of Fort Jamrud on the Frontier, a major of the Maharaja Holkar's Infantry posed before the palace at Indore. It was a small education for an English child to scrutinize those illustrations and to absorb the information printed on their backs, which told me, among other things, that Hyderabad was the chief Indian Princely state, that Jodhpur possessed an up-to-date aerodrome, that Tehri-Garhwal was a Hindu state of 350,000 inhabitants in the Himalayan foothills, that the ruler of Nawanagar was a nephew of his predecessor 'who was better known in this country as the great cricketer Ranji'. I could have composed my adventure story after fantasizing over my tab cards and nothing else.

But my subconscious had also been electrified by Gunga Din. I hadn't come across the poem so far as I know, though I was certainly reading Kipling's prose when I was ten (and a judgement I instantly formed, which I haven't needed to revise, is that *Kim* is one of the most marvellous books I ever opened). Gunga Din, however, entered my life across the cinema screen a couple of years before I tackled anything of Kipling in print, and whoever wrote the script enlarged very considerably on the five verses of the inspiration. I still get the sweats when I recall how the Thugs held Victor McLaglen over the snake pit in an effort to make him say which way over the mountains the Highlanders would be coming to attack their stronghold. I was amused by Cary Grant's knockabout version of another British sergeant, and the third member of this leading trio, Douglas Fairbanks Jr, had an enviably dashing quality that I hadn't much noticed among the NCOs who thronged our church every Gallipoli Sunday. But it was dear old Sam Jaffe who stole the picture, trudging along in the dust with his waterskin behind the marching columns, getting the battalion bandboy to let him practise on the bugle and finally, with blood spurting from his knife wounds and bagpipes skirling distantly in the soundtrack, clambering inch by inch to the topmost pinnacle of the temple, to sway there heroically while he blew the Retreat and warned the troops to take cover. I wept buckets during the last few moments of that film, when the regiment stood around Din's grave and the Colonel recited Kipling's final lines. Yet if a great part of it was a caricature of what actually happened during the previous century in India, the screen version of Gunga Din at least gave me a new and intense feeling for the place, with its spectacular scenery and the throbbing menace of heat over lonely telegraph wires strung out across an empty plain. Even if – as it may well have been – the film had been shot in some blistering part of the American West, the director had managed to convey some truth about the India I was to discover for myself much later on.

One way and another, by the time I reached my Pennine grammar school, with ourselves and our cousins and our Dominions beyond the seas fighting the war side by side and back to back, I must have known quite a bit about India for a boy of my age whose family had never been connected with it. Almost every particle of that knowledge would have been strictly limited to a British version of India and especially to the campaigns of her soldiers there. What's more, as my education in this arcane topic continued during my schooldays, the teaching of it moved upon lines I was already familiar with. I don't recall any formal history lesson dealing with the sub-continent, or even Asia as a whole, our obsessions being ancient Greek-cum-Roman and modern European, with a token of North American in the Upper Fifth. India cropped up only in asides. As when the classics master introduced the Latin perfect tense and, forever on the lookout for some anecdote that might redeem the arid pages of Kennedy's primer, mentioned Sir Charles Napier's famous one-word signal to the Government after he had conquered the Sind territory in 1843: '*Peccavi.*' – 'I have sinned' (a myth without substance, for the pun was composed three years after Napier's conquest by some anonymous contributor to *Punch* and erroneously attributed by his readers to the general).

Apart from the family recollections of Mr Gandhi there was nothing at all to balance these legends of imperial possessiveness. There may have been books which would have told me more useful things than I was learning about India, but I can't think the local public library would have stocked them even if my elders had suggested them to me, which they didn't. There was no television and even if the wireless did broadcast the equivalent of today's informative documentaries, they never came within my hearing. There were newsreels at the cinema which one watched fascinated as the war drew on and which, from time to time, offered glimpses of Indian soldiers fighting with us for the Cause. One year they were hauling field guns with the aid of mules up the mountainous spine of Italy, some time later they were doing the same thing over muddy jungle ridges in Burma. Never was there a hint of Subhas Chandra Bose and the defected troops of his Indian National Army who were fighting alongside the Japanese, hoping that if the war went the right way for them they would recover their country from the British by force of arms instead of continuing to wait for the imperialists to leave gracefully. So I was always left where I came in, with the feeling that these magnificent fellows were without exception our loyal henchmen from our devoted Dominion beyond the seas; and this was, indeed, a great comfort between 1939 and 1945.

Nor was there, in those days, any Indian I could inspect in the flesh and speak to even if I'd had the necessary courage. I daren't say that Indian restaurants or shops were unknown to the British Isles outside London forty years ago, but they had not yet been heard of in our vicinity, though there may have been something of the kind in Liverpool, where a colony of P & O lascars was reputed to live. I didn't clap eyes on anyone from the brightest jewel in the imperial crown until the war was over and the peaceful euphoria of 1946 included a tour by the Indian cricket team. I watched Vijay Merchant begin a big innings in the county game at Old Trafford and borrowed somebody's binoculars so that I could observe more closely every mannerism of Merchant's captain, who was nothing less than the Nawab of Pataudi – which was romantic history come to life if ever there was such a thing. I went to the match, mind, not because

I was preoccupied with India but because I was mad about cricket. That team, after all, was not only the first official touring side to appear from anywhere for seven seasons; it was also a rather good one whose Sarwate, of Holkar, and Bannerjee, of Bengal, had between them hit an astonishing 249 for the last wicket against Surrey a few weeks earlier, which remains to this day a record for first-class cricket in England. I don't doubt that some of the hoarier county members in pavilions up and down the country wondered why these chaps wanted Independence when they could play so splendidly with things as they were. As for me, had I still been tempted to think conventionally of Indians as natives, that touring side would have taxed my credulity. A native, clearly, was a brown or black man reduced at least to a pair of ragged breeches (soldiers in ceremonial smartness were part of India's mystery and a separate case) but those cricketers were if anything even more impeccably dressed than our own players, blazers edged with piping and spotless white flannels creased so sharply that you could have cut your finger on them. That I was no longer thinking in the clichés of race may have had something to do with a wartime admiration for what were then termed our gallant Soviet allies, which induced me to study some persuasive literature about the wider world we lived in, disseminated by the Anglo-Soviet Friendship Society. Besides, cricket itself did not allow that particular simplicity to enter its calculations. Although it could be snobbish in the extreme, it had already taught me that the game in England – as in almost every other part of the Empire – was blessedly colour-blind.

I was not at any stage of my boyhood studying India in any formal sense. What trifles I knew about the country, its people and its rulers were no more than the magpie acquisitions of a lad who mentally pocketed anything that hove into view. In this process, however, I was collecting impressions which marked me as a child of my own peculiar and transforming historical age. Though it didn't dawn on me at once, I was among the last of those who knew themselves to be the ruling elite of the British Empire; a notion, I may say, that would have produced much cynical mirth if it had been uttered among our neighbours, most of whom had been out of work at one time or another since the day I was born until the war rescued everyone from the dole queues. Nevertheless, even among the unemployed of the industrial north, there was conscious acknowledgement and gratification that we were a superior nation whose power extended over His

Majesty's other subjects spread across the globe. It was solace for the chronic casualties of our society to know that they were not quite at the bottom of the heap, as the evidence around them too often suggested. Somewhere out there was an even lowlier underdog in the form of the native, obliged by divine authority and His chosen British instrument to know his inferior place and keep it, just like a millworker in South Lancashire.

In the time that passed between my rudimentary awareness of India and my first chance to go there and see it for myself, the world was politically turned upside down. The British Empire's dissolution had almost been completed, and we old imperialists were briefly enjoying a new role as a second-class power without responsibility, London being widely regarded as one of the swinging cities of the world with a lot of splendid history going for it, too. India had for twenty years been independent by the time I got there, as had its twin Pakistan, and the only political ties attaching either nation to the British were the nebulous, scarcely more than nominal ones of the Commonwealth. I was still offspring of the age I lived in, which meant that my attitude to British imperialism had evolved from juvenile acquiescence, through adolescent hostility, into a detached curiosity. I was also somewhat better informed about India than I had been when my sources were restricted to Rudyard Kipling, Player's cigarette cards, comic serials, school-room asides and family folklore. This did not mean that I could consign the lot of them to the rubbish bin, merely that I could appreciate them more thoughtfully in the perspectives of wider knowledge. In some ways they had served me well, far better than might have been supposed by a lofty critic of such juvenilia. I had discovered, for example, that the writer who invented Clicky Ba and all those lurid doings on the North West Frontier, had probably been more faithful to the mood of his chosen period than some shuddering academic would have wanted to allow; that some of the British who fought and ruled in India in the nineteenth century had themselves written of their experiences in an exuberant prose scarcely distinguishable from that of my first comic. Such a man was Herbert Edwardes, whose exploits were conducted up in the hills where the lands of the Sikhs bordered those of the Afghans. Many years later, when he had been knighted for his services to the Raj, Edwardes had this to say about the period when he was making his reputation as a 30-year-old lieutenant. 'What days those were! How Henry Lawrence would send us off great distances:

Edwardes to Bunnoo, Nicholson to Peshawar, Abbott to Hazara, Lumsden to somewhere else etc, giving us no more helpful directions than these, "Settle the country; make the people happy; and take care there are no rows!"' Had I known that such boyish originals existed when I was a child, I might never have touched a comic.

When I reached India at last I was, like everyone else going there for the first time, intoxicated by the strangeness of this new experience and staggered by the scale of everything happening there. The inklings I had of what to expect had not nearly prepared me for the powerful flavours of the country itself. The contrasts were tremendous, between poverty and wealth, between gentleness and violence, between beauty and ugliness, between the entrancing and the shocking. There were moments when one wished to linger there for the rest of one's days, and others when one wanted to fly home without delay. India, I found, was erotic carvings on the lonely temples at Khajuraho, centuries old but cut in stone so untouched by time that they might have been sculpted the year before: it was the bustees of Calcutta where multitudes dwelt without drainage, without sewerage, without running water, without light, in conditions that animals would have been spared in Europe. India was exhausted men straining like galley slaves to pull rickshaws, and it was languid men dressed like the more dandified officers on my cigarette cards and surrounded by retainers not much less splendidly clothed. It was the bewitching peace of the Garhwal hills above Tehri, where the only sound was the pattering feet of Bhotia women bearing brass vessels full of water from the infant Ganges, and it was the aching din of Chandni Chowk in Old Delhi, a medley of honks and clangs and clatters and rumbles and shouts, with transistored *obbligatos* on the sitar. It was working elephants gaudily decorated with crayon as though for some carnival; it was a bear being led on its hind legs by a busker not a mile from Palam International Airport; and it was a train of camels loaded with Mirzapur carpets as they plodded along the Grand Trunk Road to the bazaar at Benares. The only thing India was not, was bland. It was the only country I had known where superlatives were as much in order as adjectives anywhere else.

It had proudly become the biggest democracy in the world and it was tacitly leader of what the jargon identified as the underdeveloped nations. But it was an industrial country as well as a peasant one, which was organizing its own atomic power within a generation of imperial rule. At the same time, India remained what it had been for at least five centuries, a hybrid land spanning the cultures of the Middle East and those of Asia, while being supremely and inimitably itself. And yet, in the midst of its strangeness and its towering scale of people and events, there was a haunting familiarity awaiting an Englishman there. Part of this was the essence of India itself which he had sniffed in tantalizing samples from infancy, half the time without having been conscious of doing so, and another part consisted of elements from his own native root which had been transplanted and could sometimes seem comically out of place. My people had marked India to a degree that startled me, and India had marked us. Some of the things my predecessors had done there, as I knew by then, were rotten and others were noble. Mostly they were a mixture of the well-meaning and the selfish. Every visit I subsequently made to India was to confirm what I had only conjectured before I first went there; that the history of the British in India is something more than an account of conquest and submission, of rebellion and imperial retreat. It is also the story of a complicated love-hate relationship that no other two peoples, so vastly different in origins and cultures, have ever known. Indians must speak for themselves about the relationship today. But they should know that their country haunts the British still, as nowhere else ever did, as no other place in the future possibly can.

ONE

A QUIET TRADE –
AND A PROFITABLE ONE

India was an imperial possession long before the British made it theirs, with the notable difference that it had not become a component in an international mechanism, the rulers having simply moved in from their native soil and put down their roots afresh. The ancient conglomeration of Hindu states under their rajas had first known alien occupation at the end of the twelfth century, when Turkish-speaking Muslims invaded the sub-continent from the north and settled around the thriving city of Delhi. More warriors, coming from the same direction and of approximately the same origin, descended at intervals over the next three hundred years, until a lasting dynasty was established with the arrival of the adventurer Babur, who was proclaimed Emperor after winning the battle of Panipat in 1526. He was the first of the Mughals, a people whose blood was a mixture of Turkish, Mongolian and other strains which had fused in the haphazard breeding that accompanied the perpetual warfare of medieval Asia. Babur himself claimed the Turk Tamerlaine the Great as a direct ancestor on his father's side, and the Mongol Genghiz Khan on his mother's. He recognized Samarkand as his family home, but had made his own base in the area between Kabul and Kandahar before venturing with his soldiers over the mountain passes of the Hindu Kush into northern India. This first Mughal took his new domain by the sword (from occupying Afghans) and held it by military might (against resistant Indian Rajputs); but he swiftly demonstrated a number of gifts not normally associated with the swashbuckling leaders of his day, who were forever on the move, restlessly pitching their tents anew as they rode from one conquest to another. His first act on reaching Agra was to create a formal garden in the Persian style which meant, in effect, imitating as best he could something that figures in every Muslim's image of paradise. He was also a considerable poet and diarist, whose autobiography is one of the great classics of Oriental literature.

The Mughal Emperors who followed Babur extended their dominion in every direction from his first settlement in the north-west. The imposition of their rule and the savagery of its punishments were tempered by achievements in the arts and crafts that we still admire as magnificent today. Among other things, they introduced much that was culturally derived from Persia, including its language, which in time became the speech of courtiers and other well-to-do, just as Norman French at one period held a distinction over Anglo-Saxon. The brutal aesthete became something of a stock character among these potentates. Babur's son, Humayan, revenged himself upon a treacherous brother by blinding him, but spent most of his time collecting illuminated manuscripts and came to his death aptly enough by falling down the steps of his library. A frequently drunken Emperor, Jahangir, increased the empire with much cruelty and boasted that his addiction to hunting had cost the lives of 17,000 animals and nearly 14,000 birds, but at the same time he was a generous patron of painters whose miniatures in gouache, illustrating court life, love life and natural history are among the most refined bequests to civilization from the East or anywhere else. A very ruthless Emperor was Shah Jehan, who executed all possible rivals the moment he reached the throne but is now recalled only for the tranquil perfection of his Taj Mahal, the shrine he built to his beloved wife Mumtaz. The mightiest Emperor, Akbar, established an efficient bureaucracy in the wake of conquests which put the frontier of the empire three-quarters of the way down the sub-continent; but he also fostered the arts on a grand scale and left us Fatehpur Sikri, his capital for a few years until the water supply dried up, to dream over, the most enduring, elegant and perfectly preserved ghost town that man ever abandoned.

The native Hindu Indians in time accommodated themselves to the rule of the Mughals, and this was largely due to Akbar's remarkable talents. He was a brilliant general and an outstanding administrator, but his greatness depended on a form of benevolence and sharp common sense. Almost uniquely in the annals of Islam, he did not forcibly convert his new subjects to his own faith, nor did he vandalize the extensive cultural monuments of the Hindus. Instead he abolished the pilgrim tax on their ancient holy city of Mathura and, by marrying a Rajput princess from Jaipur, offered an alliance which made it easier for the native population to accept his rule. Loyalty was rewarded with positions of responsibility, sometimes of great influence, in Akbar's administration, and by the time he died in 1605 the Mughal empire in India was both powerful and thoroughly incorporated into the life of most people. The writ of the Muslim overlords never ran right down to the southern shores, so that an uneasy peace was maintained along a frontier line. There were other deposits of Hindu independence where local rajas were prepared to pay tribute in exchange for virtual autonomy, which enabled them to rule their own subjects on long-established feudal principles. Generally, the mass of the people everywhere lived as they always had done. They cultivated their small parcels of ground and hoped that neither scorching heat nor raging flood would at the very least ruin them, or, in a bad year, cause them to starve to death. They wove textiles, they fashioned implements and ornaments from metal, they lent and borrowed money at crippling interest rates, they traded in merchandise, they paid their exactions to whomsoever the gods had placed in authority over them; and at the level of the peasant majority it really didn't make much difference whether that authority answered to the one true god proclaimed by the Prophet, or to the myriad deities their ancestors had always worshipped. Their life was neither more nor less pleasant, fruitful and inspiring than that of people living in Europe at the time; it was simply shaped differently. This was the society which awaited a new invasion from across the seas.

The European vanguard had, in fact, shown its face even before the Mughals arrived and it came in the person of the Portuguese, the greatest and most daring navigators at the end of the fifteenth century.[1] Six years after the hired hand Christopher Columbus had crossed the Atlantic to America on behalf of the Spanish, Portugal's own Vasco da Gama had made landfall in 1498 at Calicut on India's south-western coast, and in both cases the sailing instructions had been the same: to rediscover the fabled Indies of Marco Polo's travels two hundred years earlier, to convert the natives there to Christianity and to bring home spices which had enormous value in the markets of Europe. In those days it was the habit to slaughter cattle every autumn in the northern hemisphere, there being no grass to feed them on in winter and no method yet devised to store fodder that would see them through to the following spring. In England there

[1] We are thinking here in terms of colonizers. The ubiquitous Romans had visited India by sea, and Indian archaeologists today are still liable to find denarii on the sites of their southern trading posts.

would be no solution to this problem until, in 1730, Lord Townshend retired from politics to his Norfolk estate and began to grow turnips, not as a garden vegetable but in huge crops for winter cattle feed. Meanwhile, spices not only disguised the taste of rotting meat; they also acted, with salt, as a preservative. Such was the demand for this asset that when the Dutch sailed East in 1595 and made a beeline for Java and the Moluccas, the first of their boats, returning home laden with cloves and other spices, made a profit on the voyage of 2,500 per cent.

The Portuguese, meanwhile, had entrenched themselves at a number of places around the Indian coast. Their headquarters were at Goa, which they captured in 1510 and which they were to hold without interruption for the next four centuries and more, until some years after the British had returned whence they came. They had secured the spices they sought from South India, the only part of the country where these things grew, and their sailors had preyed profitably upon shipping in the Arabian Sea. But the imperatives of the Catholic Church were what drove the Portuguese most of all. They were also incidentally responsible for the first recorded Englishman setting foot on Indian soil – the Jesuit Thomas Stephens, who sailed from Lisbon in 1579 and laboured for forty years as a missionary in Goa. And it was the proselytizing instinct that rapidly earned the Portuguese a bad name among Hindus and Muslims. The new colonizers not only forbade every faith but their own in the territories they acquired, but imported the Inquisition to help conversions. Worse, they assumed it was unnecessary for a Christian to keep his word with non-believers. As a result they were regarded as people whose cruelty was matched only by their treachery.

It was not to be expected that Elizabethan Englishmen, with well-developed tastes of their own in buccaneering and trade, would sit idly at home as rumours came in of colossal profit in the East, and we may wonder only what kept them so long behind the Portuguese and the Dutch in getting off the mark. This they did in September 1599, when a group of London merchants pledged themselves to raise £30,000 in support of a voyage to the East Indies and sought royal permission for a monopoly of commerce with that part of the world. The charter came to them from the Queen's hand on the last day of 1600, and with it the East India Company was launched; the start of a much larger enterprise than any of its founders anticipated, with a lasting effect on history that not even an ambitious Elizabethan could have imagined. The merchants were intent only on 'a quiet trade' with no trouble for anyone, least of all for themselves, and certainly didn't see their organization as a springboard for military adventures. At the outset they weren't especially interested in India, either, regarding it merely as one of several ports of call they might canvass while pursuing most of what they were after farther East. The news coming out of Amsterdam was what made them lick their lips most greedily in anticipation, and they had determined to make the bulk of their fortunes in the same area the Dutch had been plundering so fantastically. They went forth initially in the naïve assumption that the Dutch would countenance rivals in the East Indies, found themselves fighting more battles than they had ever bargained for around Java and the Moluccas, and, after substantial losses in manpower and property at the Massacre of Amboyna in 1623, beat a retreat to India, where they had known less hostility in their early inspections.

The first English vessel there had anchored at Surat on the north-west coast in 1608, shortly after the Emperor Akbar had been succeeded by Jahangir, and William Hawkins went inland to the imperial court at Agra to obtain trading concessions on the coastline. He was received pleasantly enough but was kept hanging about for a couple of years. He gathered that the Portuguese had at least half an ear with the Emperor and were whispering malicious things about the English into it, and finally left empty-handed. So did Sir Henry Middleton, who turned up some time later in another ship, but his response to imperial indifference was not to cut his losses and go home; he stood his vessels off to sea and held to ransom every Indian trading craft that crossed his bows. A subsequent Company mariner, Thomas Best, improved on this by thrashing four Portuguese men o' war with his two merchantmen, and this cumulative display of English sea power produced the desired result. A document bearing the imperial order, the vital firman, was issued in 1612, allowing the English to set up a trading post at Surat, and the Company factors erected their first factory, which was a series of buildings for administration, for quartering their men, and for the storage of goods.

The rest of the seventeenth century was spent in gradually expanding this foothold into a chain of factories around the sub-continental coast. This was but a local version of what the Company was doing in the same period over a much wider area of the East; its operations stretched as far as China before the eighteenth century arrived. In India the east coast was breached in 1640 with the acquisition of some land at Madras, leased by one of the last Hindu rulers to retain his sovereignty in the face of Mughal advances. English quarrels with the Portuguese having been patched up (to some extent because the Dutch threatened both) and friendship being solemnized in matrimony, the Company's position on the west coast was strengthened in 1665 when it was handed Bombay as an item in Catherine of Braganza's dowry at her wedding with King Charles II. By 1690 the chain was, for the time being, completed when, after years of trying, the Company set up a permanent colony on the Hooghly River in Bengal, near a village which the Hindus knew as Kalikata in deference to their most fearsome deity, but which would soon be Anglicized into Calcutta. The trying had not been without bloodshed; a series of disputes with the regional Muslim officials caused the Englishmen to shunt up and down the river for some time before Admiral Nicholson's ships sailed up and established title to the settlement with superior fire power. This was not the only occasion when Englishmen were involved in hostilities. They successfully defended themselves in their fortified factory at Surat in 1664 when Sivaji, Hindu chief of the warlike Marathas who were to plague both Mughals and Europeans until well into the nineteenth century, attacked the port and sacked most of it. There were other bouts of friction with Mughal rulers at a local level, sometimes started by English arrogance, sometimes not: the new-comers could go out of their way to avoid giving offence, as when they built themselves a chapel at Surat bare of any religious images or paintings, which they knew were anathema to Muslims. As for the Emperors who sat in Delhi or Agra according to whim, they tolerated the English presence for the most part, a quid pro quo for the English undertaking to protect all Mughal shipping from whatever hazards sailed the adjacent seas. Officially each side acknowledged the other's sphere and abided by this tacit agreement, though often enough there were infringements of one sort or another far from the immediate reach of the imperial court. It was a curious and haphazard relationship, but we must not expect the India of that period to supply the tidy arrangements we have come to demand of the twentieth century.

The build-up in trade was steady rather than spectacular in those first few decades of the Company's Indian adventure. Pepper and other spices could be obtained directly from the Malabar coast, or second-hand from Indian traders plying between their own shores and Ceylon or the East Indies. Cotton yarns and cloths came from a number of areas, both east and west, Madras supplied sugar and Gujarat indigo dye, while Bengal specialized in silks and saltpetre. In exchange for this the Indians would accept all manner of metals (tin, lead and quicksilver were in great demand) as well as tapestries and ivories and any kind of mechanical novelty. What their merchants sought most of all, however, was silver bullion, and great quantities of this were shipped from England, whose biggest home product of that age, woollen broad cloth, could not be expected to attract Indians in the sort of weather most of them knew. So much silver was exported from London – more than twice the value of all other commodities combined – that the Company teetered on the brink of financial disaster, and for the first of many times in its history became the target of attacks in Parliament, which took the view that the spending of precious metals abroad was distinctly unpatriotic.[2] It not only survived this drain on its treasury and the accompanying unpopularity, but in the long run benefited from the experience. It had to diversify its operations throughout the East, discover fresh markets and new sources of goods, juggle its trade around half the globe and learn how India could be fitted most profitably into the network without leaning too heavily on silver. We shall shortly see how it successfully adapted itself to current market forces, so that, before long, its employees were indeed acquiring riches beyond the dreams of avarice.

The structure of this enterprise, whose techniques, power and influence were not to be paralleled until the birth of the multi-national corporations in our own times, was also gradually evolving into a hierarchical shape. From the group of original subscribing merchants in London a Court of Directors had emerged, with twenty-four members elected for four years in office, after which each had to stand down for twelve months before putting himself up again. Below them at home came the shareholders, and after that a considerable point of growth in the domestic economy. It was not long before the Company was one of the largest employers of labour around London, with dockyards of its own at Deptford and Blackwall, as well as warehouses, foundries, cordage works, sawmills

---

[2] Oddly enough, the historian Pliny complains that ancient Rome's bullion resources were also drained by her Indian trade.

and even slaughterhouses where cattle were butchered to victual the Company's growing fleet of East Indiamen. All this was supervised from a sequence of headquarters until in 1726 a splendid new building went up in Leadenhall Street, from which the Company functioned for the rest of its days. Its coat of arms over the front door was embellished with the motto 'Auspicio Regis et Senatus Angliae', which had a fine imperial ring.[3]

By the end of the seventeenth century India, for Company purposes, had been divided into three Presidencies; Madras, Bombay and Bengal, each independent of the others and corresponding directly with London on its own behalf. Local control was exercised in each case by a President (alternatively known as Governor) supported by a council of ten senior merchants who had settled in the presidency town. Below these Members in Council came other senior merchants at the top of a carefully regulated ladder of status and promotion. By 1706, this system saw a man acting for three years as junior merchant before becoming a senior, three years as factor before becoming a junior merchant, and five years as a writer before achieving the position of factor. The writer was nothing more than a clerk, whose days were spent wearily on a high wooden stool scratching interminable entries into a ledger with a quill pen, but so numerous were these poor hacks that the Writers Building in Calcutta, where the men of the Bengal Presidency worked, became one of the community's most conspicuous landmarks; as it still is today, when it houses the secretariat of the Indian state government of West Bengal.

Although conquest was still far from the Company's thoughts, there was a conscious attempt to transplant familiar institutions to this developing colony in the East. Law courts and civic Corporations were established in each Presidency, and Madras went so far as to equip itself with a silver-gilt mace to be borne on ceremonial occasions ahead of dignitaries, who were clad in scarlet serge robes and who rode – as nearly as they could – in the same order of precedence as the Lord Mayor and Aldermen of London. Bombay opened its court, where Mr Wilcox would sit as the first Presidency judge, with a procession from the factory, through the bazaar, to the guildhall, which must have impressed onlookers as much as did the Lord Mayor's Show at home. It started with fifty flunkeys in green

[3] The Company had earlier flourished an even more extravagant motto, 'Deus Indicat' – 'God Points the Way!'

livery, marching two by two, as were the twenty Gentlemen, twenty Mooremen and twenty Christians representing 'their several casts or sects' immediately behind. Then came His Honour's horse of state, led by an Englishman, two trumpets and kettle drums on horseback, the English and Portuguese Secretary carrying His Majesty's letters patent to the Honourable Company, and a long trail of functionaries on foot, on horse or in carriages and palanquins – attorneys, churchwardens, Constables, servants, the keeper of the prison with two tipstaffs, and other Gentlemen. Somewhere in the middle of the parade the judge rode on a horse blanketed in velvet, a little way behind the Governor, who was carried in a palanquin by four English pages in rich liveries, 'bare headed, surrounded at distance with Peons and blacks'. Such panoply, not quite as gorgeous as anything the Mughals and the Hindu princes could provide, but trying very hard to compete, was to become a familiar sight as the Raj – the rule – of the Emperors was overtaken by that of the British.

We must call them British from now on, rather than English, because the Act of Union between England and Scotland was sealed in 1707 with a service in Wren's distant St Paul's Cathedral. Henceforth the Union Jack was the national flag of the united kingdom and the bunting which announced British advances all over the earth, even though these might be – as they almost invariably were to start with – of a purely private and usually mercantile nature. In India it now flew over the three chief Company outposts that were beginning to take shape as recognizable communities built to distinctly European specifications. These were always at some distance from the Black Towns where the natives lived, even though dwellings and ancillary buildings – Calcutta had the first of many theatres by 1745 – began to appear outside the pukka battlements of the first fortified factory. Pukka buildings were made of masonry or a combination of brick dust, lime, molasses and cut hemp, which was said to be as hard and firm as conventional brick or stone; the majority of natives made do with kutcha constructions of mud bound together with fragments of straw. But efforts to reproduce the amenities of home were no protection at all against the biggest hazard that faced the British in India, which was to their health.

Sickness in Europe at the time was on a scale to dismay our own pill-popping and deodorized society, but in India it was of an order to defeat the imagination. Any disease that thrives on heat and moisture was rampant there and the mortality rate among Company employees was little short of devastating. Fourteen out of twenty-one people in the factory at Surat had died between the winter of 1630–1 and the spring of 1633, and this was only a small foretaste of what was to come wherever the British settled below the hill-country of the sub-continent. Bengal, by far the lushest of the three Presidencies, with a sopping climate of heat haze even outside the monsoon season of June to September, was the worst place of all for a man to gamble on his chances of surviving to see the English Channel again. The area around Calcutta was largely swamp, and the death rate among Job Charnock's men there as they struggled to establish the Company settlement was so high that they called it Golgotha, the place of the skulls. Captain Alexander Hamilton, who was constantly sailing in and out of the new port at the turn of the seventeenth and eighteenth centuries, reckoned that of 1,200 Englishmen alive there one August, 460 had been buried before New Year's Day. And it was to be a long time – not until well into the nineteenth century – before such figures were significantly reduced. It has been estimated that between 1707 and 1775, no fewer than fifty-seven per cent of Company employees died of sickness in Bengal; in the worst decade, from 1747 to 1756, the toll stood at seventy-four per cent. Whole families could be wiped out, as one nearly was in the case of William Thackeray, who lost five out of six sons in India, though not before the fourth had fathered William Makepeace Thackeray the novelist. But graveyards everywhere were almost as busy as the Park Street Cemetery in Calcutta, sometimes because these British ate and drank far more than was safe for them in a climate that exacted much higher penalties than their own from the self-indulgent. They shifted food as if at a banquet every time they sat at table, and poured after it large quantities of wine or, even more damagingly, punch, whose name they picked up from the Marathi word for five, which was the number of ingredients in the concoction – sugar, lime-juice, spice, water and arrack, the local spirit. By the time newspapers began to appear in 1780, they regularly carried warnings every June about the dangers of over-consumption in the desperate weather ahead.

In spite of hearing about these dreadful conditions every time an Indiaman sailed up the Thames from the East, there was no shortage of young men wanting to board her on the return journey to try their own luck out there. For one thing, the Company's business was expanding and more recruits were needed to run it; for another, greater opportunities than ever before were opening up for individuals to line their pockets, irrespective of obligations as Company employees with a fixed salary for their work. The expansion in business was generally achieved with the full sanction of Mughal authority, which was well accustomed to distributing favours for services rendered. The Bengal Council despatched the merchant John Surman to Delhi in 1714 to seek a variety of trading concessions and, though he was kept waiting there for three years, the time his party spent in the imperial capital was well occupied and very worthwhile. The Emperor Farruksiyar was suffering from venereal disease, which Surgeon Hamilton somewhat laboriously cured, and the reward was permission for the Company to purchase thirty-eight villages as well as to trade freely in Bengal with customs dues fixed at 3,000 rupees a year (£341), whatever the turnover or profit. Local governors, the Nawabs, were similarly well disposed from time to time, making concessions for a variety of assistance from the British, most often military, which was useful in putting down insurrections or stamping out the banditry that threatened the ample coffers of Mughal officialdom. On the other hand, a governor might perversely ignore the imperial firman and try to extract whatever he could in impositions on the Company trade for his private use, and the Nawab of Bengal did exactly that in the matter of the customs dues.

The opportunities for gain that were now inducing young men to come out from England by the boatload had existed only since the 1660s, when the Company relaxed its strict interpretation of the monopoly it had been granted by Queen Elizabeth. Earlier, it had fought against any semblance of private trade by its own countrymen, certainly by any of its employees, but had been obliged to drop this rigid attitude simply because it couldn't be enforced. The Company could try to crack the whip over its own people, though that was difficult enough at long range when the round voyage between London and India could take up to 18 months, but it could do nothing at all to hinder those Britons who started to ship themselves to Asia on foreign vessels. With such men beginning to operate freely on their own account – sending their trade goods to continental markets in Europe and transferring the cash by devious methods to the London banks – pressure mounted within the Company's own ranks for permission to do likewise and it became harder and harder to refuse this in view of the pittances paid to Company servants. Even as late as 1744, the chief of the factory at Dacca received no more than £40 a year, his junior merchants £30, factors £15 and writers £5.

Though, in each case, a number of allowances lifted these sums somewhere above the minimum rate, they were princely salaries compared with what Indians received from the Company. There were seventy-seven native employees of the Benares District Council in the last decade of the eighteenth century, working as clerks, local tax collectors and the like, and their total wages bill was £102, while the British judge received £220.

The Company devised a neat way of preserving its monopoly while at the same time allowing its men to wade into private profit – and in doing so it was more generous by several decades than either the Dutch East India Company or its French counterpart, which had started operations in 1668. British employees were still forbidden to trade directly with Europe, but the Court of Directors in London said that they might make what they liked of business opportunities on the side within Asia. This became known as the country trade and its extent by 1777 may be judged from the fact that in that year exports from Calcutta alone were being shipped westwards as far as Basra, Muscat and Suez, eastwards to Sumatra, Penang and China, as well as to the Coromandel Coast below Madras and the Malabar Coast south of Bombay. Some of the shipments were carried by East Indiamen in the increasingly complex operations of the Company, others were part of Mughal commerce, or represented the activities of free merchants, of whom there were dozens in Bengal by then; but many of those exports had been shipped by Company officials on their own behalf. In every case of country trade an invariable ally of the European dabbling in it – and the biggest dabblers were the most senior men – was the Indian banian, or broker, whose knowledge of the local language, of rumour in the bazaar and of ways and means, made him indispensable for success. And, unlike native employees of the Company, the banians came out of these operations very well indeed, some of them (like Gokul Ghosal and Cantu Babu towards the end of the eighteenth century) becoming as rich as any Englishman and almost as powerful. The banian was Mr Fixit in Calcutta, Bombay, Madras or the up-country settlement, while the European provided the outlay, frequently by borrowing from Indians at eighteen per cent, though this was nothing to what the poor peasant cultivator had to pay the money-lenders, who might extort anything up to 150 per cent. The European also had to cope with the complicated matter of landing his ultimate prize. The authorized method was by bill of exchange, the Company allowing

33

individuals to pay money into its various Indian treasuries, in return for bills which could be drawn later in London at dates and rates set by the Company. As this sometimes involved waiting four years for cash to be safely banked at home, many men turned to the method the free merchants had always used and remitted their profits delicately through French, Dutch, Danish and Swiss concerns, sometimes in the form of specie or jewels.

They were, for a start anyway, mostly the Company's covenanted or civil servants (the expression originated here) to distinguish them from a growing collection of men who were employed to bear arms. The first move towards soldiering was the arrival in 1662 of four companies of British troops in Bombay – still a Portuguese possession, though shortly to be a wedding present, with a Company outpost going up. The men came as soldiers of the King on the understanding that, if they needed to take up arms in India, it would be as Company troops. Then, in 1675, the Surat factory received orders that its civil servants were to be drilled in military disciplines so that if they were attacked, as they had been by the Marathas nine years before, they would be the better equipped to defend themselves. In the event of hostilities, they would be commissioned and paid like military officers, with their Indian employees and anybody else who could be pressed into service providing the army of other ranks who would bear the brunt of whatever fighting occurred. Similar orders were executed wherever Company factories were built until, about the turn of the century, East Indiamen were sailing out with a number of young men heading not for the lowliest grade of writer in the civil service, but for a career as Company soldiers starting as cadets. In the early 1700s, there were 200 men under half a dozen officers in Bengal to guard the trade and factories there, and it was no more than prudent of the Company to take such precautions. India was not, and never had been, a sublimely peaceful land. Tribal wars had always flared up, banditry had long flourished, rulers of whatever denomination had been liable to quarrel. Two groups in particular had struggled for ascendancy from the beginning of Hindu history; warrior kings, the rajas, for territorial and Brahmin priests for social advantage. It was well understood by everyone on the sub-continent, from the Mughal Emperor down, that if you wished to safeguard your possessions and even your life you had better be prepared to fight from time to time. The Company was doing no more than that. 'All war is so contrary to our interest', the Directors declared in 1681, 'that we cannot too often inculcate to you our aversion thereunto.' This was a genuine cry from the pocket of men bent on commercial speculation and nothing but, and it was to be repeated time and again for at least another hundred years.

War, nonetheless, was what they got by the middle of the eighteenth century and, typically, it was with the French at first. Though they were latecomers to India, the French had prospered almost as much as the British, whose Company trade in 1740 represented over ten per cent of the entire public revenue of Great Britain. The French trade by then, having started half a century behind, was already worth half as much and catching up so fast that it was distinctly possible it might overhaul the British share in India within a few more years. There was ample reason for each to come to blows but hostilities actually broke out because, far away in Europe, the War of the Austrian Succession began, with Britain and France on opposite sides, as they quixotically were again when the Seven Years War erupted a little later with most of the original alliances reversed. The upshot in India was that a French fleet attacked and took Madras in 1746 while the British unsuccessfully besieged the French settlement at Pondicherry, though in the pause between the two European wars Madras was restored to the British in exchange for Cape Breton Island in North America. The French governor Dupleix, however, having got the bit between his teeth, did not wait for the second European war to start before he moved once again on his rivals in India. His excuse came, providentially, with a purely Indian dispute to two important positions in 1750 – that of the Nizam of the Deccan, the Emperor's deputy over an enormous area lying between the south-western and south-eastern coasts, and that of the Nawab of the Carnatic, the governor of the province which included all the European settlements along the Coromandel Coast. In each case the British backed one Indian candidate for the succession, the French another. Aided by two useful assassinations, Dupleix saw his man safely on to the Nizam's throne (receiving land grants and a splendid title in return) then marched his troops to Trichinopoly, where the British client for the Nawab's office was under siege from his rival. The matter looked as if it might well end as Dupleix intended, with a second puppet installed and French influence so increased in southern India that the British would shortly be squeezed out altogether. But the British played a trump card by sending 200 of their 350 soldiers, with 300 native sepoys and three small field-guns, in an unexpected dash from Trichinopoly to Arcot, the Nawab's capital. They took it against a force twice the size of their own, then held it for fifty days while both the French and Indian besieging armies tried to get them out again. When British reinforcements arrived the besiegers were beaten off, pursued, and defeated several times with the aid of Maratha troops and a native army from Mysore, both of whom sprang to the side of Mohammed Ali, the British nominee for Nawab, when they saw the tide turning in his favour. This was, effectively, the end of French political ambitions in India. Dupleix was recalled to Paris in disgrace in 1754 and, although other skirmishes occurred until the end of the century, the French who remained had neither the vigour nor the military skill seriously to challenge British power again.

From Arcot in 1751 there emerged a name the British would hero-worship as long as they contemplated India. It was that of Robert Clive, who had persuaded his commander at Trichinopoly to let him take a chance on seizing the provincial capital and who covered himself in glory for the rest of the campaign. Clive had come out from England in 1744, son of a hard-up country gentleman and bound for a grinding start as writer in the civil service at Madras, with the prospect of a reasonable substance one day if he moved up the Company ladder assiduously and was lucky with his country trade. He was a manic-depressive youth of eighteen when he arrived, who had been noted for ebullient exploits like steeple-climbing at home, but who twice tried to blow out his own brains during the first few weeks of loneliness in India (and would eventually die, vastly rich and a Baron to boot, by cutting his throat in Shropshire). His Company superiors thought him a competent worker but a bad mixer and he might never have been heard of again except by meticulous researchers into East India archives, had Dupleix not attacked Madras, from which Clive escaped with his face blacked, disguised as an Indian interpreter. He promptly applied for an ensign's commission and by the time Arcot was over and done with he was a captain with a brilliant reputation for tactics and daring leadership. He then resumed the mercantile post he had been offered just before the siege, as supplier of provisions for the Company troops in Madras, and within two years had made such favourable contracts that he was sailing for England with a wife and £40,000 in his account. His partner in the provisioning business, Robert Orme, wrote a glowing version of Clive's military prowess which helped make him the toast of London and Member of Parliament for one of the notorious rotten boroughs of the time (he won by 5 votes, all bought, in a total poll of 55). Yet after only eighteen months at home he was on the way back to India as a lieutenant-colonel posted second in command of Company forces in the south. The British still felt threatened by the French, but Clive's first action was in alliance with Maratha troops against a stronghold of pirates who had been pillaging Mughal and Company shipping indiscriminately. And then came the call from Bengal.

For years even before Clive first went to India, the Mughal empire had been splitting at the seams for reasons which had little if anything to do with Europeans. It had been shaken by invasions from the north which continued through the middle of the century, mostly by Afghans, once by Persians. There had been internal disputes, like those in the Deccan and the Carnatic which first brought Clive to notice. Some of the subject Indians had revolted, the Sikhs and the Jats among them, but the most difficult people had been the Marathas, from Maharashtra in the west, whom nobody liked or trusted because they could be fighting alongside you one minute and throwing themselves upon you the next. The Mughals were starting to wilt under all this pressure and had begun to lose their sense of mission, although the British were to recognize the Emperor's authority right up to the nineteenth century. Among the imperial possessions, Bengal still paid tribute but virtually went its own way, which meant among other things that the Nawab did as he pleased in imposing customs dues on the Company there and interpreting other clauses in the Emperor's firman. The year after Clive returned to India, friction with the British in Calcutta came to a head when the young and reckless Siraj-ud-Daula succeeded his grandfather as Nawab of Bengal, picked a quarrel with the Company and marched on the settlement with 30,000 foot soldiers, 20,000 horsemen, 400 trained elephants and 80 pieces of cannon. Most of the British fled at the sight, as well they might, but a handful remained and were captured. The young Nawab may have been arrogant but he was not a bloodthirsty monster and all he did with the British captives was to relieve them of their valuables and have them locked up for the night in the brig at Fort William, which had always been known by the British as the Black Hole, though it was nothing worse than a room with a window opening on to a verandah. Unfortunately, the night of June 20, 1756 was probably the most oppressive of that year, because the monsoon broke the following day. When the brig was unlocked in the morning many of the prisoners had suffocated or died of heat exhaustion – perhaps 43 out of 64, which was bad enough but not nearly as bad as the Black Hole's self-appointed hero, John Zephaniah Holwell, made out in subsequent accounts. He claimed that 146 people had gone in, of whom 23 survived, and those figures still tend to circulate in some British history books though they have long been proved a nonsense. The brig was far too small for the numbers lodged there; but it didn't have elastic sides.

From Madras, Robert Clive came north with a punitive expedition and recaptured Calcutta without difficulty in one sortie. He then sailed his force further up the Hooghly River and bombarded the French settlement of Chandernagore which, like the British downstream, had been quietly getting on with business as usual during the stirring encounters between their compatriots in South India. After that he took the step which was against all the Company's instincts; indeed, it was against many explicit instructions to avoid political involvement in the affairs of India, and he defied them just as the Governor of Madras had done a few years previously. Aware perhaps of what Dupleix might have achieved for French prosperity had he succeeded as puppet master in the south, Clive decided to play kingmaker in the north and put up an elderly Mughal general, Mir Jafar, to supplant Siraj-ud-Daula as Nawab of Bengal. On the battlefield of Plassey, a year almost to the day after the Black Hole of Calcutta, Clive's forces defeated the Nawab's again and Siraj-ud-Daula fled towards Bihar, where he was caught by Mir Jafar's son and murdered. In just twelve months of military display and dealing that was as unscrupulous as any on the sub-continent at the time – but no worse than that – Clive had made himself the master of the richest province in the land, so fertile that the Mughals called it the paradise on earth, so bountiful to commerce that in any normal year of the eighteenth century sixty per cent of all British imports from Asia came from Bengal. In doing so, Clive effectively founded the British Empire in India. From this point, although no-one recognized it for the moment, there was to be no going back to the notion of East India Company chain stores around the margins of the country, which is what the Directors had been carefully building for nearly 150 years and what they still wished for in Leadenhall Street. From now on the British were in the position of rulers and would only expand from a provincial to an imperial dimension. Clive saw this very clearly. He wrote to the elder William Pitt – himself the son of a man who had gone to India as a Company seaman and come home with a fortune – urging that the Crown should replace the Company in the three Presidencies, which 'would prove an immense source of wealth to the kingdom'. The suggestion was ignored.

The British response was entirely local and one of unmitigated greed. They had some very fanciful notions of the accumulated wealth at the disposal of a Nawab, one estimate in 1757 assuming that Mir Jafar could lay his hands on £40 million as soon as the British placed him on the gubernatorial throne. It was nothing like that amount, but the British queuing up for a share in his loot could not have been too disappointed by what they individually received from putting him where he was. Clive himself came at the head of the beneficiaries with a present of £211,500 and Governor Drake (who had fled from Calcutta and missed its Black Hole) collected £31,500. Then there was Mr Watts 'who had run very great risks and played a vital part in the Plassey revolution', obtaining £117,000, Major Kilpatrick (£60,750), Mr Walsh (£56,250), Mr Manningham (£27,000), Mr Scrafton (£22,500), Messrs Boddam, Frankland, Mackett and Collett (£11,367 apiece), Messrs Amyatt and Pearkes (£11,366 each), Major Grant (£11,250) and poor Mr Lushington who had to make do with a mere £5,625. All this was on top of the £187,000 the new Nawab was required to pay the Select Committee of the Bengal Council for the trouble to which it had lately been put, and the £275,000 he was obliged to hand over to the army for sorting everything out to the benefit of all and sundry. In both those transactions many individuals, Clive most of all, took another cut; in addition to which, 18 months later, Clive also obtained a grant of revenue from the Nawab worth £27,000 a year which was paid for the rest of his life. When, thirteen years later, a committee of the House of Commons investigated what had been going on in Bengal at this time, it concluded that presents paid to Britons in 1757 alone amounted to £1,238,575 and that between then and 1765 sums exceeding £2 million had been disbursed to individuals in specie and jewels. By 1781 the figure would have risen to something approaching £4,750,000.

This fantastic windfall was only the start of what was to be shaken from the tree in the next few years. By having the Nawab in their pocket, the British were able to arrange trading conditions in Bengal exactly as they pleased in the knowledge that the Emperor was too far away to interfere and, anyway, had too many problems of his own to bother about even if he had wished to be obstructive. Far from being difficult, the Emperor Shah Alam recognized the realities of the transformed Bengal and in 1765 made the Company his Diwan there, responsible for the collection of his imperial revenues in the province. So long as the British paid him his dues they were at liberty to enjoy whatever surplus they might extract from the countryside, by trading imposts or any method they fancied, which had been the traditional licence enabling many generations of Mughal officials to make themselves rich. The concession was almost superfluous for by this time trade was totally dominated by the British and their Indian middlemen, and individual fortunes were being made at a rate and size to take the breath away. In 1776 the political economist Adam Smith thought that between eight and ten per cent was a good profit in England, but ten years before that the normal profit in the internal trade of Bengal had been between twenty and thirty per cent and up to seventy-five per cent in some commodities such as salt, betel nut and tobacco. For a dozen years after Plassey, profits of twenty-five per cent were regarded as a sign of the moderate man, and there were to be few of those around for some time to come. Instead there were free merchants like Archibald Keir, who employed 13,000 men to manufacture 12,000 tons of salt in one year. There were Company officials coining money on the side, literally in the case of William Marriott, who was appointed Resident in Benares and immediately began to run the mint there on his own account. There were very highly placed functionaries, like Henry Vansittart, Governor of Fort William in 1761, whose share in the salt trade was reckoned to match that of all other Company servants put together and who was presented with £225,000 for his part in replacing Mir Jafar with another puppet, Mir Kasim, who also ceded to the Company the districts of Burdwan, Midnapore and Chittagong. Vansittart was quite brazen about his opportunism in India. 'We are men of power, you say', he wrote to a correspondent in England, 'and take advantage of it. Why, man, what is the use of station if we are not to benefit from it?'

These were the Nabobs, a word that started to appear derisively when the first of them reached England with their plunder in tow and that went into general circulation after a play with that title was staged in London in 1768. They were not much cared for at home, being lumped together as an ill-mannered and ostentatious gang along with Caribbean sugar planters, African slave traders, government war contractors and others who were doing well out of the construction of British interests overseas. Most of the dislike sprang from sheer envy of their sudden wealth, for the majority of Nabobs had left England as the sons of tradesmen or gentry in straitened circumstances and had come home able to buy up almost anything in sight. There was also a very real fear of them among the country squires, as the Nabobs acquired property and began to change the traditional pattern of land ownership and social patronage. Usually they set themselves up as country gentlemen and lived off the income of an estate, or investment in government stock, or by lending their plentifully spare cash to deeply rooted neighbours who needed a mortgage; very few invested their money in further trading ventures or in the manufacturing enterprises of Britain. Paul Benfield was an exception, a Cheltenham shopkeeper's son who went to India as a civil servant and made enough money at it (£500,000 by all accounts) to buy an estate in Hertfordshire and establish his own bank, which failed so badly that he died a pauper in Paris. The Nabobs also antagonized a lot of people who were in no sense their social or economic rivals, whose lives for generations had been regulated by a form of feudalism which could be distant but familiar, stern but benevolent. The upstarts rudely interrupted this, accepting none of the old squire's responsibilities towards his tenants, protecting their land from trespassers much more fiercely than the gentlemen they displaced.

All over the British Isles expensive property changed hands at an unprecedented rate as the Nabobs sailed home with their treasure. Eyre Coote, after two periods in India, bought large places in Ireland, an estate in Wiltshire, a country house in Hampshire and a residence in London. John Zephaniah Holwell, who had gone to Calcutta as a timber merchant's son, returned with £96,000 and purchased Chilton Lodge near Hungerford. Richard Barwell, known even by contemporaries in the Company hierarchy in Bengal as an unscrupulous rogue, bought Stanstead in Sussex from the Earl of Halifax, had it landscaped by Capability Brown and altered by the architect James Wyatt. William Watts, who had run very great risks before Plassey, procured two properties in Berkshire – one bought from the Duke of Kingston for £40,000 – and a town house in Hanover Square. Bisham Abbey near Maidenhead, West Park near

Fordingbridge, Caversham Park, near Reading, Somerford Hall near Brewood, Hook House in Hampshire – these were but a clutch of the homes that fell into the hands of the Nabobs or were built by them. Their land hunger was so great that, in catering for it, a lottery in Calcutta was offering an estate on the Hertfordshire and Middlesex borders as first prize. Their speculations also included Parliamentary seats, thirty Nabobs taking their places at Westminster between 1760 and 1784, several treading the same path as Major Scott, who bought the pocket borough of West Looe for £4,000 from the nephew of Lord Bathurst and consequently became its MP. Four rotten boroughs in particular, Hindon and Cricklade in Wiltshire, New Shoreham in Sussex and Shaftesbury in Dorset, saw a regular traffic in returned profiteers from India. General Richard Smith, once a cheesemonger's son, emerged from Company service to take the seat at Hindon by the simple expedient of marching to the Market Cross before polling day and promising five guineas to everyone who voted for him. The best paid workmen in England, who didn't have a vote, would be earning less than ten shillings a week at the time. Yet diamonds were beginning to fall in value because of the quantities brought in by people like Francis Sykes, who returned from Murshidabad to buy Basildon Park in Oxfordshire, a Parliamentary seat and a baronetcy to cap the lot.

A small impression was made on the social life of London, where the town houses of the Nabobs were clustered around Mayfair. The arrivistes popularized Madeira which they had found to be the only wine that improved and kept in a hot climate. Curried food was introduced in their wake, a speciality of the Norris Street Coffee House in the Haymarket from 1773, and advertised within a few years by Sorlie's Perfumery Warehouse as something that 'renders the Stomach active in Digestion, the Blood naturally free in its Circulation, the Mind vigorous – and contributes most of any Food to an increase of the Human Race.' But the greatest effect of the Nabobs on the British, apart from disturbing the equilibrium of ownership of the land and power around the country towns, was in tempting a much wider variety of people to follow them to India in the hope of equally immense capital gains. The Company now found that the upper classes, for the first time, were interested in providing it with recruits. Soon Calcutta would be holding annual dinners of old boys from Westminster School – twenty-seven attended in 1784 – and East Indiamen outward-bound from the Thames would include in the passenger list the occasional young sprig steeling himself for initial drudgery as a writer after coming down from the heights of Oxford or Cambridge. The risks were high in the business speculations ahead, highest of all in the matter of health, but the prospective gains were a powerful counter-attraction to any hazards that might be in the offing. On Clive's imperial foundations a great army of prentice craftsmen were ready and willing to build.

TWO

ORDER
OUT OF CHAOS

The most envied of the Nabobs was Clive himself who, by his own calculation, had accumulated £401,102 by the time he sailed for home a second time in 1760, swollen with the profit that accrued from Plassey. He left Bengal because his health was failing and, on reaching England six months later, he quickly took himself to Bath for the cure, with large doses of opium to relieve the pain of gout. He returned to a mixture of acclaim and jealousy which was precisely reflected by his having to make do with an Irish peerage, always regarded as inferior to an English one. But nothing could diminish whatever money could buy, and with his wealth the new Lord Clive repaired Styche Hall, the family home, bought another one a few miles away, purchased an Irish estate and a London house in Berkeley Square, and obtained a Parliamentary seat at Shrewsbury. He also dealt generously with his parents, his five sisters and a number of aunts, and settled an annuity of £500 on Stringer Lawrence, the old soldier who had taught him everything he knew about warfare before the siege of Arcot. After that Clive turned his attention to the internal politics of the Company, whose Directors were dismayed by what he had let loose in Bengal. As they contemplated Clive's own fortune and the others being amassed in his wake, they reasonably wondered whether there would be anything left for them to take out of the province if individuals were stripping it as thoroughly as appeared; and bills of exchange on private trade were now mounting so rapidly in London as to threaten seriously the Company resources there.

Clive was locked in acrimony with the Directors on his responsibility in these issues when news followed him from India that the Bengal Council had fallen out with Mir Kasim, and that a breach with the Emperor himself seemed imminent; that, in short, the avarice of Company employees out there might very well wreck the Company's operation altogether. 'And this is the way your Gentlemen behave,' complained Mir Kasim.

They make a disturbance all over my country, plunder the people; injure and disgrace my servants . . . Setting up the colours and showing the passes of the Company, they use their utmost endeavours to oppress the peasants, merchants and other people of the country . . . They forcibly take away the goods of the peasants, merchants etc. for a fourth part of their value, and by ways of violence and oppressions they oblige the peasants to give five rupees for goods which are worth but one rupee, and for the sale of five rupees they bind and disgrace a man who pays a hundred rupees in land-tax . . .

Some Englishmen were uttering the same unpalatable home truth, among them Edmund Burke, who described Company servants in these terms to the House of Commons;

animated with all the avarice of age and all the impetuosity of youth, they roll in one after another; wave after wave; and there is nothing before the eyes of the native but an endless hopeless prospect of new birds of prey and passage, with appetites continually renewing for a food that is continually wasting.

Hastily the quarrel in Leadenhall Street was soothed and Clive sailed East yet again, this time to represent the Company's interests with all the vigour that lately he had applied only to his own advancement. Straightaway he forbade the further acceptance of presents and put down a mutiny of British officers who were not prepared to fight for the Company if the Company discontinued, as it now did, the special allowances they had collected for service away from their garrisons. Clive then set about healing the friction that had arisen in his absence between the Council and the Emperor Shah Alam, and secured the Company's right to act as Diwan in collecting the imperial revenue from Bengal. He was to do nothing more in India. His health collapsed again, needing fifteen grains of opium a day now, and in January 1767 he left Calcutta for the last time, to enjoy his riches painfully for another seven years before he committed suicide.

His last gesture in Bengal was not nearly enough to stop the rot that he had started there, and the Company came within an ace of bankruptcy before genuine principle was at last applied in India and began to produce some sort of order out of chaos. It appeared first of all in the guise of Warren Hastings, who went to Calcutta as a young writer in 1750 and returned to England fourteen years later as a junior member of the Bengal Council who, exceptionally, had failed to make a fortune. He was still so poor when he was appointed Second Member of the Madras Council in 1769 that he had to borrow the money for his passage from England and throughout his long service in the Company he conspicuously refused to make what personal profit he might have done from the opportunities available. This is not to say that he turned his back on everything that came his way. He engaged in private trade, like every other official, especially in silk and opium, and he regularly sent diamonds to England, one of which he tried to sell to Catherine the Great of Russia. But when he finally retired in 1785 he had no more than £75,000 in his account, and he had been a Governor-General in Calcutta for thirteen years by then, with salary and allowances amounting to £30,000 per annum for the last decade. In part, his failure to amass the wealth expected by then of such a powerful figure could be put down to a form of laziness, for he lacked the accountant's mind and application of Clive. Moreover, even his enemies – of whom there were many – admitted that Hastings was an open-handed man to those he liked who were in need, and when he left India much money was owed him that he never bothered to collect. But his moderation in financial matters was also part and parcel of his character, which was determined, subtle, sympathetic and more honourable than most.

The enmities began within the Council in Bengal and were led by his junior colleague Philip Francis, whom Hastings fought and wounded in a duel, and they continued beyond his retirement, when he was impeached at Westminster but acquitted of the corruption charges Francis had inspired. The intrigues against him inevitably spread to Leadenhall Street, even though the Company had appointed him Governor of Bengal to clean up the mess there in 1772, and he could be seen to be doing that. Patronage was the name of the game in London and many complicated gambits were played on the board at any given time, with high officials in India often reduced to the status of pawns. At the least significant level, two or three thousand pounds might change hands if a Director of the Honourable Company would but nominate so and so's son for a writer's position in the East, and Henry Dundas, a Scottish lawyer whose mounting activities in British politics earned him the nickname of 'King Harry the Ninth' and the ultimate position of Secretary of State for India, became notorious for sponsoring many a youth whose parents had the necessary cash. But patronage came high as well as low. The office of Commissary General of Musters had been created by the Directors for the bankrupt Lauchlin Macleane, who owed a great deal of money to a leading Company politician,

Laurence Sulivan. A special paymastership was created in Oudh for a relative of Sir George Wombwell when he was the Company Chairman. Hastings himself was obliged to find positions for people urged on him by two different Lords Chancellor, the Lord Chief Justice and the Archbishop of York. It is not surprising that, operating inside this jungle of collusion, he made enemies among his superiors in England as well as among his subordinates in India. A relatively honest man, in the age of the Nabobs, was liable to attract as much spite as applause.

He was greatly assisted in what he set out to do because the Company was so near insolvency just before his Bengal appointment that it had gone cap in hand to the Bank of England for a £1 million loan. It was bailed out of its difficulties at the price of a Regulating Act of Parliament in 1773, which was the first time the British Government took a hand in what had become the political matter of India. At the suggestion of Hastings, this Act stipulated that Company officials who collected revenue or dispensed justice should no longer be allowed private trade, and that neither civil nor military servants could accept presents from Indians. Clive had ordered the second of these provisions, of course, but presents had changed hands again the moment his back was turned. To these curbs on individual plunder, Hastings added another of his own. He abolished the dastak on private trade: exemption from the Emperor's normal customs dues which had been granted to the Company by Farruksiyar over half a century before and which individuals had gradually assumed for their own benefit as well, at the cost of much bitterness from the Nawabs and competing Indian merchants. At the same time Hastings, searching for reasonable solutions, reduced duties within his power to a low level in order to stimulate trade. He also proposed that wages paid by the Company should be much increased to reduce the temptation to profiteer on the side. The Regulating Act took care of that, too – Hastings's own salary and allowances being raised to £25,000 a year at first. Some of this went in paying for the small army of servants and the official entertainments that went with the position – and of all the public figures in Great Britain, only the Lord Lieutenant of Ireland collected as much.

This first Government intervention in India helped Hastings in his immediate objective of declaring war on corruption, but otherwise it added to his burdens by removing the autonomy of the Madras and

Bombay Presidencies and making them answerable in the first place to him. He would henceforth function from Calcutta not only as Governor of Bengal, but as Governor-General of all the Company's Indian holdings. An instant result, apart from acquiring two more sources of jealous intrigue, was that he inherited military adventures which the Madras and Bombay governments had separately started, the Marathas running true to form by having a hand in each. The Bombay campaign, which was to drag on for three years until Hastings managed to arrange peaceful terms, should have been a purely Maratha affair all through, because it centred on that perennial pastime of Indian rulers, a struggle for succession, with tribal factions ranged behind an uncle and a posthumous son. The Madras folly was much more serious, the government there having provoked three parties against it – the Marathas, the Nizam of Hyderabad, and Hyder Ali of Mysore – and, before peace came, a French fleet was adding its weight to their side. Only by suspending the British governor of Madras and throwing his own best resources across the country from Bengal, did Hastings extricate the Company from this crassness in the south, and he didn't achieve that until the year before he left India, 1784, which was also the moment when the British Government took a second step towards its total rule. The younger William Pitt's India Act of that year sprang from Government alarm that Company recklessness in the East might easily draw the nation as a whole into a number of political positions it could well do without. The Act imposed a body of six commissioners above the Company Directors in London, known as the Board of Control and consisting of the Chancellor of the Exchequer and a Secretary of State for India, together with four Privy Councillors appointed by the monarch. The Company still had the power to hire and fire its servants in India, and it was still at liberty to pursue its trade there as before. But the Board of Control could now overrule Leadenhall Street on any matter touching politics, which meant that in future the Governor-General in India was much more its man than the Company's. Although no-one had yet grasped the fact that an empire was being built, the structure of the British Raj was starting to rise from the trenching dug by Robert Clive.

Hastings had twice resorted to arms on his own account, with little to be said in his favour on either occasion. He backed the Nawab of Oudh, another puppet of the Company, against the Rohillas in the

European officer under a tree with his servant; gouache by a Bengali artist 1775.
It is a deferential view of the British, who had lately become rulers of Bengal as a
result of Clive's victory at Plassey. The Indian servant is depicted as somewhere
between the stature of the officer and that of his pet dog.

View of East India Docks; watercolour by William Daniell 1808. The docks had
been constructed a couple of years earlier, on the Thames below the Isle of Dogs,
between Blackwall Reach and Bugsby's Reach, to serve the East India Company's
thriving interests in India and other parts of Asia. East Indiamen plied between

here and Calcutta or other Indian ports, laden with the merchandise of two
civilizations. The docks were only part of the Company's organization at home,
where it was one of London's biggest employers of labour.

Lord Wellesley; oil by Robert Home c. 1803. The future Duke of Wellington's elder brother, Wellesley was responsible for the great annexations of territory that firmly established British rule throughout India. At the same time he founded Fort William College, whose educational influence was to inspire Bengalis with ideas of independence long before other Indians began to campaign for it.

Lord Cornwallis; oil by Arthur Devis 1795. Cornwallis had surrendered to George Washington at Yorktown in the American War of Independence before Pitt asked him to become Governor-General in India. Like Hastings before him, he took a stand against corruption among Company employees but is remembered most for the Permanent Settlement he imposed on Bengal in 1793. Though well-intentioned, this method of tax collection produced social upheaval in the Presidency.

Warren Hastings; oil by George Romney 1795. He had been recalled to England to face impeachment, but had not yet been acquitted, when Romney painted this picture. The charges were mischievous. While Governor-General in India, Hastings had taken the first steps in cleaning up the corruption Clive began, and consequently made many enemies among the British in Bengal and their patrons in London.

A European Gentleman with his Munshi or Native Professor of Languages 1813. By this time books containing such illustrations regularly appeared in London, picturing the conditions in which East India Company servants made their living. The habit of hiring a local teacher for instruction in a native language had at last taken hold. Earlier Company employees had rarely bothered to learn a local tongue, leaving communication to a bilingual Indian in their pay, usually the banian who acted as middleman in all their transactions.

The Writers' Building, Calcutta, engraving by the Daniells 1798. This was the administrative headquarters of the East India Company in the Bengal Presidency at the time, where its writers (clerks) kept the books balanced. It subsequently served the same purpose for the Government of India until 1912, and today it functions as before for the state Government of West Bengal. The obelisk in the foreground commemorated those who died in the Black Hole of Calcutta.

A suttee; oil by Tilly Kettle c. 1770 – 1771. Suttee was the process by which a Hindu widow was burned alive with the corpse of her husband. Lord William Bentinck proscribed the rite in Bengal in 1829, though it lingered elsewhere in India for several more years. Many Indians welcomed the change, others opposed it fiercely. Kettle's painting dramatizes the moment when, before the young widow is put on her husband's funeral pyre, she says farewell to her relatives.

Taylor's Emporium, Calcutta; watercolour by Sir Charles D'Oyly c. 1825-1828. By the middle of the nineteenth century, British women had at last come to settle in India in some quantity. One consequence was the rapid growth of large shops run on European lines, like Taylor's, which memsahibs and their gentlemen patronized in person, instead of leaving their servants to do all the shopping in the native bazaar.

A study at Haileybury c. 1880. The photograph might just as well have come from an illustrated edition of *Stalky and Co,* though the school Kipling had in mind when he wrote the book was in fact in Devon. A pupil at Haileybury not so long after the photo was taken was Clement Attlee. In 1947 he was the Prime Minister presiding over the dissolution of the British Indian Empire which his old school had been founded to provide with administrators.

Fledgling burra sahib and memsahib with their Indian syce (groom). British children born in India were supported by bevies of servants from birth. These two were luckier than most, because the habit was to send them home to England at about the age of five to be educated properly. Many, like Rudyard Kipling, didn't see their parents again until they had reached their late teens.

The Massacre at Cawnpore; tinted lithograph by T Packer. This was one of the most notorious events in the Indian Mutiny. Nana Sahib offered safe conduct down the Ganges to British survivors of the Cawnpore garrison, but had them

butchered as they set off in boats. Most of the dead were women and children, and British emotion at their deaths in particular was largely responsible for the appalling punishment of mutineers later.

Grand Durbar at Cawnpore
1859. There is little good to be
said on behalf of either side in
the Indian Mutiny. One man
who does emerge with credit is
Lord Canning, who had been
appointed Governor-General
just before the Mutiny began
and was to be the first Viceroy
of India. He put a stop to
British acts of revenge, and
when he left for home in 1861
Indians generally were sorry to
see him go. Here he is pictured
in some gesture of
reconciliation at Cawnpore, the
year after the Mutiny finished.

Queen Victoria with her Indian
servant 1895. She formed a
strangely intense relationship
with Abdul Karim, her Munshi
(teacher), in spite of much
disapproval from her Ministers,
who regarded him as an
upstart.

The Durbar Court of the
India Office, London.
Opened by Disraeli in 1868,
the India Office in Whitehall
was the home headquarters
of British rule over India.
The Durbar Court, under its
glass roof, was the scene of
receptions for visiting
Indian princes and
politicians.

District Officer at his
paperwork on an upcountry
tour c. 1920. The Indian
Civil Service was the greatest
pride of British India,
renowned for its efficiency
and its incorruptibility.
There were never more than
1000 men in this elite body,
whose foundations rested
on the work of the D.O.,
who supervised all that
happened in an area whose
average size was 4430
square miles.

Queen Victoria proclaimed Empress of India, Delhi 1877; oil by Val Prinsep.
Victoria had been ruling India directly for 19 years by this time, following
the end of the East India Company's suzerainty after the Mutiny. But Benjamin

north; worse, when the Raja of Benares refused to meet a military commitment he had made to the Company some years before, Hastings judged him a rebel and put him down with force. But warfare is the last thing for which Warren Hastings should be remembered, although his generals in the southern campaign had demonstrated that British troops with a backing of native sepoys could hold their own against a combination of fierce Indian forces without having to call on help from home. (None, in any case, would have been forthcoming, for the thirteen colonies in America had revolted against the King and any reinforcements that might have been available from England had been needed across the Atlantic while Hastings was buttressing the British position in India.) Warfare was still something the Directors shrank from, for commercial rather than moral reasons, because it damaged trade and cost a lot of money to conduct. It was also inconsistent with all the policies that Hastings had privately set his mind on. He was bent on restoring trade to its old stability, and succeeded so well that in the decade starting in 1783 the recently impoverished Company made nearly £13 million clear profit from its Indian operations. Besides trade, and after cleansing the Company of local excesses, he was most of all intent on leaving a civilized administration behind him that others would have difficulty in dismantling. His greatest gift was that he didn't for a moment believe that the British, or any Europeans, held a monopoly of civilized values. 'The people of this country,' he said, 'do not require our aid to furnish them with a rule of conduct or a standard for their property.'

He applied this philosophy in his overhaul of the legal processes under his control, by setting up courts under British judges without trying to substitute English law for the existing codes of the Hindus and Muslims, his intention being 'to found the authority of the British Government in Bengal on its ancient laws, to point the way to rule this people with ease and moderation according to their own ideas, manners and prejudices.' This was easier said than done, especially where Hindus were concerned. Their ancient law, the dharmashastra, was not codified like that of the English, based upon precedents established by earlier cases; the Hindu pundit could interpret matters as he thought fit according to the general precepts of Manu in the light of present conditions. Islamic law introduced by the Mughals was, at least on paper, much more regular in its approach because it derived its authority from specific instances in the Koran and the presiding maulana could refer to them in making his judgements. But in many parts of the Mughal empire the entire system had become corrupt, with disputes being settled in favour of the party which could produce the bigger bribe. Among Hindus it was common for people to force an issue in their favour by various forms of blackmail; they would sit and fast on their adversary's doorstep, knowing it was well understood that their death in the process would leave a curse on the opponent; Brahmins would get their own way by promising to disembowel themselves or dash out their children's brains if they were thwarted.

What Hastings drove towards was a system by which an Englishman would adjudicate on the advice of a pundit or maulana sitting by his side, with penalties remaining as they had been before the British came to India. He renounced a right the Company had assumed, to a commission on all debts and property recovered by its court decrees, and he stopped the habit of paying law officers out of fines and court fees. He also instructed every officer to set aside part of his day for the hearing of complaints, which were to be deposited in a padlocked box outside the court house to which the officer alone had the key, and read out in open court. The big problem, of course, was the one that had hampered the British ever since their first incursion into India: their own failure to come to terms with the local languages and consequently to understand properly the local customs. It was Warren Hastings who broke through that self-imposed barrier, in the first place by instructing one of his bright young men, Nathaniel Halhed (not long out of Harrow and Oxford), to translate whatever he could discover of traditional Hindu law. Another man, Charles Wilkins, was told to supply the need for official documents printed in Oriental scripts. By 1778 these two had so far followed their chief's cast of mind as well as his initial instructions, that Wilkins had published Halhed's *Grammar of the Bengali Language* on the first vernacular printing press in India. Within a few years, India would contain a sprinkling of Company men who were not obsessed with trade or preoccupied with profit, but with administration and with disinterested knowledge of the complex culture surrounding them on every side. Wilkins, still running the government press, would, at the suggestion of Hastings, have made the first European translation of the *Bhagavad Gita*, one of Hinduism's most sacred texts. Jonathan Duncan would be Resident in Benares, reforming the most corrupt place in the northern lands and turning with relief each night to his studies in Persian. Henry Colebrooke would be assistant Collector of revenue in Tirhut and grateful to be away from the quarrelsome society of British Calcutta, with the peace and quiet that enabled him to become a major European scholar in Sanskrit. William Jones, brought out to sit as judge in the High Court in Calcutta, would be weaving his knowledge of Sanskrit, Persian and Arabic into the startling theory that there was a common and Aryan source of Indo-European languages. It was Jones who presided over the Asiatic Society of Bengal, which Hastings founded in 1784, and began to form its reputation as one of the outstanding centres of scholarship in the East, which it still retains two centuries later. These men, and a growing band like them over the next few decades, became known as the Orientalists, and were to defend Indian traditions in a great battle for cultural supremacy before British India was very much older.

When Hastings left India in 1785, to face his long ordeal before the Parliamentary tribunal at home, Calcutta was so advanced and relatively sophisticated that it would shortly be known as the city of palaces on account of the number of opulent buildings the British had erected there. It was virtually their creation, unlike Bombay and Madras, and it was the capital of a Presidency that had grown throughout Bengal and Bihar, and along the River Ganges beyond Benares into the client state of Oudh. The southern Presidency was so far confined to Madras itself and a few outlying districts, the western Presidency still consisting of little more than Bombay on its marshy island. Enormous expanses of India had not been visited by Europeans, yet by the end of the eighteenth century people sitting in London would have very clear visual images not only of the British settlements but of Hindu antiquities, Mughal architecture, and the strange wild landscapes of the sub-continent. Artists had been attracted there by the prospect of gain like everybody else, though in the first place they saw their opportunity to cash in on the booty of India by painting the portraits of those already successful in commerce, extortion and war. Tilly Kettle, whose work was often mistaken for that of Sir Joshua Reynolds, was in Madras and Calcutta just after Clive retired. It was he who tipped off John Zoffany, a painter with his origins in Central Europe who had ingratiated himself with George III, to come out and share this bountiful new market; which Zoffany did as thoroughly as any

Nabob by charging 1,000 rupees per person appearing on his canvases, taking care that these consisted for the most part of groups of Britons with their retainers in the background. Landscapes were ignored until 1780 when William Hodges, who had been the official artist on Captain Cook's second Pacific voyage, toured parts of central and northern India and became the first man to introduce this rare new topic of art to the connoisseurs in London. He was soon, and forever after, to be upstaged by the Daniells.

Thomas Daniell was an innkeeper's son who had learned the elements of drawing and brushwork when apprenticed to a coachbuilder whose carriages he decorated. He had a flower painting accepted by the Royal Academy, produced illustrations to Spenser's *Faerie Queen*, and began to picture well-known English 'sights' like Wookey Hole and Mother Shipton's Well. Landscapes and buildings, he decided, were his forte, but art in England at the time was dominated by portraiture, particularly by that of Reynolds and Gainsborough. So he would go to India, taking with him as assistant his dead brother's son William. The Daniells arrived in Calcutta in 1786, and while they kept body and soul together for the first few months by odd jobs of repairing and cleaning oil paintings, Thomas began to create twelve of his own views of the city which he would engrave and sell as aquatints: William's part in the process was to fetch and carry while he picked up techniques of draughtsmanship and printing that would one day make his name almost as celebrated as his uncle's. That very first collaboration was an instant hit with the local Company people and their hangers-on, and orders poured in for the pictures, especially after William Hickey – Irish lawyer, diarist and gossip about town – had bought a complete set and spread word of his pleasure around. By the time the 1788 monsoon was finishing, the Daniells had made enough money to start the first of their journeys into the interior of India, Thomas having readied himself by joining the Asiatic Society and picking the brains of everyone there who could tell him something of what might lie ahead.

They set off with a couple of Portuguese half-breeds and five native servants on a long voyage up the Hooghly and into the Ganges aboard a budgerow, a passenger boat that could be rowed or sailed, in appearance a bit like an Oxford college barge. As well as reams of paper, rolls of canvas, pencils, brushes, easels, stretchers, paints and camping equipment, they took with them a perambulator, which was a large wooden wheel with a mile counter attached, so that they could make crude maps wherever they went. In the next three years they took themselves farther to the north-west than any European had been before, reaching Srinagar up in Garhwal, where they presented the local Raja with two pistols and a watch in return for three beautiful birds they couldn't identify, some musk and a yak's tail. They had surprisingly little trouble on the way, though they were attacked by thieves once and their host in Srinagar tried to enlist them in a war against his brother. Somewhere they were invited to join a tiger hunt, somewhere else they picnicked beside hot springs which tasted, they thought, better than the waters at Bath. Wherever they went, Thomas sketched and painted furiously – buildings like the Taj Mahal and the Red Fort at Agra, Akbar's fortress at Allahabad, the Jama Masjid and the Qutb Minar in Delhi, Hindu temples at Brindaban, Gaya and elsewhere, as well as bare ranges of Himalayan foothills, lush stretches of the Ganges and the Jumna. Always he included unobtrusive figures alongside the buildings or in the otherwise empty landscapes (the Daniells themselves occasionally) in order to give scale or relieve monotony in the composition. Some of his sketches were sold as they went along and he had high hopes of commissions from Asaf-ud-Daula, the Nawab of Oudh, but when they reached Lucknow the Nawab's patronage had already been exhausted on a number of itinerant artists, Zoffany among them. It was, none the less, an extremely successful trip for the Daniells, with 150 new pictures to offer their public in Calcutta when they returned at the end of 1791.

Four months later they were off again, this time sailing down the east coast to Madras before beginning a second overland journey – conveyed in palanquins with forty-eight servants now – which took them to the southern tip of India at Cape Comorin. The Mughals had never made much impression so far down country, though the British had already fought over it more than once and the Daniells encountered a convoy of wounded on its way back from an engagement with Hyder Ali's son, who was in combat with the Company across the state of Mysore. Yet again they escaped trouble apart from being robbed once, and after eight months on the road they were supplying the British public of Madras with pictures as busily as they had supplied their compatriots in Calcutta. On the proceeds of these sales they took ship to Bombay, spent a few weeks sketching in the town and its immediate vicinity, then headed home by way of China. They saw London again after nine and a half years which were remarkable whichever way they are looked at. For this tireless pair of craftsmen, this highly talented but otherwise very ordinary uncle and nephew, had equally wandered round a sub-continent which was known to be rife with various dangers from human beings, animals and disease, and they had come through all their experiences virtually unscathed. They had returned from a saga that they had reduced to the nearly homespun, yet the evidence they brought back with them was to English eyes exotic in the extreme. They had hundreds of pictures in their portfolios when they docked and before long these were not only hanging framed in fashionable English homes; they were also providing the motifs for other forms of decoration, from Staffordshire pottery to wallpaper. One way and another, the Daniells created a visual impression of India such as the British at home had never had before; this formed many of their distant attitudes, and it has lingered up to our own day.

Their arrival in Calcutta had coincided with that of a new Governor-General, and during those years when the Daniells were painstakingly sketching their way round India, Lord Cornwallis was preparing nothing less than a social revolution there. He was, at first sight, an unlikely figure to be following in the footsteps of Warren Hastings and to be continuing some of the ambitions that Hastings had held. Here, for the first time, was a British ruler who had not come up from the ranks in the service of the East India Company. Cornwallis was an aristocrat, a soldier who had begun his career as an ensign in His Majesty's First Regiment of Foot Guards, and his professional stock was still high after he had surrendered his forces to George Washington at Yorktown in the final act of the American War of Independence. It was William Pitt, appreciating qualities not always obvious in a defeated commander, who pressed him to accept the Governor-Generalship of India when Cornwallis would have much preferred to stay home and be what most of him was at heart: a country landowner with domestic political interests on the side. Pitt knew him to be a strong-minded zealot who had waged war in America not only on Yankees, but on Britons who had made outrageous profits from their contracts with the army. He was by breeding and application a lofty man, who came to India in the conviction that every native was irreversibly corrupt; that most of his fellow-countrymen were almost as defective, better only insofar as they might be civilized if one tried hard enough to propel them along the straight and narrow. While he was clearly not the fellow to duck military solutions, it is significant that in two periods of rule in India, amounting to nine years, he only once went to war, against Tipu Sultan in the campaign the Daniells had encountered in the south, and that was the residue of a long-running sore. Cornwallis, like Hastings before him, was not intent on expanding British interests in India; he was damned well going to knock into respectable shape what was already there.

He differed fundamentally and crucially from Hastings in his attitude to Indians, his predecessor having seen administration as something to be conducted in partnership with the natives. Cornwallis would have nothing to do with such nonsense and reversed an earlier decision that would have left much of the day to day business in the hands of the old Indian official class, who had been performing it since the Mughals arrived. With the exception of a single judge, all Indians were removed from high posts. At the same time, like the old-fashioned squire he really was, Cornwallis vowed that the conduct of his own men should be exemplary and he added extra rules to those included in the first Regulating Act, which finally and completely separated those Company officials engaged in trade from those having anything to do with the administration in any form. From now on the recruit could opt to serve in the commercial or the political sphere, but he couldn't have so much as a toenail in both. Nor could anyone other than a Member in Council or a humble writer come out to India as a result of patronage at home, all other offices from now on being filled by promotion and on ability from within the ranks of the presidency where vacancies occurred. Auditors were appointed to scrutinize all expenditure, and one Collector soon afterwards was warned that if he failed to submit his monthly accounts punctually, he'd be liable to instant dismissal. Cornwallis had, in effect, founded the Indian Civil Service which was to be the greatest ornament of the British Raj, though it would not be known as the ICS for another half century. He also continued a number of legal reforms that Hastings had started. There was still to be Hindu law for Hindus, Islamic law for Muslims, but many of the savage punishments the Mughals had introduced were now abolished, and in some respects Cornwallis left behind him a criminal code more humane than the one existing in England. And, for the first time in India, government itself was liable to be summoned before a court to answer for its activities, whether a charge was brought by a

European or a native. No form of authority known either to Hindus or Muslims had ever had to submit to such a thing before.

Nothing Cornwallis did, however, was to affect the life of Indians more than his approach to the method of collecting revenue in Bengal. This was traditionally based on the agricultural produce of the land, and in that sense it bore some resemblance to the old European custom of tithing income to the Church. It involved three parties; the peasant cultivator, the zamindar and the ruling authority. The zamindar was in every way the central figure in the operation, the landholder-cum-tax gatherer who squeezed out of the peasant as much as he could, passing on to the ruler only as much as he was forced to, armed retainers often being used in the transactions between all three. These relationships might be bruised by brutality but this never went beyond certain bounds of realism, there being little point in beating a peasant to death when his crops had failed, if only because that would result in a shortage of labour the following year; and it would be senseless to dispose of a zamindar who alone knew the potential wealth of a locality and how to extract it. There was, though, extreme uncertainty for the ruler about the annual expectation of revenue, which might vary according to the weather or the smartness of the zamindar in serving his own interests. But the Company had retained the system and many of its Nabobs had fattened themselves by screwing the zamindars for all they were worth in its name, to the ruin of some. Lord Cornwallis had little time for variable factors, even less for powerful people abusing the person and property of individuals. He decided that in future the revenue required by his government should be permanently fixed, based on the average paid over several previous years, and collected by his own officials who (he would make sure of this) would be absolutely incorruptible. The zamindar would be treated like an English country gentleman, yielding the same taxes year by year, with no opportunity to belabour the poor peasant for more than was just and at no risk of being thrashed himself for failure to supply an inflated demand. This new order in 1793 was to be known as the Permanent Settlement and Cornwallis thought, like the good Whig he was, that it would bring a fine stability to Bengal. He assured the Board of Control in London that the principal landowners would be

restored to such circumstances as to enable them to support their families with decency and to give a liberal education to their children . . . that a regular foundation of ranks may be supported which is nowhere more necessary than in this country for preserving order in civil society.

He formulated a new regulation for the Presidency, which surmised that land would become the most desirable of all property 'and the industry of the people will be directed to those improvements in agriculture which are as essential to their own welfare as to the prosperity of the state.' He hoped that waste land would be broken in and cultivated under his incentives. His Lordship had a benign and scrupulous vision of something he was familiar with on his own estates at home: an orderly rural society with acknowledged sequence of rank, in which every man would prosper strictly according to birthright and diligence. In Bengal it failed to come off, partly because it didn't make nearly enough allowance for the sometimes devastating effect on harvests of the Indian climate.

Under the old order, people might be the worse for wear if unable to tip up their dues but they had rarely been dispossessed of their place on the land, which was seen as their hereditary right. But now land became a commodity like opium, salt, textiles or anything else. Let anyone fail to pay the required revenue under the Permanent Settlement and his land would be put on the market to raise the necessary funds, or he would have to resort to the moneylender, which simply delayed his loss and made it more expensive in the end. A result was that the moneylender's grip on the country, which had always been pernicious, became deadlier than ever. Many of the old zamindars were ejected from their traditional position in the rural society and in their place came a rising breed of absentee landlord from Calcutta – Indians whose financial speculations had been placed on an unassailable footing when they were enlisted by Company traders to act as banians. A society which had already been seriously undermined by the steady decline of Mughal order and authority now lost one of the remaining forces which bound it to its past: the indigenous power of the traditional landowners, which embodied patronage and welfare as well as punishment and exploitation.

It is clear that Cornwallis never intended to damage Bengali society in such a way, but this happened all the same for a reason that would recur throughout the advance of the British across India – their assumption that what had worked in previous experiences would work in new ones. Their initial approach in Bombay had been modelled on what they already knew of Madras; they began to administer Benares on the basis of two decades in Bengal; when they got to the Punjab they would set about things as though they were dealing with the same social conditions they had just mastered in the North-Western Provinces. Often these assumptions were socially disastrous and always it took the British many years to realize that the habits of Indians were not remotely uniform across the country. India was certainly not the place where you could assume that what was time-honoured in rural Wiltshire would be feasible here. This was a sub-continent where fourteen major tongues and over 800 distinctly different dialects were spoken. There were not just the four great varnas, or social categories, that the strangers had quickly understood – the Brahmins (priests), the Kshatriyas (warriors), the Vaishyas (merchants), and the Shudras (servants). These levels were then subdivided into castes, something over 2,000 of them, with tortuous subtleties of occupation, breeding and domicile separating each, all loaded with perilous infringement and dire penalty. It was a long time after Lord Cornwallis before the British would finally appreciate that in almost every way of life the Punjab was less like Mysore, say, than Scotland was comparable to Spain.

Certainly no such nuances afflicted the vision of Lord Wellesley, whose rule straddled the turn of the eighteenth into the nineteenth century. His background was the Irish gentry with some small experience of Indian affairs on Pitt's Board of Control in London, and he was the first Governor-General to attach much importance to Sunday observance, to disabuse the natives of the notion that the British had no religion. But he came to India above all with a profound hostility to all by-products of the French Revolution, whose effects he had seen at first hand as a young man in Paris; the experience had turned him into a Francophobe, although he had lived with a Frenchwoman for nine years, and had children with her, before they married. Lord Wellesley arrived in Calcutta just as Napoleon's army was marching into Egypt and his imagination told him where Bonaparte might be heading for next. The French had not yet quit India – any more than had the Portuguese, the Dutch and some Danes – and in the south they were still flirting with Tipu Sultan in Mysore, as well as commanding 14,000 native troops in Hyderabad. Almost before he had his land legs again, Wellesley exchanged his Governor-General's hat for that of commander-in-chief and led an expedition south to put down potential French ambitions once and for all. In two short months he had defeated Tipu Sultan thrice and seen him die trying to defend his fortress at Seringapatam, had annexed half the state of Mysore and had placed the rest under the nominal rule of a client child-prince. For the first time, British control over South India was similar to that they had held in the north since Plassey forty-odd years before.

This was the opening phase in the great British expansion across India. Wellesley was an imperialist down to his spurred boot heels, even more than his young brother Arthur, the future Duke of Wellington, who was soon in India with him, fighting as a colonel in a campaign against the Marathas. Having blooded himself on Tipu's alliance with the French, Wellesley abandoned all pretext of saving British settlements from the far-fetched chance of Napoleonic invasion and went full tilt for British supremacy wherever it could be asserted and at anyone's expense. Fighting obstacles were battled into submission, helpless states were coolly annexed under treaties that offered protection but little else, states that were fearful of their neighbours were guaranteed independence provided they let the British run their external affairs. India was ripe for this plucking, as it had not been since the Mughals moved in. But Mughal power was finished. Although an Emperor still sat in the north, he was reduced now to the limitations of a minor Indian prince, his resources squandered, his might exhausted by successive invasions and revolts. Politically, India was back to where it had been in the twelfth century, a bundle of feudal territories with neighbours perpetually at odds, collectively little but an appetizing prospect for any acquisitive power that had cohesion and a disciplined army at its disposal. So Wellesley proceeded to satisfy his appetite, and his masters in London were now far too worried by the very real threat Napoleon was offering the whole of Europe to pay much attention to or to keep up with the rapid changes going on in India. Communications were still poor and Lord Wellesley's habit was to act first and seek confirmation afterwards. By the time the Government decided matters had gone much further than was advisable, and recalled Wellesley in 1805, the British stake in the sub-continent was enormous. The whole of the north-west – Sind, the Sikh lands and those of the Rajputs – was still untouched, as was a great tract of Maratha territory in the middle. Ceylon would not be totally a European colony until 1815. Otherwise India was almost evenly divided between British possession and the protected states.

It is tempting to pigeon-hole Wellesley as a freebooting adventurer on a grander scale than Clive's and consign him to the military essayist, but there was another side to him which played a significant part in the development of British India and the advance of the Indians themselves. He revealed it first in his anxiety for the character of junior Company employees in the alluring atmosphere of Calcutta. The city may have struck some people by now as a larger and steamier version of Bath, but it was throbbing with all manner of purely local species, from exorbitant moneylenders to beguiling nautch girls, that Lord Wellesley thought his young men, innocent from England, could well do without. He wished his writers to become reliable functionaries of administration and power, and he concluded that the best way of achieving this was 'to fix and establish sound and correct principles of religion and government in their minds at an early period of life'. He would therefore create on the banks of the Hooghly River something comparable to the ancient institutions of Oxford and Cambridge, and knowing that the Company Directors would tolerate no such fancy that cut into their profits, he would finance it from a levy on all the civil servants in India. So Fort William College arose, its teaching staff drawn not only from the growing number of British Orientalists but also from scholarly Brahmins who were starting to drift into the city from their ancestral properties in rural Bengal as the effects of the Permanent Settlement began to tell. Soon the young students were writing essays on such subjects as whether the Asiaticks (sic) were capable of as high a degree of civilization as the Europeans. They were sitting at the feet of Indians whose whole lives had been steeped in Sanskrit poetics, sacred literature and Puranic mythology. They were attending disputations in Indian languages on 'the best method of acquiring a knowledge of the manners and customs of the natives of India,' and these events were held in the gorgeous new Government House that Wellesley had built (without letting on to Leadenhall Street until it was necessary to present the bills) at a cost of £140,000.

By 1805 the Directors had decided that the European part of the curriculum was better presented in the English countryside before their recruits were exposed to the vices of Calcutta, and they created Haileybury College in Hertfordshire for this purpose. Boys were admitted there at the age of fifteen and for the next three years (apart from rudimentary instruction in Oriental languages) studied mathematics and natural philosophy, classical and general literature, law, history and political economy – this last under Thomas Malthus, who occupied the first chair in the subject ever known in the British Isles. But Fort William continued to function for another generation and in that time it became much more than a forcing house for loyal civil servants; it became a centre of Bengali literary patronage and a depot of linguistic research. In the first five years of its existence it published more than a hundred original works in oriental languages and by 1818 it boasted the largest collection of orientalia in the world: the Escorial had 1,851 volumes, Oxford 1,561, the Seraglio in Constantinople 7,294, but Calcutta then had a total of 11,335 printed and manuscript sources. In the process of all these activities it played an unpremeditated part in restoring to the Bengalis something of the self-esteem that Cornwallis had broken in 1793. Bright young Indians were involved at various levels in a number of the college's offshoot enterprises, like the Hindoostanee Press which the Urdu instructor John Gilchrist began, or the Calcutta School Book Society which one of Fort William's first students, William Bayley, inspired; and increasingly, local young men were engaged as assistants to the British and Bengali teaching staff alike.

From this stimulating atmosphere these youths emerged with a confidence that their fathers had just lost, and with it they embarked on a period in their people's history which has been glorified as the Bengal Renaissance. One of their leaders was Rammohan Roy, son of a newly impoverished zamindar, who fell under the spell of the British Orientalists and from them acquired many dizzying European notions about the rights of man and suchlike, which must have seemed rather inconsistent to him at first. But these caused him to write a famous tract denouncing suttee at a time when, in three consecutive years, a total of 983 women in Calcutta alone were known to have been burned alive with their husbands' corpses. He also launched a new Hindu sect which eventually evolved into the liberal Brahmo Samaj, started a school for both races, compiled a Bengali grammar, and lobbied Lord Wellesley to drop press censorship, which the Governor-General had imposed when he scented a whiff of revolutionary thought in the newsprint. Some twentieth-century Bengali scholars have with hindsight crowned Roy the Father of Modern India, which may be taking local pride too far. The importance of the Bengal Renaissance, however, is beyond any doubt. It was nothing less than the start of a racial pride that would develop the strongest opposition to British rule in India until Mahatma Gandhi, from the other side of the sub-continent, came along and marshalled forces that Indians have never dreamt of before. The ruler who detested the French Revolution above all things had unwittingly introduced his Indian subjects to its English apostle Thomas Paine. The conquering Lord Wellesley's apparatus for the production of reliable governors had begun a process of education that would lead one day to their downfall.

THREE

A MORAL DUTY
TO PERFORM

For all but a decade after Lord Wellesley left India there was a pause before the British resorted to arms again. Then they marched against the Gurkhas, an aggressive people who for years had raided the lands below the northern hills from their strongholds in Nepal. After four pitched battles spread over fourteen months, the two sides made a treaty that neither was ever to infringe in the slightest particular, and even before it was signed Gurkhas were enrolling to fight henceforth for the British. A few months later they were included in the army which began to put down once and for all the predatory Marathas, who had been everybody's foe on and off for two centuries and were now in alliance with the Pindaris, a large gang of marauders without tribal or religious allegiances, who responded to nothing but the chance to pillage, and worshipped only loot. By the spring of 1819 this formidable combination had been broken up for good and although it had surely provided the British with a pretext for further territorial gain, no other Indians were disposed to lament the defeat, least of all the Rajput states which had suffered most from the Marathas and now hastened to make treaties under which they could live peacefully in tribute, as at the height of Mughal power. As for the British administrators who moved into new districts lately ruled entirely by the sword, they were not so much exhilarated by their expanded power as depressed at the prospect of having to revive areas which had been wasting away under a long succession of wars. The officials who were installed in the territories Wellesley acquired had reacted in much the same way. The gradual decline of the Mughals and the accompanying struggles for local supremacy in the imperial twilight, had left much of India in physical decay and social disorder.

Thus began a period of British rule which in some ways is the most attractive one in the whole of their association with the sub-continent, certainly to the romantic. It is full of upstanding figures like Charles Metcalfe, Mountstuart Elphinstone, John Malcolm and Thomas Munro, whose rectitude was beyond anybody's patronage, whose courage in holding to principle was abnormal, and whose delight in working among Indians is infectious. Of these four – and there were many less exalted like them – Munro was the senior, having served under Cornwallis in his Mysore campaign before rising to be Governor of Madras. It was he who saved India from total submission to the Permanent Settlement, arguing that what might do for Bengal would not necessarily be suitable elsewhere. His policy was that the state's demand for tax should never exceed one third of the value of the land's produce, and that it should be collected directly from the peasant, not the landlord, making the cultivator feel he had a bigger stake in improving India's potential. London at last conceded Munro's point and allowed other revenue settlements to be made in keeping with local custom, though twentieth century scholars have attacked Munro's ryotwari system on the grounds that its chief effect was to reinforce the position of the dominant castes.

John Malcolm, who became Governor of Bombay, had a large contempt for bureaucratic remote control; dreading, he said, 'no human being (certainly no Nabob or Maharajah) half so much as an able Calcutta civilian, whose travels are limited to two or three hundred miles, with a hookah in his mouth, some good but abstract maxims in his head, the Regulations in his right hand, the Company's Charter in his left, and a quire of wire-woven foolscap before him.' Like Munro, he was one of the first Britons to understand that a ruler had to stay close to the people in India if he was to earn their respect and engage their loyalty. He used to tell with gusto a story against himself about the song his bearers once chanted as they carried him across country by palanquin:

There is a fat hog – a great fat hog – how heavy he is – hum – shake him – hum – shake him well – hum – shake the fat hog – hum.

Elphinstone, one of Fort William's first graduates, was a model of the civil servant in India who rambled around the countryside, cultivating acquaintances with village headmen, adjudicating on local boundary disputes, glorying in his paternal role and then settling down for the night beside the campfire with some calf-bound epic of the ancient Greeks or conversation about Hindu myth, consciously learning all the time. 'I shall think I have done a great service to this country', he wrote at the beginning of his career, 'if I can prevent people making laws for it until they see whether it wants them.' He did see himself as a dispenser of very rough justice, none the less, if laws were infringed. When some Brahmins in Poona plotted to murder all Europeans there, he had the ringleaders blown from the muzzles of field guns, declaring that this form of execution 'contains two valuable elements of capital punishment; it is painless to the criminal and terrible to the beholder.' If that sounds intolerably barbaric to our own sensitive ears, it is as well to remember that just before Elphinstone came along, the Marathas disposed of offenders in the same district by throwing them from a height on to a contraption of spikes.

Charles Metcalfe's attitude towards Indians is the most appealing of them all. He was an Etonian, a protégé of Wellesley, and Elphinstone's classmate at Fort William, who was given the chance to demonstrate his quality at the age of twenty-three, when he was sent to the Punjab as envoy to Ranjit Singh, the colourful leader of the Sikhs. Minus one eye, frequently stupefied on a mixture of alcohol, opium, meat juice and granulated pearls, possessor of the Koh-i-Nor diamond and an incalculable number of wives and concubines, Ranjit Singh may have been excessive in his private life but was remarkably moderate in his rule; and he had given his people a sense of nationhood which he was prepared to defend with a well-drilled army officered by mercenaries from half a dozen European countries. The likelihood of hostilities breaking out between such an independent fighter and the acquisitive British was high, but the young Englishman and the tribal warrior took to each other at once in a guarded sort of way and after six months made a treaty of mutual respect which held for a generation. Metcalfe's reward for this stripling diplomacy was to be Resident at Delhi by the time he was twenty-seven, nominally the Governor-General's representative at the Mughal Emperor's court, but as the Emperor himself was only a nominal figure now, effectively governor of an area half the size of England. And here his talents were demonstrated to the full. He satisfied his masters by raising the revenue nearly fourfold in a couple of years, eschewing the Bengal method and encouraging men who had lived by the sword to break in new ground for agriculture, which produced more tax. He stopped the death penalty in his province and instead of having petty thieves whipped, he had them trained to do more acceptable things with their hands. As Philip Woodruff has remarked, it is possible to say 'that in some ways the Delhi administration was the most enlightened in the world. In England men could be hanged for a forty-shilling theft; the United States were still to permit slavery for another fifty years. But there was no hanging in Delhi and no selling of slaves.' Yet of all Metcalfe's gifts, none is more striking than his realism when he contemplated the relationship between the British and Indians as a whole. He had become very wise and senior in the apparatus of the Raj when he wrote this:

Our dominion in India is by conquest; it is naturally disgusting to the inhabitants and can only be maintained by military force. It is our positive duty to render them justice, to respect and protect their rights, and to study their happiness. By the performance of this duty, we may allay and keep dormant their innate dissatisfaction; but the expectation of purchasing their cordial attachment by gratuitous alienations of public revenue would be a vain delusion . . .

One would need to be no more than a healthy sceptic to decide that the undiluted testimony and conclusion of Britons about other Britons, ought to be divided at least by two in order to come somewhere near the truth of the matter. The fact is, though, that voices beyond suspicion of patriotic pleading are to be heard applauding the manner in which the conquerors behaved in the first quarter of the nineteenth century, when they took most of India under their control. Victor Jacquemont, the French botanist who saw much of the country between Calcutta and Bombay, marvelled at the energy of the British and added this:

The English who inspire so much respect in the natives by their power, strength, wealth and morality (always true to their word, upright and just ninety-nine times out of a hundred) who . . . receive from them so many Asiatically servile demonstrations of respect and submission, the English are the only European people that do not take pleasure in these marks of respect. They esteem themselves too highly, they despise the coloured races too much to be flattered by their homage . . .

His compatriot the Abbé Dubois, after thirty years in India, wrote in 1823,

The justice and prudence which the present rulers display in endeavouring to make these people less unhappy than they have been hitherto; the anxiety which they manifest in increasing their material comfort; above all, the inviolable respect which they constantly show for the customs and religious beliefs of the country; and, lastly, the protection which they afford to the weak as well as to the strong . . . all these have contributed more to the consolidation of their power than even their victories and conquests.

Well, perhaps Europeans did stick together in Asia when they were not fighting each other, and the Abbé was certainly wrong in suggesting that the British left all Indian customs alone, as we shall see. But Indian voices, too, spoke well of their new rulers from time to time. Rammohan Roy's was among them in the same year as the French priest's:

Thanks to the Supreme Disposer of events of this universe, for having unexpectedly delivered this country from the long-continuing tyranny of its former rulers and placed it under the government of the English – a nation who are not only blessed with the enjoyment of civil and national liberty, but also interest themselves in promoting liberty and social happiness . . . among those nations to which their influence extends.

Rather fulsome and a bit sweeping, perhaps, from someone who had not seen other nations under British influence. But ten years later, when he was dying, Roy was of much the same mind when he considered how the British themselves had changed since the days when they dispossessed his father of his land:

Finding them generally more intelligent, more steady and moderate in their conduct, I gave up my prejudices against them and became inclined in their favour, feeling persuaded that their rule, though a foreign yoke, would lead most speedily and surely to the amelioration of the native inhabitants.

Now that has the ring of truth.

There had been another renewal of the Company's charter in 1813 and the changing attitude of the Government towards India is reflected in three stipulations it made before allowing Leadenhall Street to continue in business for a further twenty years. The most drastic by far was an end to the Company's monopoly on everything but the China tea trade, for novel theories of political economy now dominated British thinking with the widest possible commercial support. The new India Act also ordered that £10,000 should be spent on education on the sub-continent, a sum which seems less mean when it is recalled that Government spent nothing at all on education in Britain until 1833, when £20,000 was voted for the schools. The third requirement was that the Church of England should at last be established in India with a senior staff of three archdeacons and one bishop – Thomas Middleton to begin with, who laid the foundations well enough for Reginald Heber, following him, to be much gratified that his hymn 'From Greenland's icy mountains/From India's coral strand' was already extant in Bengali.

There had been clergymen in India for many years before the Anglicans officially moved in, but they had been Company chaplains restricted to the cure only of British souls. Missionary activity had been expressly forbidden until Lord Wellesley, of all people, suddenly began to patronize six Baptists who sailed up the Hooghly River in 1800 in defiance of the ban. Two of them, Fountain and Ward, actually had police records at home for supporting the French Revolution, and Wellesley would certainly have clapped them in gaol if they had not dropped anchor upstream of Calcutta at the Danish settlement of Serampore. He changed his mind, full of his plans for Fort William, when he discovered that Ward was a trained printer and that William Carey, the Baptist leader, had a flair for Indian languages which he had picked up in a previous existence as an indigo planter. Before long Carey was on the teaching staff at Fort William and Ward's presses at Serampore were able to print anything Wellesley wanted in Bengali, Urdu, Oriya, Tamil, Telegu, Kanarese or Marathi. Evangelism, however, remained a touchy subject until Lord Wellesley had left, and by then Christian fervour was issuing from several other quarters besides the Baptists. The first whiff of missionary zeal had come from the pen of Charles Grant, who had worked under Hastings and Cornwallis in Bengal, had taken to religion seriously when he lost two children to smallpox, and had returned to England, where he became a Company Director. Two years after leaving India in 1790, he had written a tract with a resounding conclusion which was to have much influence at home: 'Upon the whole, then, we cannot avoid recognizing in the people of Hindostan a race of men lamentably degenerate and base, retaining but a feeble sense of moral obligation . . . and sunk in misery by their vices.' This was the opening shot in a debate which became something of a national obsession the moment the Napoleonic threat to Europe had ended and the British could address themselves fully to the question which loomed large as a result of Wellesley's conquests: having acquired this gigantic new property in India, what on earth do we do with it?

The growing band of free traders at home were perfectly clear about the purpose of India in the British scheme of things. It was to serve their commerce, which had been hamstrung for far too long by the Company's monopoly there, and the country should be developed on sound Western principles so that Rajas and zamindars might learn to live in homes furnished with British products, while peasants could ape their European counterparts once they had the money to buy the smaller necessities of life from British workshops and mills. 'Under these circumstances', said a spokesman of free market forces in 1813, 'a trade might suddenly grow up beyond the Cape of Good Hope, to take off all the surplus manufactures that Britain can produce.' The strategists, too, knew what India's role must be every time they looked at the map. It must be a military base and springboard to counteract Russian imperialism, which was about to take over where French ambitions had failed; and they would remind anyone scoffing at this idea that in 1807 Napoleon and the Czar Alexander had met at Tilsit to discuss a joint operation against our possessions in India. But the crux of the debate was a secondary matter to the tradesmen and stiffly ignored altogether by most of the strategists. It was to do with the Indian way of life and the degree to which the British should attempt to change not just its household arrangements, but its very nature.

A key figure in the discussion was Jeremy Bentham, and it is easy to see how a sub-continent with a vast population would interest a man whose philosophy was dedicated to the greatest happiness of the greatest number of people. In 1793 he had let it be known that he was more than willing to help in reforming the law system of India, and in due course gaols were built at Poona and Ratnagiri based on Bentham's proposed Panopticon, the model penitentiary in which the warders could at all times keep an eye on the prisoners. He corresponded with Rammohan Roy about judicial reform, and books expounding all aspects of his Utilitarian ideals were placed on the curriculum at Haileybury as soon as the Company college was opened. They were soon joined by a six-volume history of India written by another Utilitarian who, like Bentham, never went near the sub-continent in person. He was James Mill, an indigent journalist who began to compose this epic in order to improve his circumstances; as it did. The Company offered him a job as a result and he rose to a senior position which was occupied after him by his son John Stuart Mill, though the younger man seems to have regarded it as nothing but a bread and butter job while he developed his own theories on liberty and other social ideals within a European framework. But James Mill had passionate opinions about India and they were mostly scathing about the state of native society there, which he saw as a Hindu despotism with little to be said for it by civilized man. Indeed, the whole thrust of the Utilitarian approach to India was, as Professor Stokes pointed out, identical with that of French colonizers who embarked later on *la mission civilisatrice* in Africa and Indo-China.

The physical and mental distance separating East and West was to be annihilated by the discoveries of science, by commercial intercourse, and by transplanting the genius of English laws and English education. It was the attitude of English liberalism in its clear, untroubled dawn . . .

Mill's passion was shared by members of another movement which did more to mould a stereotyped English mentality in the nineteenth century – we have known it as the Victorian attitude – than any other. This was the Evangelical revival, whose source lies in the preaching of Wesley and Whitefield from the 1750s on, and whose beliefs had climbed into the upper middle classes within a few decades. For Anglicans its focal point was the well-to-do Clapham Sect, whose leaders lived near each other in the same part of London, and among these, by the turn of the century, were Charles Grant and Sir John Shore, who had both been advisers of Cornwallis in formulating the Permanent Settlement, Shore succeeding him as Governor-General before Wellesley. Another prominent Claphamite was William Wilberforce, leader of the fight against the slave-trade wherever it operated and member of seventy different organizations pledged to end moral corruption in England, who declared that the conversion of India to Christianity was 'that greatest of all causes, for I really place it before Abolition.' He told the House of Commons in 1813, in the debate which preceded the new India Act, that he saw the sub-continent as a place which would 'exchange its dark and bloody superstition for the genial influence of Christian light and truth', the gods of the Hindus being 'absolute monsters of lust, injustice, wickedness and cruelty. In short, their religion is one grand abomination.' The general level of Claphamite discourse on the subject of India was steadfastly maintained at this saintly height, though Charles Grant had ventured to come down to earth in the tract he composed in 1792. After enlarging on the degeneracy of Hindostan and the saving graces of Christianity, he surmised that 'In every progressive step of this work, we shall also serve the original design with which we visited India, that design so important to this country – the extension of our commerce.'

A number of British voices were raised against the potent combination of Evangelicals and Utilitarians. In London they included those of Warren Hastings the reconciler and, more surprisingly, Lord Wellesley the conqueror. In India opposition came from the entire body of Orientalists, who had been immersing themselves in the native culture for the best part of a generation when the Company charter was due for renewal in 1813, and liked a great deal of what they had discovered. They would not quibble with some of the propositions put forward from the other camp; the Evangelical enthusiasm for education and the earnest desire to serve mankind which came from the same direction, or the sharper Benthamite principle of personal responsibility, accountability and inspectability which would propel many an Englishman and Scot through India in the years to come. But the Orientalists drew the line at much else that was being uttered seven thousand miles away and would soon be imposed from the Himalaya to Ceylon. They denounced Mill's history as the work of a bigot, and one lacking all scholarship at that. A member of the Asiatic Society, Colonel Stewart, published a pamphlet entitled *Vindications of the Hindoos, by a Bengal Officer*, which suggested that 'Hinduism little needs the meliorating hand of Christianity to render its votaries a sufficiently correct and moral people for all the useful purposes of a civilized society', and remarked that

Whenever I look around me, in the vast region of Hindoo Mythology, I discover piety in the garb of allegory: and I see Morality, at every turn, blended with every tale; and, as far as I can rely on my own judgment, it appears the most complete and ample system of Moral Allegory that the world has ever produced.

Even the Baptist William Carey resisted the notion advanced by the Evangelicals at home, that indigenous learning should be completely replaced by European knowledge taught in English. His Serampore colleague Joshua Marshman put forward the first detailed proposals for public education in India, whose object was not so much to degrade Hindu civilization as to undermine the religious elitism of the Brahmins. In 1818 he began to publish *Dag Darsan* (Magazine for Indian Youth), which was distributed free to the students of the new

Hindu College in Calcutta and informed them of European history in Bengali. It was a modest, almost a disinterested adjunct of the college's curriculum, which promoted a mixed culture and had been sponsored by British Orientalists and upper caste Hindus, twenty of whom had drawn up the foundation's charter. Within a few years Horace H. Wilson, East India Company physician and distinguished philologist, was to establish the companion Sanskrit College in the city, which taught the traditional Indian topics of rhetoric, sacred literature, law and grammar, as well as a Western schedule of science which included mechanics, hydrostatics, optics, astronomy, chemistry, mathematics, anatomy and medicine. Nothing illustrates better what the Orientalists in general were driving at.

The battle over cultural supremacy was fought, won and lost during the Indian career of Lord William Bentinck, which extended – with a great gap in the middle when he was occupied elsewhere – from 1803 to 1835. Lord William was from the Whig aristocracy, the second son of a Prime Minister (the Duke of Portland) and an ardent disciple of Edmund Burke, that compelling orator who could simultaneously be horrified by the effects of the French Revolution, gratified by the American War of Independence against the British, and deeply critical of Company rule in India. Bentinck went East when he was twenty-nine, to be Governor of Madras under Wellesley, whose views to a large extent he shared, including many of their inconsistencies. He had a low opinion of the Company Directors, but insulated himself from Indian advice. He was keen on the idea of Fort William College and sent many of his young men there for training, though he saw little point in their learning Sanskrit, which he thought a useless dead language. He persevered with Munro's form of revenue collection and viewed the oppression of the peasant, whether by Company Collector or Indian Raja, with much distaste. He believed in British glory in India, but it must be based on Indian *happiness* – that elusive idea again, which Rousseau had unleashed, which Jefferson had embraced, which Bentham was propagating, and which the improving British administrators in India were now uttering and pursuing all the time. Bentinck in Madras was priggishly eager to establish British integrity and vowed to 'keep down persons of power and influence, and to make comfortable the lower orders . . .' He was busily making a policy of this when, in 1806, the Indian sepoys at the garrison of Vellore mutinied and killed 114 British officers and men. The reason was a new regulation the local military commander had introduced to smarten up his troops, which involved the removal of caste marks from the face and the shaving of beards, as well as the wearing of a new-style turban with a leader cockade. After a court martial nineteen mutineers were executed and the rest set free. A few months later the Directors – who had heard of Lord William's low opinion of them once too often – used Vellore as an excuse to recall him to England on the grounds of negligence.

For the next twenty-one years, while Indian affairs stumbled on without him, Bentinck was engaged in a variety of tasks. He was appointed British Minister to Sicily and Commander-in-Chief, Mediterranean, which meant that he was proconsul charged with kneading an uncertain ally into shape. He sat in the House of Commons but hardly ever spoke there. For ten of the twenty-one years he worked hard as an enlightened country landowner and played a leading part in the reclamation of the East Anglian Fen country, with a great programme of ditching, draining and building roads. By 1828, political and Directorial power groupings had changed enough for Bentinck to be restored to India, this time as Governor-General of the whole country. He went with a battle cry ringing in his ears, of which he had no need. 'We have a great moral duty to perform in India', was the instruction of Lord Ellenborough, President of the Board of Control, and Bentinck knew it with both head and heart, having developed into a Benthamite with moderate Evangelical tastes. Morality hallmarked everything he did in the next seven years.

The Company was enduring one of its periodic spasms of financial difficulty when Bentinck sailed and his first act was to cut down on British allowances as an economy, which made for unpopularity at once. A few pockets of corruption were still to be found, usually among the Residents at princely courts, and he ruthlessly weeded these out, sacking Mordaunt Ricketts from Lucknow and Sir Edward Colebrooke from Delhi. Rank and file Company soldiers, on the other hand, had good cause for gratitude when he abolished the punishment of flogging – something that wouldn't be lifted from the British Army at home or elsewhere in the world for another fifty years. Bentinck also instituted an imaginative scheme of public works, drawing on the enthusiasm and know-how he had built up during that decade in the Fens. He made a start on the Grand Trunk Road that would eventually link Calcutta and Delhi, ordering it to be built 1ft 6in above the highest flood level at any point and the plantation of trees throughout its length at intervals of 60ft on both sides of the metalled surface. He put his weight behind a new plan to run steamboats on the Ganges and, within weeks of his return to India, watched the inaugural departure of the *Hoogly*, with her side paddles and her 30 tons of fuel, for Allahabad 787 miles away. Soon, improved versions of the craft were running to a timetable between the two cities. Outward-bound from Calcutta, much of their cargo consisted of wages for the imperial soldiery stationed along the river's banks (though occasionally, because bribery was intolerable, there would be large packages described on the bill of lading as 'valuable presents being returned to Nawab of Oudh'). Coming downstream, the steamers were liable to be loaded with more money, this time the land revenue collected from Indians, which was helping to pay for the public works and the now extensive schemes of education.

In his attitude to Indians, Bentinck's first notions were modified. He had arrived with the Evangelical reflex about the degradation of Hindu civilization and proceeded to attack Hindu society at two of its most vulnerable points. He conducted an inquiry into the practice of suttee, in the course of which he canvassed Bengali opinion on widow-burning, finding some in favour of its abolition, others totally opposed to any infringement of the ancient tradition. Then he prohibited it forever in British India, standing pat on the dictum that innocent blood must not be shed; but in the same declaration stating that 'I disown . . . any view whatever to conversion to our own faith. I write and feel as a legislator for the Hindus, and as I believe many enlightened Hindus feel and think.' After that he turned to Thugee, which had bedevilled central India for years, though the British had been unaware of it until they discovered that some of their sepoys, going on leave from various garrisons in ones and twos, had never reached home, had simply vanished. In fact, in every case, they had fallen in en route with a party of apparently innocent travellers moving in the same direction. And on the second or third night of the journey with their new acquaintances, when everything was hail-fellow-well-met around the campfire, someone would signal surreptitiously in the darkness and the sepoys would be strangled from behind with a cloth that had knotted into one of its corners, to give a better grip, a silver coin consecrated to the goddess Kali. Then their bodies would be tipped into a grave that had been dug while they were sharing the evening meal with their fellow travellers, who were all Thugs. Sepoys weren't the only people to disappear in this way; any Indian was liable to be murdered on the road, whether he was connected with the British or not; and, while every strangled corpse was always robbed, the object of the killing was ritual religious sacrifice. Bentinck put young Captain Sleeman to stamping it out, which he eventually did, and not until he was well into his long detective work was the full extent of Thugee apparent to the British. Sleeman caught one man who admitted to 719 strangulations with his own hands, and there were many not far behind that awful tally. In five years more than 3,000 Thugs were convicted after trial in British courts, and the only evidence regarded as conclusive by Bentinck's judges was that provided by 'approvers', people who had themselves served in the gangs. These approvers were so numerous in the end that a special gaol for them had to be built at Jubbulpore, to safeguard them against the vengeance of old associates. Some Thugs were sentenced to hanging, others were transported to penal settlements for life. Forty or fifty gangs of them had been at work, strangling maybe twenty or thirty thousand travellers a year – the overall figures were never more than roughly guessed.

It was the same Bentinck who, while systematically eradicating two extremities of Hindu practice, could be seen even by Hindus as a tremendously liberal figure in his policies towards Indians. Believing it essential, in morality as well as in imperial expediency, that the natives should be trusted more and paid better, he proposed a clause in the Company's 1833 Charter Act admitting Indians to the covenanted ranks of the Company for the first time, opening the way for them to become senior civil servants like any Briton. The Directors carefully neglected to implement the clause but did quadruple the salaries of Indian judges, which Bentinck would have raised tenfold had he been given his own way. Blocked from promoting Indians into the formal hierarchy of the Raj, he fostered their unofficial advance wherever he could, by appointing them to committees controlling education and by recommending them to the uncovenanted but none the less influential judicial and administrative posts such as honorary magistrate and deputy collector of revenue. And for a man who in part had subscribed to the condescending generalizations of Wilberforce and the other Claphamites, he was quite remarkably free from colour prejudice, going out of his way to make personal friendships in particular with Eurasians of mixed blood, who were shunned more often than not by full-blooded members of the two races that had created them. Astonishingly – in view of what would never be accomplished, what was not even to be thought of by the bulk of the British who followed him – it seems that Bentinck had some vision of a future in which large numbers of people would emigrate from home and in which intermarriage with Indians would become the rule instead of an increasingly rare exception. Two years after he left India for good, depressed by his awareness that the British were still strangers in the land – something to do with human nature, beyond the statistic that there were fewer than 40,000 of them in the midst of 150 million natives – he said this to Parliament in London:

In many respects the Mohammedans surpassed our rule; they settled in the countries which they conquered; they intermixed and intermarried with the natives; they admitted them to all privileges; the interests and sympathies of the conquerors and conquered became identified. Our policy has been the reverse of this; cold, selfish and unfeeling; the iron hand of power on the one side, monopoly and exclusion on the other.

By then the cultural pattern in which the British would try to mould India had been pretty well settled, and the man who had sealed the wax on this aspect of her fate was Thomas Babington Macaulay. Here was someone with the most severe antecedents possible, Scottish Presbyterian forebears having produced, in his father Zachary, a pillar of the slave trade abolition movement and the Clapham Sect. Young Tom, however, came gaudier than either the Highlands or the Evangelicals normally bred. As a Cambridge undergraduate he was marked as a brilliant star with a gift for expressing a dramatic imagination in vivid, sometimes intoxicating, language. There hadn't been a day when he wasn't learned beyond his years, and he had a prodigious appetite for work which he had variously satisfied as an essayist for the *Edinburgh Review*, as a student at the Bar, and in the House of Commons. He had made influential speeches on the Reform Bill in 1832 and in the East India Company charter debate the following year, when he spoke as Secretary of the Board of Control. He had, on that occasion, looked forward to

the proudest day in English history. To have found a great people sunk in the lowest depths of slavery and superstition, to have so ruled them as to have made them desirous and capable of all the privileges of citizens, would indeed be a title to glory all our own . . . there are triumphs which are followed by no reverse. There is an empire exempt from all natural causes of decay. Those triumphs are the pacific triumphs of reason over barbarism; that empire is the imperishable empire of our arts and our morals, our literature and our laws.

With his colours thus nailed firmly to his masthead, he sailed for India early in 1834 with one of his sisters as companion, to be the Fourth Member on Bentinck's Supreme Council, specifically charged with legislation. It was a new post created by the fresh charter act and he saw it as one that made him 'the guardian of the people of India against the European settlers'. He approached it with zest but at the same time made no bones about a different satisfaction that lay ahead. For all his industry and brilliance, Macaulay in 1834 was almost penniless and hoped that he would be able to save enough from his new salary to put financial worries behind him when he returned to London. It was the reason he had accepted the job.

Before reaching Calcutta, he left the East Indiaman at Madras and proceeded inland to meet Bentinck, who for health reasons was staying at Ootacamund, 7,000 feet up in the Nilgiri Hills. Finding that time hung heavy between discussions with his chief and discoveries of the local life, he began to write *The Lays of Ancient Rome* up there (and would return home three and a half years later, after discharging a heavy workload in India, with the manuscript almost finished and plans for his *History of England* beginning to take shape). A few weeks later, sailing up the east coast to the British capital, he diverted himself by learning Portuguese and reading the *Lusiads* twice. It was not the best preparation for what was to come but Macaulay, open as few people were to all forms of what he identified as civilization, had a mind curiously half-closed to anything else. He would shortly battle vigorously for the abolition of press censorship in India – used in Bombay and Madras against the European proprietors of radical English-language papers – and for the passing of a so-called Black Act, which removed a privilege that Europeans had over Indians in law, a matter of appeals to higher courts. In championing this last cause, he was threatened with lynching by a white mob in Calcutta. Yet while he was engaged in drafting both those enlightened measures, he was also beginning to scribble his famous Minute on the subject of Indian education, which powerfully demonstrated a philistine streak.

The great debate by this time had narrowed down to a purist one about the scope and the means of education. On one side the Orientalists argued that Indians should study their classical languages not only because these were enriching in themselves as an access to tradition, but because a knowledge of them – closely linked as they were to the vernacular tongues – was indispensable if anyone was to have a hope of comprehending Western science and general knowledge without a high proficiency in English. On the other side the Anglicizers, while conceding the usefulness of vernacular languages, ridiculed the argument in favour of classical teaching and suggested that any Indian youth who wished to study the *Bhagavad Gita* in full would get just as much out of it if the original Sanskrit were transliterated into the Roman alphabet. They looked to the day when English would not just be the talent of a highly qualified elite but, with the vernaculars, the native language of the whole sub-continent. Although he never had the high contempt of some for the Indian classics, Lord William Bentinck shared this notion. So did Macaulay's future brother-in-law, Charles Trevelyan, who was deputy secretary in the political department of the Government in Calcutta, and whose vision went beyond even Lord William's thoughts on intermarriage. 'The existing connection between two such distant countries as England and India,' wrote Trevelyan in 1838,

cannot, in the nature of things, be permanent; no effect of policy can prevent the natives from ultimately regaining their independence. But there are two ways of arriving at this point . . . One must end in the complete alienation of mind and separation of interests between ourselves and the natives; the other in a permanent alliance, founded on mutual benefit and goodwill . . .

No Englishman before him had been as prescient as that.

Mindful of his new Member's literary reputation, Bentinck invited Macaulay to preside over the education committee which was wrangling on the cultural issue. Macaulay was being asked to adjudicate on the two schools of thought, both of which were represented on the committee, and nominally he was re-interpreting the intention behind the educational clause in the India Act of twenty-odd years before. With this brief he produced a document which illustrated his most conspicuous gift and his glaring, arrogant deficiency. He had not found one Orientalist, he said, 'who could deny that a single shelf of a good European library was worth the whole native literature of India and Arabia.' He believed he was not exaggerating when he said that 'all the historical information which has been collected from all the books written in the Sanskrit language is less valuable than what may be found in the most paltry abridgements used at preparatory schools in England.' In his central statement of belief, he ventured to suggest that

> The question now before us is simply whether, when it is in our power to teach the [English] language, we shall teach languages in which . . . there are no books on any subject which deserve to be compared to our own . . . whether, when we can patronize sound philosophy and true history, we shall countenance at the public expense medical doctrines which would disgrace an English farrier, astronomy which would move laughter in girls at an English boarding school, history abounding with kings 30 feet high and reigns 30,000 years long, and geography made up of seas of treacle and rivers of butter?

There was little doubt which way the debate would have gone in the end, even without Macaulay's intervention. With it, there was none at all. On reading the Minute, Bentinck declared that 'the great object of the British Government ought to be the promotion of European literature and science among the natives of India.' Three years later, forty seminaries for the teaching of English were open to boys of all castes in Bengal alone, and the Calcutta Book Society had sold over 30,000 English texts in even shorter time. At the new Hooghly College, 1,100 students were attending the English faculty, only 300 the Oriental. And even Macaulay was seeing a danger in this headlong pursuit of Western culture. 'We mean these youths,' he said, 'to be conductors of knowledge to the people, and it is of no use to fill the conductors with knowledge at one end, if you separate them from the people at the other.' But the thing was done, and a new and revolutionary force had been released for good or ill.

He did, in fact, fulfil his small vanity about acting as guardian of India's people. He gave the very best of himself in drawing up, virtually single-handed, a new penal code which exhibited humane principle, common sense, clarity, remarkable knowledge and the boundless energy of its author. When Macaulay arrived in Calcutta, the country still laboured under a patchwork of justice derived from Hindu law, Islamic law and Company regulations that varied from one presidency to another. The corruption of witnesses was commonplace among Indians, particularly in matters relating to land and property, and punishments meted out by the British were often different from place to place: a petty offence (selling stamps without a licence) might incur only a fine in Bengal, but would result in a short prison sentence in Madras and up to five years plus corporal punishment in Bombay. Macaulay's first objective was to overhaul the whole system and he began by composing a minute with the axiom 'Uniformity where you can have it; diversity where you must have it; but in all cases, certainty.' It argued for a reduction in the variety of courts, it accepted that native judges were far more competent to assess the evidence of natives than British lawyers, it was adamant that pleading henceforth must be oral and that all witnesses must be examined in person by judges in open court, instead of being allowed to submit depositions which were well known to be frequently perjured. A great deal of what Macaulay proposed in the minute was innovation, but it was nothing to what he advocated when he turned to the criminal code.

He drafted this in two years of working flat out (though somehow he managed to write a long essay on Francis Bacon at the same time) and he drew on a variety of precedents, including the Code Napoleon, which had taken nine years to compile, and Livingston's Louisiana Code, which had been four and a half years in the making. 'It is indeed', he wrote to someone when he was half way through, 'one of the finest employments of the intellect that it is easy to conceive'. Every imaginable subject was covered in Macaulay's finished work: offences against the state and against public tranquillity; the abuse of powers by public servants and the contempt of lawful authority; offences relating to revenue, weights and measures, public health, religion and caste; illegal entrance to property and illegal pursuit of legal rights; breach of contracts, defamation, criminal intimidation; and, of course, murder, assault and theft. The death penalty was to be restricted to murder and treason, flogging and the pillory were to disappear.

From start to finish the work was meticulously done, with sources carefully quoted at every turn – and they came in several languages. Whenever possible, Macaulay illustrated a point by drawing on his colossal general knowledge, so that readers of his code incidentally learned how Sir Joshua Reynolds would take old pictures to bits to discover the secrets of colouring, how many famous assassins failed to kill some of their victims because they invariably thrust the blade at the heart but found it deflected by bone, how Indian craftsmen sometimes counterfeited the mark of Sheffield cutlers on knives and forks they had made themselves. Macaulay doubtless enjoyed showing off his erudition in these asides, but every illustration was there to make unmistakably plain a technicality which might otherwise have been obscure to some. Not a trace of jargon was to be found in the text, which was worded simply throughout and reduced a mountain of law and the reasoning behind it to 200 pages of octavo clearly set out. That alone was something to marvel at. So was the compassion and understanding that went into it. Whatever his faults paraded in the Education Minute, Macaulay showed none of them in his penal code. The legal document demonstrated total respect for Indian customs, whether these concerned the Muslim insistence on purdah, or the Hindu fixation with caste. It firmly distinguished between murder and euthanasia and demanded a smaller penalty for the second than for the first. It pointed out rampant inequities in Western societies ('A woman is entitled to reparation for a breach of promise of marriage, but to none for a rape.') and in suggesting the right of a woman to own property in her own person it introduced to India a law that the British wouldn't catch up with at home for another forty-five years.

The code was distributed to the senior judges throughout India when it was completed and, though their opinions differed on some points, the general verdict was that it should be adopted with some minor modifications. It then had to be ratified in London where, the processes of politicians and lawyers being what they were, adjudication took much longer. It would not be enacted until 1860, but from that time on it was the law of the land. Lord Macaulay therefore didn't live to hear of its effect on the sub-continent where he had spent a few hectic, ambivalent years. Soon after he had finished drafting his code he took passage to England, for which he had pined all the time he was away, and where he would spend the rest of his bachelor life in the financial security his Calcutta savings had partly produced.

FOUR

HIGH NOON

The emphasis on Christian morality didn't prevent the British from taking more territory under their wing in the years after Bentinck and Macaulay had gone, though their first attempt to do so led to one of the biggest disasters in military history – an inauspicious start to the young Queen Victoria's reign. It was prompted by those strategic anxieties – especially Lord Palmerston's – about Russian intentions towards India, which were manifestly uncertain to say the least. Before long the two powers would be at each other's throats in the Crimean War. The Great Game for big stakes in Asia, which was played intermittently throughout the nineteenth century and into the twentieth, had them facing each other first across the buffer zone of Afghanistan, and the Russians were thought to be pressing the local ruler Dost Mohammed for concessions that, if given, would clearly pave the way for the Czar's troops to pour south over the Hindu Kush, as the Mughal invaders had come.[1] So in 1839 an immense British army set off to forestall the threat by removing Dost Mohammed from his throne, which they did, packing him off to exile in India and installing the puppet Shah Shuja in his place. They had been through this procedure many times before, and once again the bulk of the army withdrew after its conquest, a Resident was appointed to manipulate the puppet King, and a few hundred British settled down to make what they could of the new posting in Kabul. But Afghanistan proved much less biddable than other annexed states and tribesmen in the countryside never quit fighting on a small scale – a skirmish here and there in broad daylight, a sentry knifed at the dead of night, soldiers potted off by marksmen in ones and twos from the surrounding hills. Two years after the capital

---

[1] The British played the Game from two different viewpoints. The administrators in India saw the Russian threat as one that might foment trouble on the sub-continent. The London Government, while not indifferent to this, saw any increase in Russian power and influence as a threat to Britain's European interests.

was taken, Kabul rose against the invaders with such ferocity that the British there accepted a truce and promised to withdraw under a guarantee of safe passage. Early in 1842 the retreat of 700 Britons, 3,800 Indian sepoys and their camp-followers – 16,500 people in all – began across the snowbound mountain wastes; and from the moment they left the shelter of their besieged cantonment in Kabul, they were under attack. For a week the column staggered on towards safety, shortening almost by the hour as bands of horsemen swept on them in waves, slashing people down in dozens at a time, knocking more off with musketry at night as the survivors lay exhausted and terrified. On the fourth day some women and their husbands were offered safe conduct, accepted it and disappeared (but would be found alive a year later in an Afghan fort). By the fifth day, when 12,000 had been killed, there were hardly any soldiers left in the column. On the sixth day the Afghans called a parley, and slaughtered almost all who remained as the British and Indians waited for talk to start. Ten days after the retreat began, just one person was left out of the 16,500 who had abandoned Kabul – Surgeon William Brydon, of the Army Medical Corps, who reached the British fortress at Jalalabad on a half-dead horse, a deliverance that was to be immortalized in a large painting which still stirs imperial emotions at the Tate Gallery today.

The following year the British took the adjacent province of Sind, and Mountstuart Elphinstone, retired in England, put that conquest in perspective when he remarked that it had been made in the spirit of 'a bully who has been kicked in the streets and goes home to beat his wife in revenge.' Although Sir Charles Napier did not send the Latin signal that was long associated with his name, he did utter one memorable sentiment when Brahmins newly under his power protested against the order banning suttee which, they declared, was the custom of their nation. 'My nation also has a custom,' replied Napier. 'When men burn women alive, we hang them . . . Let us all act according to national customs.' After Sind it was the turn of the Punjab, but something very curious happened there. This was tribally and religiously a strangely mixed area, a hotchpotch of Hindus and Muslims who might equally think of themselves as Rajput or Jat, Gujar or Pathan. It was also the home of the warrior Sikhs, whose religion was a refinement of Hinduism with a monotheistic tendency owing something to the influence of Islam. When that powerful man Ranjit Singh died in 1839, rival chiefs instantly went to war with each other in the normal struggle for succession, and the British moved in six years later because they were not prepared to tolerate an unstable area so close to possible Russian influence. And remarkably, after two short but bloody campaigns had been fought, the Sikhs settled down under British rule with every appearance of genuine contentment. Here again, as in the time of Wellesley's conquests, the invaders were extremely well served by the quality of the men who took over the administration in the new districts. Under the two Lawrence brothers, Henry and John, the young officers charged with pacifying the Punjab exercised their authority with a careful mixture of boyish gusto and mature consideration of local interests. It was long days in the saddle and being a judicious father to your people all over again, with justice being seen to be done and rapid material improvements made to help those who always suffered when there was fighting about; the eternal peasant cultivator scratching a living from the soil. As a success story it may have owed something to that rarest of all coincidences: the swift and mutual respect of two different races the moment hostilities are over because someone – probably by a fluke – has done the perfectly right thing at the absolutely vital moment. Whatever the reason for a peaceful Punjab under British rule by the time the nineteenth century reached its halfway mark, it was just as well for the imperialists, because a dreadful cloud was drifting up unnoticed over the rest of northern India.

Historians have advanced many reasons for the great Indian Mutiny, which happened because a number of factors made some sort of upheaving protest almost inevitable by 1857. Too many changes had been wrought by the British in the previous half century to be digested smoothly by people with ancient habits and beliefs that had never been so disturbed in such a short time before. Up to the last decade of the eighteenth century, the white men had done little to alter the fundamentals of Indian life, such injuries as the natives had suffered at alien hands being ones their ancestors had known from rulers since the beginning of time. But, since 1793, life on the sub-continent had been in a perpetual state of flux as a new philosophy appeared, bringing threats in many shapes and forms not only to the present but to eternity as well. Conquest in itself was of relatively little account, for that was familiar enough, whether by strangers or by belligerent rulers from neighbouring states. But no rulers before the nineteenth-century British had looked as though they might be planning to eradicate all distinctions of caste, had already proscribed certain existing institutions, and had lately started to change the physical appearance of the familiar with large-scale public works that included the introduction of devilish-looking objects which they called railway trains. Sophisticated Bengalis and others who were eagerly embracing Western education and the wider knowledge it brought, took all the changes in their stride because they could understand both the purpose and the limitations (it is relevant to remember that the Mutiny broke out in the year when universities were founded in Calcutta, Bombay and Madras). The fact that the British were not planning half the horrors the primitive mind shrank from was, however, entirely lost on masses of unlettered Indians, who didn't understand most of what was said in the impartial courts of law and could not be expected to grasp that even the most alarming impositions of the rulers were the subject of debate among the rulers themselves, and therefore very liable to modification or even abandonment from place to place and time to time. What they could see was startling change beginning all around. What they could feel was an overt racial condescension that the British had almost never exhibited before the nineteenth century. What they could smell was a new and passionate religious zeal.

The big puzzle about the Mutiny – and it has never been satisfactorily explained – is why it was restricted to a comparatively small area of the sub-continent. There were uprisings in Bombay, in Hyderabad and in Indore, all swiftly put down by military force before they got out of hand. Otherwise the country outside northern India never made a move, and even there the rebellion was localized. Neither the Sikhs nor the Gurkhas, the Rajputs nor the Marathas raised a hand against the British. Few of the native princes allowed themselves to become involved, and some put their resources at the Government's disposal. Thousands of Indian troops remained loyal to their officers while others were butchering anyone associated with the white regime. The revolt centred on the province of Oudh, where several things produced pressures not known to the same extent anywhere else. Lord Dalhousie, Governor-General for eight years up to 1856 and a great man for public works, had translated this area from a client state into a fully-annexed property of the Raj, and in doing so had drastically reduced the power of the talukdars, the local 'barons of Oudh', whose private fortresses had risen from 17 in 1800 to 246 in 1849. They were among the most notorious leaders of the revolt.

But the insurgence consisted of varied elements and grievances. There was a largely high-caste army of sepoys in the Bengal Army, inflamed by what they saw as a religious threat, which included their gradual displacement by lower castes in the military structure and on the land. There was a rural rebellion of peasants against social displacement caused by land reforms, which had made them more than ever the prey of moneylenders; yet the toughest peasant rebels were those who had resisted social upheaval and had complaints about taxation. There was a specifically Muslim insurrection, in which holy war was preached in Allahabad and Faizabad, and the faithful there looked for a lead to the King of Delhi, Bahadur Shah II, a man in his eighties descended from the mightiest of the Mughal Emperors and now a pensioner of the British, who treated him with great courtesy so long as he remained a complaisant figurehead. Although there was not a great deal of collusion between these various forces – the sepoys, for example, never tried to involve themselves in rural revolt, concentrating their attention on Delhi, Lucknow and Cawnpore – in combination they terrified the British in India for over a year, and not for another six months were all the rebels finally dispersed. Much of the horror for the British sprang from the fact that natives they had individually known for several years, and trusted absolutely in their patronizing way, suddenly one morning cut to pieces parents whose children they had been cradling gently only a few hours before. Many Indians, too, shared this nightmare, for the disorder of the Mutiny became a great excuse for the settling of old scores, and plenty of natives perished because they were suspected of casting spells or had given offence in some quite trifling way. What the whole episode never remotely resembled was a national struggle for independence, as some Indians in the twentieth century wished to believe.

The incident which brought the first lightning flash might have been avoided if British officers in the Company's army had been less obtuse; if they had not lost the habit of communicating with their men in the familiar manner of an earlier generation. The memoirs of Sita Ram Pande, loyal soldier of the Raj for forty-eight years from 1812, are especially illuminating on the contrast between the officers he first knew and those who came later in his career:

The sahibs often used to give nautches for the regiment, and they attended all the men's games . . . Nowadays they seldom attend nautches because their padre sahibs have told them it is wrong. These padre sahibs have done, and are still doing, many things to estrange the British officers from the sepoys . . . When I was a sepoy the captain of my company would have some of the men at his house all day long and he talked with them . . . I know that many officers nowadays only speak to their men when obliged to do so, and they show that the business is irksome and try to get rid of the sepoys as quickly as possible. One sahib told us that he never knew what to say to us. The sahibs always knew what to say, and how to say it, when I was a young soldier.

The blunder over the greased cartridges would have been much less likely in 1812 than in 1857.

Technically it happened because a new rifle had been developed, but this still had to be loaded from the muzzle with a cartridge which was now encased in paper instead of cloth. The old cartridges had been lubricated with a mixture of wax and vegetable oil, to ease their passage down the barrel to the breech, but the new ones went more smoothly with a greasing of tallow which could be compounded of various animal fats. The Adjutant-General of the Bengal Army knew very well that whereas goat or mutton fat would be unobjectionable to his sepoys, beef fat would be impossible for a Hindu to touch, pork fat for a Muslim, and he warned the ordnance suppliers accordingly. But when the production of cartridges started in India, the contractors were given no definite instructions for the composition of the grease – and that was quite enough to rouse the suspicion of religiously orthodox sepoys that they were about to be defiled *en masse*. Word went round the garrisons of northern India much faster than the British ever imagined, and discontent was already widespread when the new equipment was rejected by sepoys at Meerut, north of Delhi. Eighty-five of them were stripped of their uniforms and shackled before being led off to ten years in gaol for insubordination, and many British on the station thought that punishment, in the circumstances, far too harsh. For Indians it was the penultimate humiliation. Next day, Sunday, 10 May, when officers and their families were getting ready for Evensong, fire broke out in the Native Infantry Lines; then sepoys came running with guns, shooting at every European in sight. The long horror had begun.

In the appalling year that followed, the savagery on both sides was unparalleled in the British association with India. But the Mutiny also paraded a whole gamut of other human responses as well – heroism, loyalty, treachery, bewilderment, generosity, vindictiveness, stupidity, grief and, very rarely, blank cowardice. They were demonstrated at once when the first mutineers rushed headlong from Meerut to Delhi and killed every European there, where the Muslims among them secured the compliance of Bahadur Shah but never managed to engage his enthusiasm for their cause. From Delhi the insurgents turned towards Cawnpore, one of the most important garrisons on the Ganges, where they formed up under the leadership of Nana Sahib, a princeling who could play billiards as well as he could do anything, and who had oozed friendship for the British while deeply resenting the fact that they had not pensioned him as handsomely as they had his father before him. He offered his assistance now and, when it was gratefully accepted, turned on his patrons and laid siege to the men, women and children sheltering in buildings half a mile from the river. A thousand people were there to start with, but after a couple of weeks under fire they were reduced to a few hundred of half starved and wounded wrecks, many already demented with deprivation and strain under the blazing summer sun. Nana Sahib then offered a truce to 'all those who are in no way connected with the acts of Lord Dalhousie', and arrangements were hastily made for the survivors to go free to Allahabad in boats. They were clambering aboard these craft at Satichaura Ghat when they were raked with fire by sepoys gathered on the banks; and as people leapt for the safety of the river, horsemen dashed among them, swinging swords. One boat escaped downstream. Two women were abducted and lived, one of them, General Wheeler's daughter, emerging many, many years later on her death-bed, where she revealed that she had spent most of her life as a Muslim at the behest of the sepoy who took and married her. Otherwise, about 125 women and children alone survived the massacre at the ghat. Within two more weeks, all who had not by then died of cholera or dysentery were butchered and their bodies were pitched down a well.

At Lucknow Sir Henry Lawrence, lately ruling so masterfully in the Punjab, gathered the British community and the loyal Indian troops into the thirty-three acres of the Residency compound, which he turned into a fortress with ramparts, trenches, booby-traps and all. Two days after it came under siege at the end of June, a shell landed in his room and he was fatally injured. Another early casualty (though he would live to see Scotland again) was Dr Brydon, last man left on the retreat from Kabul. As buildings crumbled under the bombardment, the beleaguered community hung on in the hope of a relieving force coming from somewhere to their aid. After ninety days, gunfire was heard across the rooftops of Lucknow and presently Generals Sir Henry Havelock and Sir James Outram appeared with a column of Highlanders through the shattered outer walls. All to no avail. The siege was intensified and a new threat was heard – the sound of sappers working underground and laying mines. By this time, people had abandoned their attempts to lead a normal life, which had caused them to hold an auction of Henry Lawrence's possessions as soon as he was dead and buried. One of the first acts of Havelock's troops had been to loot whatever fineries remained without owners in the compound; but now soldiers were risking their lives creeping out in the darkness to find something to eat, and people were consuming small birds when they could trap them. Medical supplies ran out, surgeons amputated limbs without chloroform, and Havelock himself began to die of dysentery. But an Irishman, Henry Kavanagh, having already made a name for himself by sitting in the underground tunnels and shooting mutineer sappers as they crawled to lay more mines, now volunteered to steal out of Lucknow and find Sir Colin Campbell's army, which was rumoured to be on its way. He squirmed through the sepoy lines, swam the Gumti, and made contact with Campbell's force some miles beyond the city. On 17 November, Lucknow was finally relieved, and over the next few days the survivors of its long siege were brought out to safety at night under the noses of the mutineers.

The campaign was to drag on for months yet, and many other shocking things happened while it lasted, but Cawnpore and Lucknow were the two crises indelibly written into the history of the British in India. So was the retribution, which was vile when it came. When General Sir James Neill reached the shambles of Cawnpore not long after it was over, he was seized with an Old Testamental vision of revenge as soon as he saw the mangled bodies in the well, the pathetic bloodstained toys, the aching entries in a diary found trampled in the mud – 'June 17, Aunt Lilly died. June 18, Uncle Willy died. June 22, George died. July 9, Alice died. July 12, Mamma died.' His men needed no urging to do what came next. Captured mutineers were to be executed, of course, but first they must be made to *pay*. Each one was made to lick clean a portion of bloody ground or floor, after a native of the lowest caste had watered it a little. Then he was hanged. To break one man's caste and consign him to damnation after death, pork and beef were stuffed down his throat while he still lived. When Lucknow was finally retaken, sepoys were bayoneted on sight, whether they were armed or not; this was known, among the British troops, as giving them a Cawnpore dinner. All over northern India mutineers were hanged in droves as the fighting died down, one magistrate boasting that he had despatched a hundred in three days near Fatehgarh. Some were blown from field guns, their bodies first smeared with the blood of those they had killed. Many of the insurgents died shouting defiance at the execution squads, others seemed apathetic or simply stood their ground with dignity while the rope was put round their necks. Very few of the British protested at the sickening toll, missionaries and chaplains being as loud as anyone in their clamour for vengeance. They were loudest of all in their desire to see the most terrible things done to Nana Sahib, but he got away after pretending suicide in the Ganges and is thought to have died of fever in Nepal in 1859. The old King of Delhi was caught and put on trial for lending his status to mutineers, refused to plead one way or the other, and was transported to Rangoon for the rest of his life, which ended within a few years.

When at last the appalling time was over, the only major figure who came out of it with full credit was Lord Canning, who had succeeded Dalhousie as Governor-General just before the Mutiny began. Fairly helpless in Calcutta to stop the lynch law that prevailed briefly in the mutinous areas further west, he insisted that harshness must not be Government policy, that various reforms must be made to soothe Indian feelings, that reconciliation should be the watchword now. He was vilified by many of his compatriots in India for this approach, but a sort of healing did begin with astonishing speed under his guidance. After he had left for home at the end of his term in 1861, the Bengali writer Girish Chandra Ghosh, normally a caustic critic of the British, had this to say about Canning; 'If India grieved at the loss of one who had proved himself so worthy to rule, it rejoiced . . . at the presence in England of a friend whose mature judgment . . . would at all times offer Her Majesty's Government a true criterion by which to settle Indian questions.'

Behind much of the British thirst for revenge was a sense of outrage that the mutineers could have behaved as they did to women. The European male's attitude to females might generally have been one of sheer humbug and worse, but it did include a form of adoration, sticky with sentimentality but genuinely felt all the same. This was not a directly sexual reflex so much as a tribute to gender, expressed as strongly as anywhere in the letters and diaries of bachelor administrators who kept a tight hold on their emotions except in references to their mothers at home. One might bully one's wife in the nineteenth century without a second thought, but there were certain things no man but a cad did to a female, some violations of the code unthinkable in the presence of women, and all of them were innocuous compared with what scores of mothers, wives and daughters suffered from the mutineers. The reaction of even the most level-headed and civilized Europeans is best illustrated, as it happens, by a woman. Flora Annie Steel went to India from Scotland nine years after the Mutiny was over and she was to make a distinguished life for herself out there, on top of being a wife and mother. After 22 years on the sub-continent she produced *The Complete Indian Housekeeper and Cook*, which rivalled Mrs Beeton's epic in size and scope, and ran to ten editions, but long before that she made her mark. At the age of 29 she had designed the town hall for a small place in the Punjab, and when she and her husband moved on to another posting she was given a jewelled brooch whose every stone had been offered from their own brooches by the local Punjabi wives. Wherever the Steels went, Flora opened a school for the bazaar children in which – though she was a practising Christian – she refused to proselytize, and in due course the Government made her Inspector of Female Schools for the whole area between Peshawar and Delhi, in which capacity she also served on the Punjabi Education Board. She was that sort of person; talented, energetic, sympathetic. Yet when she composed her memoirs she remembered most distinctly how she had felt about the Indian mutineers from half a world away in Scotland. 'I burnt and hanged and tortured the Nana Sahib in effigy many times,' she wrote.

It had taken a long time for women to reach Mrs Steel's level of achievement in British India, and not many were ever to equal hers. For that matter, it had taken a long time for women to appear on the scene at all, considering that the first British landfall had been made early in the seventeenth century. Even in Clive's day, men rarely brought their wives out from England, and not until the start of the nineteenth century could the arrival of women from home be described as so much as a trickle. The earlier inhibition was partly to avoid exposing members of both races to what would nowadays be called culture shock, which lasted a long time in some places: no married man was appointed Resident in Nepal until 1843 because the Gurkhas and other locals feared that if a white woman lived among them some vital essence of the hill state would vanish into thin air. Mostly, though, married men came to India by themselves because delicate womanhood must be shielded from the hellish climate and the hazards to health; it would, after all, be only a temporary separation until a fortune had been made. But it was a far from celibate world for those early Company employees and many unions were made with Indian women inside and out of wedlock, with the happy result that racial prejudice was almost unknown until it surfaced in the nineteenth century with the assistance of Evangelical dogma.

It is to the first British women on the sub-continent that we owe much of our knowledge about the daily life of the white community from the late eighteenth century onwards, because they came out with large diaries to fill, parting presents from relatives and friends at home. Mrs Fay, lawyer's wife and dressmaker, reaches Calcutta in 1780 and quickly informs us of the extravagant and silly eating habits there.

We dine at 2 o'clock in the very heat of the day . . . A soup, a roast fowl, curry and rice, a mutton pie, a forequarter of lamb, a rice pudding, tarts, very good cheese, fresh churned butter, excellent Madeira (that is very expensive but eatables are very cheap) . . .

Other sources in the next few years enlarge on domestic details, so that we know the primitive methods employed to keep the climate as far at bay as possible. Grass screens, 'tatties', were hung over open windows and sprinkled with water to keep rooms relatively cool. To create artificial breezes the punkah (introduced by the Portuguese) was supplemented by the therm-antidote, which was a large three-sided case with rotating fans turned by an iron handle. Every family had its abdar, the servant who stayed up all night constantly moving an earthenware jar of water in a larger vessel containing saltpetre and water, which produced a chilled liquid by morning. This was the only thing akin to refrigeration until a persevering American, Frederic Tudor, solved the problem of transporting ice from a cold to a hot climate in the nineteenth century. After twenty-eight years of experiment he succeeded in shipping large chunks of frozen Wenham

Lake from Massachusetts to South America and beyond by insulating it with a packing of sawdust: in May 1833 the *Tuscany* arrived in Calcutta from Boston with two thirds of an ice cargo still solid, and thereafter life took a turn for the more convenient in India. Not that the weather itself remained anything but a trial to the European constitution – 'It is so very HOT,' wrote Emily Eden shortly after coming out in 1836, 'I do not know how to spell it large enough!' The British had become accustomed by then to recognizing only two seasons of the year in this difficult environment: the Hot Weather and the Cold Weather. The second of these, lasting from October to the middle of March, was a relative expression referring to temperatures comparable to those of the warmest springs and summers at home. In the Cold Weather you could enjoy even the plains of North India, which in the Hot Weather burned so fiercely that, from the 1820s onwards, the British fled from them whenever possible to take seasonal refuge in the cooler highlands of the sub-continent.

October also brought another phenomenon, which Lady Falkland noted in 1857 with a gleam in her patrician eye. 'The arrival of a cargo (if I may dare term it so) of young damsels from England is one of the exciting events that mark the advent of the Cold Season.' The young damsels were the daughters or nieces or family friends of officials in India and they had shipped themselves East, as much as anything, in order to see what they could make of the British communities as a marriage mart; for there always had been, and always would be, a surplus of eligible bachelors out there biding their time for a wife. Several years before the Indian Mutiny, the poet Thomas Hood was so struck by this traffic that he put it into facetious verse:

> By Pa and Ma I'm daily told
> To marry now's the time,
> For though I'm very far from old,
> I'm rather in my prime.
> They say while we have any sun
> We ought to make our hay –
> And India has so hot a one
> I'm going to Bombay . . .

Such a young lady was Sophia Goldbourne, who arrived when women were so very thin on the ground that she could immediately write home how the attention and court paid to me was astonishing. My smile was meaning and my articulation melody; in a word, mirrors are almost useless in Calcutta and self-adoration idle, for your looks are reflected in the pleasures of every beholder and your claims to first-rate distinction confirmed by all who approach you.

It would be a long time before women were expected or desired to be anything more than Miss Goldbourne made herself sound. Many demonstrated during the Mutiny that they could stand fast in extreme difficulty with as much heroism and toughness as any man, yet afterwards the majority were still supposed to be decorative homemakers and intelligent listeners; nothing more. They had arrived in India as what the waiting males cynically called the Fishing Fleet, and those with the plainest looks or the most garrulous tongues sailed back to England again the following March under the epithet Returned Empties. Of those who made their catch and stayed on, a few had enough character to resist the patronizing standards of the day and had found the husbands to match them. Generally, the ones who stood out were those who accompanied their men everywhere that duty called in India, and who would have died of boredom if they had not tried to come to grips with the country and its people instead of staying home as dutiful housewives. These were the women like Flora Annie Steel and, a generation before her, Fanny Parkes, wife of a Collector in the interior. She was endlessly curious and soon fluent in Hindi, and elation fairly steams off the pages she scribbled when she had time. 'How much there is to delight the eye in this bright, beautiful world,' Fanny wrote one day. 'Roaming about with a good tent and a good arab (horse), one might be happy forever in India!'

This was not a view taken by the majority of British wives, who settled down into the status of Memsahib – with a distinctly capital M in some cases, where these good ladies made themselves forbidding figures to Indians and lesser Europeans alike. Fortified by their Twilfit Corsetry ('Famous throughout the Empire') they would remain captive but progressively less captivating on the pedestal men had constructed for them until after the twentieth century's first world war. They yielded to no-one in their faultless instinct for the correct order of social precedence, in knowing who should sit precisely where around the dinner table, who might be safely snubbed and who should be grotesquely flattered. They were at first victims and then perpetuators of a vicious circle which reserved them

93

for their husband's pleasure alone, left them ignorant and smug within a small superior coterie, and could in time and with perseverance produce a creature who became a trial to husbands and anyone else in sight. They had a great deal of power around the home, with at least a platoon of servants to scurry for them at every beck and call – ayah (nurse or maid), bobajee (cook), chokidar (caretaker), khitmagar (butler), dewan (gatekeeper), and syce (groom) who were backed up, as often as not, by twice as many bearers and sweepers. So many servants were attached to the average British household that someone who arrived in 1844 was surprised only to find that there wasn't some menial to masticate his employer's food.

Discouraged in the first place from making real contact with India and lacking the will to pick up more than a smattering of language adequate for speaking to the servants, the memsahibs became progressively more isolated, as the nineteenth century rolled on, in a frigid expatriate sub-community of their own. They were renowned for their attempts to reproduce English gardens, complete with lawns like green velvet, in tropical or semi-desert conditions that turned all vegetation either to jungle or dust within a few months. They were notable for imitating festive celebrations of home with dogged devotion, even if the Christmas dinner did consist of pea-fowl much more often than turkey. They waited eagerly for the arrival of catalogues from the big London stores, which reached India towards the end of summer when the steamships were running in the 1870s, so that if you moved fast you might expect to order Christmas presents and receive them just in time. Otherwise you had to make do with what was offered by the growing number of stores in British India – Whiteaway & Laidlaw, Hall and Anderson, and local branches of the Army & Navy, or Timothy White's.

The memsahibs knew a great deal of heartache when they had children. Infants, of course, saw much more of their ayahs than their Mammas, which was a wilful neglect with mixed results. It meant that large numbers of Britons born in India knew and cared much more about the country than their parents had done, and were haunted by those earliest native memories to the end of their days; it could also produce a powerful self-importance in young people who had been treated from the cradle with the same deference usually shown only to adults. But five years old was the age when the local magic was suddenly withdrawn and the child was packed off to Europe, to be educated and brought up in totally British ways. After that, children very often didn't see their parents for years on end. So Mamma, bereft of the son or daughter she had scarcely allowed herself to know even when she had the chance, consoled herself with a daily routine that hadn't varied much from the time she first came out and wedded the middling civil servant, the Army captain or the rising entrepreneur. In the sort of small provincial town where many memsahibs dwelt in India, it went something like this: up at 5 A.M. with horseriding till 7 A.M.; breakfast on the verandah, followed by a cold bath before dressing to receive visitors at 10 A.M.; anything up to four hours of social chat with the visitors; lunch at 2 P.M. followed by a siesta, which might amount to lying on the bed with a book till it was time to ride again in the late afternoon; then bathe again, dress again and enjoy more social chat or a stroll near the band-stand, where the military musicians from the local garrison would play; after nightfall a supper party, with songs round the pianoforte until bedtime. This was a prescription for the narrowing even further of minds already constricted by the dominant attitudes of middle class Victorian England. Few women would follow it unwaveringly day after day without becoming quite sure that they, and those like them, were naturally superior to the mass of humanity in India. It would have had a similarly exclusive effect if it had been practised among their own people at home.

The Memsahib-in-chief never saw India, yet she pervaded its life at every point, especially after the Mutiny, when she made herself part of the great reconciliation process that Lord Canning began. There can scarcely in all history have been an absentee monarch who touched as many distant subjects as Queen Victoria did with a sense of mystery approaching the divine; certainly there can have been none representing alien rule whose own person seemed increasingly exempt, as time went on, from the natural resentments of a conquered people. When the tide of Indian nationalism first began to flow towards the end of the century, the Queen herself was never associated by its leaders with the policies of her Government they had started to reject, and in this they showed a fine appreciation of where power really lies in a constitutional monarchy, whatever lustre is carefully maintained on the figurehead itself. By that time the awe in which the Queen was held was such that many Indians would swear they had actually seen her, just as they would vouch for some personal contact with any one of their native gods.

And there is no doubt at all that this remote ruler had, in return, a strangely intense feeling for the people of India. The Mutiny was only a few months old, but had already produced the nightmares of Cawnpore and Lucknow, when she informed Canning that 'the Indian people should know that there is no hatred to a brown skin, none; but the greatest wish on their Queen's part to see them happy, contented and flourishing.' When peace at last came in 1858, and the rule of the East India Company was finally brought to an end, the Queen's own attitude was more strongly emphasized. Her ministers of state had drawn up a proclamation which would explain to Indians how the circumstances of their government had now changed, and Victoria was outraged by the tone of the first draft. She insisted that certain parts of it must be altered, and one passage in the final document was clearly and importantly all her own work.

Firmly relying ourselves on the truth of Christianity and acknowledging with gratitude the solace of religion, we disclaim alike the right and the desire to impose our convictions on any of our subjects . . . We do strictly charge and enjoin all those who may be in authority under us that they abstain from all interference with the religious belief or worship of any of our subjects on pain of our highest displeasure.

At the same time she let it be known that she wanted Indians to be given every opportunity to take part in the administrative machinery of their country at whatever level an individual's 'education, ability and integrity' qualified him for. She did not pretend that this benevolence was a disinterested one, her proclamation making the point about her Indian subjects that 'In their prosperity will be our strength; in their contentment our security.'

Victoria gloried in her own status and when, in 1877, this was amplified into Empress of India (at the suggestion of that florid man Benjamin Disraeli) she relished the added weight attached to her signature on official pronouncements; not only Regina, but also Imperatrix. But expediency and self-satisfaction cannot by themselves explain her attitude to India and its people. She took a constant personal interest in events on the sub-continent that she never showed to the same extent in other parts of her Empire. She once made a Prime Minister (Lord Salisbury) apologize for referring to Indians as 'black men', and she complained that not enough Indians had received awards in her 1898 Birthday Honours. She fostered a campaign to reduce the death rate among Indian women during child-birth and one public indication of this was the award of no fewer than five Kaiser-i-Hind medals to women doctors in 1900. She had no illusions about the failings of some fellow-countrymen out there. 'The future Viceroy,' she wrote to Salisbury when a new appointment was in the offing in 1897, 'must really shake himself more and more free from his red-tapist, narrow-minded Council and entourage. He must . . . not be guided by the *snobbish* and vulgar overbearing and offensive behaviour of many of our Civil and Political Agents . . .' She was an uncommonly astute monarch as well as an imperious one.

Nor can her sympathy for India be accounted for by her peculiar attachment to an Indian servant in the royal household, for that didn't start until 1887, when Abdul Karim appears to have been appointed a groom of the chamber as a gesture related to her Golden Jubilee. The Queen's Scottish retainer John Brown had died four years before, and whether or not Victoria consciously sought a substitute figure for the departed Highlander, the Indian plainly began to occupy a comparable role in her life. From the outset she encouraged him to teach her Hindustani and, although she never acquired more than a rudimentary knowledge of the language, the lessons continued up to her own death, supplemented from time to time by curried meals that Abdul eagerly cooked. He was much less popular with senior officials of the royal household, who regarded him as an upstart with a tendency to lie for the sake of self-advancement. He had been a junior clerk in the administration of Agra gaol before entering the Queen's personal service at the age of twenty-four, and let it be known that his father was a Surgeon-General in the Indian Army. This was false; his father was no more than a hospital attendant who mixed medicines for sick prisoners in Agra. By the time court officials had found this out, it was too late to dislodge Abdul from the Queen's favour. She rounded on them angrily as a deeply prejudiced gang, reminding them that she had known two Archbishops who were the sons, respectively, of a butcher and a grocer. The Indian continued to flourish under her patronage. He was given the title Munshi (teacher), and after one of her language lessons she noted in her diary that he was 'a vy strict Master . . . a *perfect* Gentleman.' She arranged for his portrait to be painted in oils. He accompanied her on a number of royal progresses to the Braemar Highland Gathering and to the theatre, and she issued instructions that he was to have a place of honour at her funeral procession, whenever that might be. She lobbied her Viceroy to secure a land grant in Agra for the Munshi's father, and she flew into a paddy when the Governors of Bombay and Madras icily returned Christmas cards the Munshi had sent to them on his own account. He had become so sure of the Queen's acquiescence and protection after a few years in her service that the Keeper of Her Majesty's Privy Purse was writing to the Viceroy how 'I have now got to think it lucky that the Munshi's sweeper does not dine with us.'

There was, in fact, a valid reason for disquiet about the Munshi's proximity to the throne. Soon after their relationship began, Victoria invited him to assist her in dealing with her Indian correspondence: the sometimes highly confidential state papers that shuttled regularly between the Palace, the India Office and Government House in Calcutta. The Munshi was a Muslim, and one reason for official anxiety was the knowledge that a close friend of his in London was a Muslim law student suspected (erroneously, it turned out) of passing information to Kabul when Anglo-Afghan relations were going through one of their periodic strains. That apart, there were signs from India that the Hindu community was becoming indignant that a member of the chief rival faith was so close to the levers of British power. The Queen was apt to dismiss such warnings from her ministers as further examples of their racial or social prejudice, and was not dissuaded from sharing her correspondence with the Munshi until Lord George Hamilton, the Secretary of State for India, told her that he would be unable to supply the Palace with confidential material in future if she continued to let the Munshi see it. So, for once, she submitted; but in the same breath ordered that the Munshi must henceforth be known as her Indian Secretary.

Victoria maintained her intense interest in Indian affairs to the end of her life, urging her Viceroys to pay attention to what 'respectable native people' had to say, warning them not to be hedged in by *red-tapeism*, which she obsessively scorned. 'Red-tapeism is, alas, our great misfortune,' she advised Lord Curzon in 1900, 'and exists very strongly in the India Office.' She corresponded with Curzon or telegraphed him very nearly every week, until eleven days before her death. Shortly after the funeral, the new King Emperor of India, Edward VII, ordered the Munshi to burn all the papers in his possession, and this was done at Frogmore Cottage, one of the

Munshi's several homes. Then Abdul Karim returned to Agra, and when he died there in 1909 there was a second bonfire of his correspondence, with the exception of a few letters in the Queen's handwriting, which his widow was allowed to keep for their sentimental value.

FIVE

CROWN IMPERIAL

The Queen's proclamation, announcing the new system of government under her own majesty, was made at every British station
throughout India on 1 November 1858, accompanied by church
services of thanksgiving and firework displays. The East India
Company's association with the sub-continent was at once brought
to an end, in spite of a petition of protest drawn up by its chief
executive, John Stuart Mill. From now on, India was incorporated
into the growing machinery of Whitehall, which was conveniently
and symbolically situated in London between the royal Palace and
the Houses of Parliament. When, ten years later, Mr Disraeli opened
some splendid new government buildings there, they included
dramatic premises allocated to the India Office. This institution
revolved around its Durbar Court, a spacious area shielded from the
English rain by a large glass roof, with a Wedgwood blue frieze
running along its four walls, and niches on which the marble busts of
senior administrators were perched and added to as time went by.
Not far away was the room occupied by a full Secretary of State –
and India was to be the only country in the British Empire ever to
have such a personage to itself. He sat within oak-panelled walls
decorated with Indian miniatures which had been filched from the
Mughal Emperor's Red Fort in Delhi; his furniture had seen earlier
service at the Company headquarters in Leadenhall Street. He had a
pair of identical doors to his room, set side by side on a curving wall,
an obliging device so that if he had to receive in audience two Indian
princes of the same rank, they could step across his threshold
simultaneously, neither yielding an inch of precedence to the other.

India matched this building with Government House in Calcutta,
which Lord Wellesley had ordered without bothering to consult
his Directors. This looked exactly like an English stately home,
Wellesley's architects having modelled it – with one or two
modifications to take account of the climate – on Kedleston Hall in

Derbyshire; and by a curious stroke of history, a Curzon of Kedleston would be ruling India from it before the nineteenth century was out. Lord Curzon, indeed, added a row of urns along the roofline so that the similarities between Government House and his ancestral home should be more complete. But from the beginning the copy had imitated the original in most other respects, down to a Marble Hall containing the busts of twelve Caesars, and a main staircase terminating in a pair of sphinxes whose breasts were amputated shortly after installation on the orders of a discreet aide-de-camp, who thought they might offend the unpredictable Wellesley. Functionally, Government House was a cross between Buckingham Palace and the India Office. It was the home of the British ruler in India, and it was also the headquarters of his Government. It was regularly the scene of entertainments which dazzled even by local standards, and its multitude of offices housed the cogs and wheels of senior administration, a perpetually busy place which the nonsense rhymester Edward Lear, who stayed there in the 1870s, immortalized as Hustlefussabad.

Before the Mutiny the ruler had been known as the Governor-General of India, but now he was the monarch's Viceroy as well, to convey the rare distinction of his position. In the whole of the British Empire this official had only one superior: the monarch herself. Even the Prime Minister in London deferred to him on any occasion when they were together, for the Viceroy was uniquely the monarch's deputy, a deliberate creation to signify the Crown's special attachment to Indians and interest in them above all others. Yet the Viceroy's rule was much more nearly supreme than that of the Queen he represented, for there was nothing remotely like an elected Parliament, which India wouldn't enjoy until after the First World War. The only local checks on the Viceroy's authority were provided by his Executive Council and the Legislative Council. The first consisted of his senior officials in the Government of India; the second combined these men with officials from the three presidencies and a number of non-officials, among whom were princes and other Indians the Queen would have regarded as 'respectable people'. Neither council had more than an advisory role, and the presence of Indians at the hub of British power was certainly more of psychological than practical value to them. It did, nevertheless, demonstrate a willingness to include natives of the country in the pattern of authority, and the British went out of their way beyond that to conciliate the Indian princes in particular, with guarantees of semi-autonomy and other material benefits, as well as a proposal at one stage to create an Indian peerage. This was, in short, Akbar the Great's prescription for successful imperialism all over again.

The men who ruled from Government House had always been and would remain a collection of individualists, having in common only a determination to provide strong leadership. They could be as bumptious as Lord Amherst, one of the Governor-Generals before the Mutiny, who never moved from one room to another without being preceded by a column of mace-bearers and who, during his morning exercise, would not suffer his wife to approach closer than his horse's backside. They could be as homely as Sir John Lawrence, the third of the Viceroys and surviving brother of the Lawrence killed at Lucknow, who worked in his shirt sleeves with his collar off and played croquet on his lawn until long after dark, with great crowds watching by lamplight through the railings. They could be as nonconformist as Lord Lytton, who shocked the exclusive society of Simla by smoking cigarettes between courses at dinner. They could be as thrifty as Lord Lansdowne, who told one of his successors that he had managed to save £20,000 in six years out of his salary of £16,700 per annum. While their own ambitions varied in intensity, they were all well aware how much their position was coveted by others. Sir Herbert Kitchener was so crestfallen when he had expected to be made Viceroy and was not, that he went into hiding for ten days to conceal his disappointment. Austen Chamberlain was one of the rarities who, on being offered the post, refused it.

The Viceroy sat at the apex of a colossal pyramid of power, and British rule was founded on an idea of hierarchy as baffling in its complexity as the caste system of the Hindus themselves. It is arguable that the love-hate relationship which developed between the British and the Indians more strongly and more enduringly than anything formed between the British and their other subject peoples around the world, did so above all because they had this fundamental attitude in common before ever they met. Each grasped the other's basic social premise and not only understood it but subconsciously respected it as a curious variant of their own. The Hindus had their castes while the British had their classes, and in each case very fine distinctions sometimes separated one social level from the next. No Indian would ever have thought preposterous, as some modern Englishmen have, George Orwell's careful dissection of his own social antecedents which led him to the conclusion that he was precisely lower-upper-middle class. Nor would an Indian today be outraged, as a contemporary Westerner might be, by the story of the Governor's daughter who shocked the first-class passengers en route from London to Bombay by dancing through most of the ship's fancy-dress ball with a second-class steward she fancied, and cut him dead shortly after leaving his cabin in the morning with the remark 'In the circle in which I move, sleeping with a woman does not constitute an introduction.' An Indian might be shocked, like the first-class passengers, because she had flouted her caste rules on the dance floor and in bed.

The subtleties of the British class system became elaborately codified in the Warrant of Precedence, which was designed as an infallible guide to hierarchy in India, indispensable to the proper arrangement of ceremony, conference or even of a mere dinner party. Aides-de-camp practically slept with it under their pillows and memsahibs might panic if they could not lay their hands on the blessed thing before the table was laid. First devised early in the nineteenth century, it was altered and expanded at intervals to take account of the passage of time and the consequent invention of new positions, but its basic structure held good from the original listings to the last ones at Independence in 1947. In the edition of 1817 only fourteen different levels of status were recognized but towards the end of the Raj there were sixty-one, some reserved for one person, others shared by a number of people.

At the top came the Governor-General and Viceroy, all alone. In second place were Governors of Presidencies and Provinces 'within their respective charges'. Third were the Governors of Madras, Bombay and Bengal (when each was out of his own domain). Fourth, another solitary figure, was the Commander-in-chief, India. Shortly after that, the full complexity set in like this: 7 – Chief Justice of Bengal. 12 – Chief Justice of a High Court other than that of Bengal. 14 – Chief Commissioner of Railways, General Officers commanding Northern, Southern, Eastern and Western Commands and officers of the rank of General. 17 – The Residents of Hyderabad and Mysore, the Chief Commissioner of the North West Frontier Province, and comparable figures. 27 – Vice-Chancellors of Indian Universities. 33 – A medley of people, including the Director of the Intelligence Bureau and the Commissioner of the Northern India Salt Bureau. 39 – Presidency Senior Chaplains of the Church of Scotland. 41 –

Collectors of Customs, Collectors and Magistrates of Districts, Collectors of Salt Revenue. 45 – The Assay Master, Bombay, and others. 47 – The Political Secretary, Aden (because the Government of India also took care of British interests up the Persian Gulf). 49 – Chief Commissioner of Stores and Clothing in Cawnpore, Commissioner of Labour in Madras, and ten others. 54 – Sheriffs within their own charges. 56 – Another assortment, ranging from the Managing Director of the Opium Factory at Ghazipur to the Deputy-Director-General of Archaeology. And finally, on the lowest level recognized by the Warrant, in position 61, a great variety of people which included Assistant Directors of Public Health, the Director of the Vaccine Institute at Belgaum, the Protector of Emigrants and the Senior Income Tax Officer in Bombay.

The Warrant confined itself to official appointments and in time, therefore, included a leavening of Indians among its horde of Britons, A separate announcement offered guidance to the hierarchy of ruling princes and chiefs in India, who were distinguished by the number of field-gun salutes each was entitled to on ceremonial occasions. Only five men were allotted a full 21-gun salute – the Maharaja (Gaekwar) of Baroda, the Maharaja (Scindia) of Gwalior, the Nizam of Hyderabad, the Maharaja of Jammu and Kashmir, and the Maharaja of Mysore. Six were entitled to a 19-gun salute – the Nawab of Bhopal, the Maharaja (Holkar) of Indore, the Khan (Wali) of Kalat, the Maharaja of Kohalpur, the Maharaja of Travancore, and the Maharaja of Udaipur. After that the table went like this. 17-gun salute: the Nawab of Bahawalpur and twelve others. 15-gun salute: the Maharaja of Alwar and sixteen others. 13-gun salute: the Maharaja of Benares and fifteen others. 11-gun salute: the Maharaja of Ajaigarh and thirty others. 9-gun salute: the Nawab (Babi) of Balasinor and twenty-nine others. Most Indian rulers had to make do with smaller public deferences than those provided by field guns. There were 562 princely states in all and they occupied one third of the land area of the sub-continent, which never came under direct rule by the British. Amicable arrangements were made to ensure that these private enclaves did not obstruct the vital workings of the Raj: the British Posts and Telegraphs Department operated throughout the princedoms and the railways crossed them without interruption. In exchange for such concessions, the princes were allowed to raise their own state military forces, some of which were virtually extensions of the regular Indian Army, with weapons supplied gratis by the British. In the tiniest states – and some were no bigger than one town and a handful of dependent villages – the ruler's troops were mostly employed as beaters and bearers when he entertained the British Resident and other guests to a weekend of big-game hunting, a pastime which accounted for the innumerable tiger skins that furnished British India, and the other trophies that might be found about a house (the elephant's feet made solid umbrella stands, its penis an intriguing golf bag).

There were two forces for the maintenance and exercise of British power in India and, implicitly, the Army was more necessary than the civil service. In fact, compared with its regular use in the first half of the nineteenth century, it rarely saw full-scale action after the Mutiny. It fought a second Afghan War in 1878–80, a third Burmese War in 1885, and battled with the Afridis on the North West Frontier in 1897. A third Afghan War came in the twentieth century, but that was to repel an Afghan invasion of India which had been urged by mullahs preaching jihad. Otherwise, military activities were confined to suppressing riots from time to time and regular skirmishes with tribesmen on the Frontier, which were seen by both sides as more of a blood sport than warfare. The Frontier engagements provided the most gripping tales in the huge mythology of British arms in India. It is said that Pathans sometimes applied to the nearest British Political Agent for the appropriate decoration after particularly exciting scraps with troops he had ordered against them. During a tribal uprising near Gilgit, in 1891, the garrison ran out of conventional ammunition and thereafter fired bullets made of garnets encased in lead. On another occasion the Khyber Rifles put down an insurrection of the Zakka Khel with great difficulty after a long sortie in the foothills of the Hindu Kush, and when the defeated tribesmen afterwards asked the British commander whether he thought they had fought well, he replied 'I wouldn't have shaken hands with you unless you had!' Then there was the time when a raiding party of Pathans was being pursued by Indian Army troops and matters had reached a stalemate, with each side sniping at the other for hours along a mountainside. The troops were aiming badly on the whole, until one of the Pathans stood up and signalled them to raise their sights, as though he was the marker at target practice on a firing range. The Frontier stories are endless: swashbuckling yarns full of honour and treachery, bravery and comradeship, danger and dash, all calculated to make adolescent blood run wild around the heart.

One of the first things the British did after the Mutiny was to reorganize the old Company's Army, to reduce the chances of such a catastrophe ever happening again. Before the great revolt, the proportion of European troops to Indian sepoys had been one to nine. By 1863 there were 62,000 British soldiers and 125,000 Indians wearing the Queen's colours, with a proportion of one to two carefully maintained throughout the Bengal Presidency, where the Mutiny had occurred; a proportion of one to three being allowed in the presidencies of Bombay and Madras. Other precautions were taken. An Auxiliary Force of India was raised, which every European male civilian was expected to join for part-time training, in case his full-time services should ever be needed. No Indian troops were allowed to man field guns from 1861 until the First World War, the only concession towards their use of artillery being the formation of Indian mountain batteries, whose light guns and other equipment were carried by mules and therefore took some time to assemble and fire. There was also a powerful school of thought which advocated the mixing, as much as possible, of tribes and castes in Indian regiments so that it would be difficult for any potentially mutinous leader to obtain the cohesion he needed to produce a serious threat. In some cases this happened, so that the 62nd Punjabis, for example, even into the twentieth century contained a company of Rajputs, a company of Sikhs, a company of Muslims from north of Rawalpindi, and another company recruited from the Frontier. Where such mixtures occurred, the strict dietary and other differences observed by the various groups within one regiment provided problems which made the quartermaster's job in any other army on earth seem like extended leave in comparison. Mostly, though, Indian regiments which had stayed loyal to the British during the Mutiny were allowed to continue as they were; and gradually, as tension relaxed, the Army as a whole developed on local regimental lines, in which regional and tribal pride became a powerful force for efficiency.

Most of the European soldiers in India after the Company's Army was disbanded belonged to traditional regiments of the British Army with their own local appeal, like the Lancashire Fusiliers, which would each send a battalion out to the sub-continent for five years at a time to reinforce (and act as watchdog over) the Indian Army. The equivocal attitude of the British to this part of their Empire is perfectly illustrated by their approach to the manning of the Indian regiments. At first these were totally officered by British soldiers, but it became a matter of policy to reduce their quota and replace many white officers by commissioned Indians. At one and the same time, therefore, the rulers were taking all possible steps to undermine any organization of another Mutiny and they were demonstrating trust by putting Indians in positions of command. Deservedly or not, the concoction worked. The new Indian Army's chief role was destined to be one of ceremonial splendour but when put to the test it was an immensely effective fighting force. More significantly, it remained absolutely loyal, a corollary to Sir Bartle Frere's remark when he was Governor of Bombay shortly after the Mutiny, that if the British could hold India only by a foreign army of occupation they had no business to be there at all. It was probably more reliable in the service of an alien rule than any other body of colonial troops whose first duty was to preserve a colonizing power from insurrection by the colonial people.

It drew the bulk of its manpower from what the British, by the mid-nineteenth century, had shrewdly assessed as the chief martial peoples on the sub-continent – Baluchis, Brahmins, Deccan and Madrassi Muslims, Dogras, Garhwalis, Gujars, Gurkhas, Hazaris, Hindustani Muslims, Jats, Madrassi Hindus, Marathas, Mers, Pathans, Punjabi Muslims, Rajputs and Sikhs. The regiments they served in were often designated by their local names (the Garhwal Rifles, the Dogra Regiment, the Mahratta Light Infantry, the Hazara Pioneers etc.) but in other cases (the Royal Bombay Sappers and Miners, and the Punjab Regiment among them) an outsider could only guess at the racial mixture they contained. There was, naturally, a pecking order of regiments, too. Among the infantry, the Gurkhas were regarded as incomparable by the British, with the Sikhs not far behind. Another crack outfit was the Corps of Guides (which also included horsemen) – the first military unit in the world to abandon gaudy uniforms in the field and wear khaki for better concealment. Cavalry has always thought itself superior to mere footsloggers, and the Indian Army's was no exception. Given his pick, any young British officer intent on a career out there would probably have opted for Skinner's Horse, the famous Yellowboys, whose title was changed six times under various reorganizations until it recovered the original, but always remained the senior regiment of

Indian cavalry. But for hauteur and devil-may-care, there was little to choose between a dozen or so – the Central India Horse, Probyn's Horse, the Scinde Horse, the Poona Horse and others. And all of them made for a brilliant display when advancing at the trot on a full-dress parade.

A fairly bright young Englishman seeking a future in India, however, would think soldiering rather beneath him and hope to be recruited by the ICS. Entry to the civil service had been thrown open to competition just before the Mutiny, which meant that Haileybury students no longer had the field to themselves, having in future to pit their wits in examination against young men who had issued from other schools as well as the Universities of Oxford and Cambridge. Some schools were to become much greater sources of supply as time went on, with Cheltenham, Marlborough, Clifton, Bedford Grammar School and Kingston (Ireland) well in the lead by the end of the nineteenth century. The formidable Dr Jowett, subsequently Master of Balliol, was especially pleased by the advent of the open competition because he thought the Indian Civil Service would help to solve the worries of Oxford graduates who were wondering what to do with their lives. For the first four years after the open exam started in 1855, some 60 per cent of the successful entrants were Oxbridge men; but then the figure dipped to 10 per cent for a while (the Mutiny had doubtless produced an attack of nerves in many prospective examinees) before picking up again. Of the 1,600 recruits selected between 1858 and 1897, virtually all came from the British middle classes; being sons of either professional men, businessmen, farmers or lesser gentry. They were not certain of an ICS career until they had gone through an investigation stretching across a couple of years. First came the open examination, which was overwhelmingly literary in the early decades, but which had, by 1900, become more evenly divided between language, literature, history, the sciences and mathematics. Then there was a probationary period in India, after which the young officials were tested on topics more closely related to their new vocation. Right up to Independence, horse-riding was a compulsory subject in the final test, as it was bound to be, given the nature of Indian topography and the scope of a young civil servant's potential work. But it was probably the only time he would need to jump a five-bar gate with his arms folded and his stirrups crossed.

The amount of responsibility carried by junior officials after probation could be quite extraordinary. The basic unit of administration was the district, and eventually this became established at an average of 4,430 square miles, or four and a half times the size of an administrative county in England. The burden of work there fell upon the District Officer, who dispensed justice in his role as Magistrate and attended to the revenue in his position of Collector. He might or might not have a younger ICS assistant; he would certainly have an assortment of Indian subordinates to help with clerical and other matters. He was on the move a great deal, for a regulation 90 days a year in a small district, 120 days in a larger one; and these tours around the country would provide the majority of ICS officials with their most marvellous memories of India, fondly recalled when they were old men retired in Dorset or Hants. They were, sometimes very consciously, playing God among the people they administered on those tours. An ICS man not yet thirty years old might have to deal with a petition to allow human sacrifice as a special concession because the crops were suffering from drought; the district magistrate of Ganjam had to deal with such an approach from the Khonds in South India just after the turn of the century. A man serving up on the Frontier might find himself addressing a tribal jirga – the council of elders – which was something between a jury and a parliament, two thousand men sitting round him in a circle while he expounded a point of Government policy; knowing that if he failed to win their confidence in a running debate conducted wholly in Pushtu and depending for its effectiveness, from the British point of view, on his own fluent ability to quote tribal myth and proverb, there might be local upheaval with hot blood flowing down the hills. And when he returned to his desk in the town where his office was, a vast amount of handwriting awaited him, for it was an axiom of the ICS that everything must be committed to paper and carefully filed – petitions, statements, judgements, applications of every kind.

From its beginnings in the richly varied routines of a country district, the career of an ICS man might proceed upwards in different ways. In fits and starts the service evolved into three separate departments. By far the largest was the Executive branch, which supplied the manpower for the districts and whose senior officials rose to work in the secretariats of the provincial governments or that of the Government of India itself. The Judicial department provided the district judges who tried cases of much greater weight than a magistrate was allowed to handle, and the senior men sat in the High Courts of the provincial capitals. Third, and most dazzling in career terms, was the Indian Political Service staffed by a mixture of Army officers and ICS officials. This was, effectively, the Viceroy's corps diplomatique and the external affairs department of the Government of India. Officials working in the former capacity became Residents and Agents attached to the courts of the Indian princes, to maintain relations between them and the Raj; while men working in external affairs administered the North West Frontier or attended to British relations with Central Asia, the Persian Gulf, Afghanistan, Tibet and Nepal. Politicals were the cream of the cream, in their own estimation at least; ICS men in general being regarded as the elite of the British in India, somewhere above the soldiers or the uncovenanted civil servants like the police officers, the doctors of the Indian Medical Service, or the men of the Indian Forest Service. Inevitably, there was a well-recognized spectrum of superiority between the different Indian provinces in which a non-Political might spend his working life. The Punjab and the United Provinces of the north were thought to have a cachet that, for example, the increasingly bothersome province of Bengal – additionally handicapped by a filthy climate of high humidity and heat – quite lacked.

For integrity and efficiency, the ICS was almost certainly the finest civil service that man has yet devised. Its incorruptibility became a byword among Indians and a source of sometimes overbearing pride among the British. No member of the service was allowed to accept any presents other than flowers or fruit, and we may be as certain as can be of human beings that scarcely anyone ever did. A story from early in the twentieth century shows just how much the word of an official Briton was relied upon by then. A young Political officer ran out of money in the Pamirs and borrowed the equivalent of £50 from a yak owner, in exchange for an IOU on a sheet of notepaper addressed to a bank in Karachi. Almost a year later the IOU was presented in Peshawar with the marks of many transactions on it, having passed through several hands all over Central Asia as a piece of currency that would be honoured when returned to its source. The ICS bred honourable men, even when it had not acquired them in the first place, and it produced more than its share of eccentrics, too. One of these, Huish Edye, gloried in his unofficial title as originator of the Gambit of the Second Reminder, which was an elaborate and witty ploy to delay action at district level on some unwelcome instruction issuing from the provincial secretariat. Another, Frederick St G. Tucker, resigned after five ICS years in the Punjab, joined the Salvation Army, and later returned to India as Fakir Singh, holy man and beggar. The service also spawned many scholars, like William Herschel, who pioneered the science of finger-printing in Bengal long before Francis Galton recognized it as a reliable method of identification; Allan Octavian Hume, who became a distinguished ornithologist, leaving his collection of 82,000 birds and their eggs to London's Natural History Museum in 1885; and Brian Hodgson, Resident in Nepal, where his international reputation in philology, ethnology and zoology grew so high that the French gave him the cross of their Legion of Honour. The one breed the ICS did not often tolerate was the hearty who might have found his level in the Army mess, where High Jinks or High Cockalorum and other boisterous activities released energies that were less and less tapped by military excursions in the field.

The ICS was not, however, faultless. Lord Curzon, acknowledging it as the most honourable and the proudest service in the world, also observed in it some of the meanest and most malignant types of disappointed humanity it had ever been his misfortune to meet; a view doubtless arrived at when his own transcending arrogance had collided with something similar in one of his officials. A more serious wholesale defect lay in the service's concentration on the needs and problems of the country districts rather than those of the bigger towns and cities. ICS men generally preferred to work among simple villagers rather than among educated and sophisticated Indians, who were less susceptible to the semi-divine approach. The emphasis in administration was on the paternal tour around the countryside, which was brilliantly carried out, but no-one ever thought of offering the same attention to the masses in the cities; and it was in the cities that discontent with British rule was always most seriously to be found. The biggest fault of all, perhaps, was the reluctance of British ICS men – and it echoed that of politicians at home – to admit Indians equally to their own ranks. The Company Charter Act of 1833 had anticipated the day when Indians would share in the government of their country up to the highest level, and even the diehard Company Directors had on that occasion expressed their aversion to anything resembling 'a governing caste' on the sub-continent. Yet in 1870 only one Indian (from the famous Tagore family in Bengal) stood among the 916 members of the ICS; and when he was joined by three other Bengalis in that year, the event was so remarkable that the successful candidates were given a special civic reception by their compatriots in Calcutta. Almost up to Independence the process of 'Indianization' in the ICS was conceded with great caution by the British and was a perpetual source of irritation among educated Indians. Any number of proposals were put forward to satisfy both sides but most of them foundered because, at bottom, there simply was not enough will on the part of enough Britons to see them through. By 1915 there were still only 63 ICS Indians, or 5 per cent of the service. Three years later a plan was adopted that would have produced 48 per cent by 1930, but by that year only 367 Indians occupied ICS posts – not much more than one third. Indianization of the civil service was a concentrated example of the general British dilemma in India; a genuine recognition that one day India must be restored to Indians, with a deep need – born of selfishness, fondness and fear – to delay the moment for a little longer yet.

Quite the most astounding thing about British rule was the annual manoeuvre whereby the central government machinery was shunted, virtually en bloc, from the capital city up into the hills before summer began – and back again when the hottest weather was over. The hill stations of India generally attracted Europeans in the first place as refuges from the worst of the climate, where, if necessary, their health could recover its old vigour in temperatures comparable to those they had known at home. When Lord William Bentinck bought a strip of land round Darjeeling from the Raja of Sikkim in 1835, it was with the express purpose of building a sanatorium there, though the community was to become much better known as the centre of extensive tea plantations. Ootacamund, 7,500 feet up in the Nilgiri Hills between Bombay and Madras, performed similar functions as well as reminding excessively nostalgic (and imaginative) Englishmen of the landscape along the Sussex Downs. In time, every hill station contrived to become a home from home to which the white people could repair for three or four months and pretend that India had receded from their lives. Ooty's town centre was named Charing Cross and most of its houses bore far-fetched signs identifying them as Harrow-on-the Hill, Runnymede, Bideford and so on; while the Ootacamund Hunt in due course boasted one of India's best packs of fox-hounds, delicately bred to pursue jackals instead of their normal prey.

Of all the hill stations, Simla was supreme. The British first ventured into the highlands that far north of Delhi during their wars against the Gurkhas, but did not drop anchor until Captain Kennedy made his headquarters there as Superintendent of the Hill States in 1822. Lord Amherst was the first ruler to visit Simla a few years later but it was, again, Bentinck who acquired the 'middle-sized village' for the Government; after which Britons regularly headed for the refreshing slopes around Mount Jakko, where strawberries, raspberries, apricots and cherries grew wild at about the same altitude as Ootacamund. Not that all visitors fell for Simla's natural charms. Lady Canning thought 'the beauty of this place very questionable', and Lord Dalhousie (who suffered from nose bleeds up there) also declared it much overrated. He did, however, improve its communications with the outside world by including it on his ambitious Great Hindustan and Tibet Road, along which all traffic proceeded until the arrival of the railway in 1903. By that time the annual migration of the Government of India was a well established event. It was Sir John Lawrence who decided, in 1863, that he and his officials would function more efficiently during the summer months if they shifted 1,170 miles from Calcutta to Simla, in spite of the logistic difficulties this produced. Not only did the Viceroy and his Executive Council make the move, together with his secretariat, his Army headquarters, his external affairs department, representatives of the Indian princes and foreign envoys. There was also a horde of attendants and guards (the Viceroy alone had two or three hundred of them), as well as attached memsahibs and children, tradespeople who supplied goods by appointment to the Viceregal household, and intermittent delegations nominated by numerous Indian interests. And, of course, the wherewithal to function efficiently: many bullock carts creaking under the weight of packing cases full of files as they laboured slowly up the Great Hindustan and Tibet Road. Hannibal's army crossing the Alps had nothing on the British Raj ascending to its summer retreat.

Gradually the middle-sized village expanded into a fair-sized town under this great imperial patronage, so that by 1903 there were 1,400 European dwellings there, as well as the native settlement lower down the hillside. Lord Dufferin had built a grandiose Viceregal Lodge, five storeys high and furnished by Maples of Tottenham Court Road, which could accommodate eight hundred people for a state ball. His successor Lord Lansdowne had laid out a formal garden around it, importing a horticulturalist from England to supervise the work. The final effect was, according to the American Lady Curzon, something that a Minneapolis millionaire might revel in, though her own very English husband didn't much care for the building at all. When Lord Curzon's Viceregal duties took him to Simla, he preferred to establish himself in a huge tent thirteen miles away among the hills, where he worked through his files and exchanged necessary messages with the town by heliograph or flashing lamp. Nothing approached the Lodge in size or anything else. The gothic shape of Christ Church (with the frescoes around the chancel window designed by Lockwood Kipling, the author's father) resembled a discreetly suburban place of worship. This was one of several cultural introductions effected by the British. Another was the Gaiety Theatre, where amateur dramatics flourished especially during the Viceroyalty of Lord Lytton, who had three gilded boxes installed – for himself and his successors, for the Commander-in-chief, and for the Lieutenant-Governor of the Punjab, in whose province Simla was situated. Presently there were several hotels, including a Metropole and a Grand. There were a couple of newspapers, the *Himalayan Advertiser* and the *Simla Advertiser*. And there was the Simla Lending Library, which had accumulated 6,000 novels before the twentieth century was much advanced.

Time, you see, hung heavy on many hands – mostly feminine – during Simla's peak season of the year. While husbands were busy about the world's work, the memsahibs enlarged a little upon the routines they normally followed wherever the Queen's service had based them in India. Croquet was quite the rage in the 1860s, and sketching was a pastime that never seemed to fade. At weekends, many people dropped down to Annandale, a pleasant valley to the south of the town, where archery contests or gymkhanas or Fancy Fairs were held amidst thickets of pine and deodar; and this was a favourite site, too, for picnics which might be part of some palpitating flirtation. There was a highly romantic side to Simla, exaggerated by its warm and starlit nights, the silence of its surroundings, and its background of mountains illuminated by a full moon. Into this potent atmosphere many women arrived alone during the hot season, their spouses remaining down on the plains, indispensably discharging their duties; and there was usually a handsome surplus of young subalterns in the Viceroy's supporting cast, ready and willing to relieve any unofficial boredom. The resulting liaisons were more often languid than dramatic or harmful, though some Indian Army colonels became sufficiently alarmed at the possibility of scandal that they forbade their young men to spend leaves up in the hill stations, lest they earn the title of 'poodle-fakers'.

The social life was so eventful, it absorbed everybody for so much of the time, that it was sometimes difficult to appreciate amidst all the tittle-tattle and the swirl of ballroom gowns how serious Simla's primary business actually was. True, red liveried Government messengers were perpetually hurrying with their precious despatches along the Mall to this or that office up and down the town; but they might easily have been characters in the gorgeous charade that many people played in Simla for those few months in every year. Anyone wondering about the ultimate purpose of it all, however, in the last quarter of the nineteenth century, might have done well to ponder the gossip which attached itself to the owner of a curio shop there. His name was A. M. Jacob and his fame was not broadcast until it was realized that he had been the model for Lurgan Sahib in Kipling's *Kim* ('A black-bearded man with a green shade over his eyes', who taught O'Hara's boy the Jewel Game and much else). No-one visiting the shop, and rummaging for bargains among its dusty stock of devil masks, prayer wheels, Buddhas and spears, knew much about the mysterious Mr Jacob's antecedents. But people had seen him perform amazing conjuring tricks, had heard tell that he was a mesmerist as well and – quite confidentially, of course, because the authorities hadn't been able to prove anything – it was *said* that the fellow was really a Russian spy.

SIX

A WORKSHOP
IN THE EAST

Coming distinctly lower down the British caste system than the civil servants and the military officers, were the civilians who settled in India for purely business reasons. Only the non-commissioned British troops, the lowest form of white humanity in everyone else's eyes, stood between them and inferior natives of the sub-continent. The business civilians, known as 'box wallahs' to those above them on the social scale, were themselves as acutely aware of status as anyone. They were keen to emphasize, when they legitimately could, that they were in commerce rather than trade; the distinction being roughly one between those who sold commodities by the ton and those who sold them by the pound weight. The first were regarded as respectable; the second were thought to be trying a bit too hard to be acceptable – and if you were merely the manager of a shop you might hear pukka memsahibs refer to you, not quite out of earshot, as a 'counter-jumper' into the bargain. The clubs which dappled British India for social relaxation maintained the demarcation lines with the most careful rigidity, being specifically designed to exclude from membership anyone not wanted on grounds of race, status, table manners or occasional mispronunciation. The majority of clubs were not founded until well after the Mutiny, until the tide of Indian nationalism was beginning to flow strongly. They were places where the British could discuss their ruling preoccupations in secrecy without fear of offending Indian business contacts, provoking a riot or being subsequently outmanoeuvred by some native eavesdropper. A young box wallah arriving in Calcutta during the heyday of the Raj would be admitted forthwith to the Saturday Club (founded in 1880) and in due course, as he proceeded upwards in commerce and substance, he might expect to achieve the Tollygunge club (founded in 1895), which generally had a waiting list several years long. But only if he became extremely influential in business could he hope one day to hob-nob with senior Government officials in the Bengal Club (a curiosity in being established as early as 1827), where the atmosphere was more rarefied than anywhere else in the city apart from the Viceroy's residence half a mile away.

All this was strangely perverse, even for the whimsical British, whom trade and commerce had caused to come to India in the first place, and were the paramount reason why they remained there as long as they did. Far more than strategy or any civilizing mission they assumed for themselves, the profit margin was the main British interest in the sub-continent; the one constant in over three hundred years of activity there. They set out to make money from India and, although their ledgers showed financial losses from time to time, British shareholders in the long run emerged well on the credit side and British factory workers at home were offered a scale of employment they would not have known without such a captive market in the East. From 1880, India was the largest single customer for British manufactured goods, and after the First World War she took more British exports than Canada, Australia and South Africa put together. In the process of these benefits to Europeans, the industrial face of India was revolutionized, the social and economic pattern altered rather less. Long after the British had gone, India remained a predominantly agricultural society, which is what she had always been, the basis being the small and virtually self-sufficient community (at the lowest possible level of self-sufficiency) whose peasants farmed meagre plots of ground in a fashion that began to disappear from most of Europe soon after the Middle Ages.[1]

Industry had been very limited before the British arrived. Luxury goods in metal, minerals and textiles had been produced in many towns for sale to noble patrons, who alone could afford them. Benares had a thriving mass of workshops making brass and copperware for religious or domestic purposes, and these circulated widely. There was little else in the way of wholesale manufacture, every village's needs being provided by its own potters, its own carpenters, its own weavers, its own smiths. One powerful factor in localizing all forms of manufacture was the poor state of communications on the sub-continent until well into the nineteenth century. Roads were rare and little more than crude cart-tracks where they existed at all.

---

[1] Karl Marx was thinking wishfully when he wrote in 1853 that 'English interference . . . dissolved these small semi-barbaric communities, and thus produced the greatest, and to speak the truth, the *only* social revolution ever heard of in Asia.'

Things and people were usually transported along river systems, or else they didn't budge more than a few miles.

The first attempt to exploit India's resources – as distinct from simply trading in whatever raw materials and commodities were already marketed there – came towards the end of the eighteenth century, when the British established indigo plantations in Bengal. Hitherto they had obtained the highly-prized vegetable blue dye from the relatively small indigo growers of Gujarat on the west coast, whose almost cottage industry was soon extinguished by the new and much better organized competition on the other side of the country. The East India Company brought in experienced planters from the West Indies, and by extortionate contracts with Bengali peasants it rapidly and profitably expanded the Indian output of indigo into a major industry which flourished until, in 1897, German chemists developed the aniline substitute dye which knocked the bottom out of the indigo market. This was but one example of how forces outside British control affected the course of Indian economy under their rule. When the Napoleonic Wars drastically cut supplies of raw silk from Italy to Great Britain, the Company responded by starting the large-scale growth of silk in Bengal. The Irish potato famine in 1846 led to the vastly increased production of rice in Bengal and Burma for export to Europe. The Crimean War, by stopping the shipment of Russian hemp to England, transformed India's growth and manufacture of jute from the level of the handloom to that of the power-driven mill. Within a decade, India's export of raw cotton began to rise to unprecedented heights and in three years trebled in price because the American Civil War had suddenly left Lancashire without its own means of making textiles.

Planting, in one form or another, is where the industrial transformation of India began, and tea was even more of a British innovation than indigo had been. The Chinese variety of the beverage had been supped in London for over 150 years before the bush was found growing wild in Assam in 1820, but the Indian industry did not get going until Dr Campbell of the Indian Medical Service brought China tea seeds from the Kumaon and planted them at 6,000 feet near Darjeeling in 1841. Within 25 years there were 39 separate gardens covering 10,000 acres in that area alone, which by 1874 was producing nearly four million pounds weight of tea a year from 113 gardens. By then a mania for tea-planting had seized the British in every part of India where the bush could be persuaded to grow, and expatriates who had failed in everything else they set their hands to were being recruited to manage gardens from Assam in the extreme north down to the hill country of Cochin in the far south. In 1888, when the total crop was worth about £4 million a year, Britain's import of tea from India exceeded that from China for the first time; a lead that was never to be lost, mostly because China tea wasn't as skilfully rolled and dried, or as well packed for the long journey by sea. Throughout this period the expertise and the profit was almost monopolized by Britons (the first tea company managed by Indians was formed in 1879) but the labour was supplied by local natives in conditions that were as indefensible, for the most part, as those that existed on the indigo plantations. Coolies were recruited by the hundred in every tea district on the promise of wages that were not paid in full, they were despatched from the recruiting towns to the gardens in unsanitary conditions which produced many deaths, and they were liable to flogging for petty offences or merely for failing to work hard enough. Bounties were offered for those who absconded while their contracts still tied them to the gardens, and even at the end of the nineteenth century some 'coolie catchers' were notorious for their brutal efficiency in retrieving missing workers. One such creature named Saboulle, who operated in Bengal, drove the first motor car seen in those parts on petrol that was sent up from Calcutta for 10 rupees a gallon, at a time when an official report estimated that a labouring family of three would expect to earn no more than 14 rupees in its most profitable month of the year.

Much fouler conditions, though rather less cruel, were to be found in the jute industry. The word jute is Bengali in origin and the plant was cultivated there before the British came to India, its fibres providing the ropes and cordage that other parts of the world made from hemp. The village handloom weavers also made a rough cloth from it and the British patronized them a great deal for purely local needs until, in 1833, they began to ship home large quantities of the raw fibre to supply a new industry that had begun in a town whose fortunes henceforth would be inseparable from India – Dundee. The Douglas Foundry there had developed a spinning machine that could handle jute as well as it could process flax, and so Dundee became a great centre for the production of jute sacks among other things; a trade that expanded fast after the repeal of the Corn Laws and the consequent demand for more bags to carry grain in. When, shortly afterwards, the Crimean War cut off the alternative hemp supplies, the action moved back to India with the installation of Dundee machinery in a mill near Serampore. Power-driven looms were quite possible there by then, for coal had been discovered in Bengal in 1820 and the first mine was sunk at Raniganj a little later. From that original Serampore mill in 1854, the jute industry in India moved forward at a steady rate that was never equalled by any other form of manufacture, for it was the only one that never knew poor years as well as bountiful ones. It was, moreover, the only industry that remained entirely under British control right up to Independence. It became the especial province of Lowland Scots, and most particularly of Scots who came out from Dundee to manage the labour force of Indians, who toiled for pitiful wages in gloomy sheds, where the atmosphere was not much less thick with dust than the workings of a coal-mine; and did so, once the electric light bulb had been invented, in 10- or 12-hour shifts that continued right round the clock every day of the week. One reason for the steady growth of the Indian jute industry was that the woven material was perfect for making sandbags, and there was always a war going on somewhere around the world. By 1882 there were 20 jute mills – all but two in Bengal – employing 20,000 hands, and by 1885 Calcutta was exporting so much jute to the United States that the Dundee Chamber of Commerce itself was complaining of slave labour conditions in India. Nevertheless, the expansion continued. In 1908 there were 38 companies employing 184,000 Indians and 450 Scotsmen in Calcutta alone; in 1914 there were 61 mills in Bengal; by 1919 (after four years of the Great War) 76 mills; and by 1940 there were 110 mills. The profits were colossal. An analysis in 1927 showed that of 51 jute mills quoted, no fewer than 32 had paid dividends of more than 100 per cent in one or more years since 1918, and ten had never paid less than 40 per cent in any of those years. Approximately half the shares in the year of the analysis were in wealthy Indian hands. But many a braw lad from Dundee had also fattened himself on the sweat of Indian labour by the Hooghly River, and on the bloodshed of war all over the earth.

The classic example of India's economy being manipulated at the whim of local interests in Great Britain is that of the cotton industry. Up to the end of the eighteenth century there had been a regular flow of Indian textiles to Britain, with fine muslins from Dacca and chintzes from Lucknow figuring largely in the cargoes shipped out aboard East Indiamen. The Industrial Revolution in Europe changed all that to the extent that between 1814 and 1832 the export of Lancashire cotton goods to India rose by a fabulous 7,500 per cent, while the muslin industry in Dacca was practically destroyed because its handloom weavers simply couldn't compete with their power-driven rivals 7,000 miles away, who could produce cloth more cheaply and in much greater quantity. Lancashire's source of raw cotton was then chiefly America, whose Mobile and New Orleans staples were both stronger and cleaner than anything India grew, and not as frequently adulterated by the producers in order to boost the selling weight. Until 1846, the cotton towns around Manchester relied on the United States for 75 per cent of their supplies, India providing under 13 per cent. But when, in that year, the Americans had a disastrous harvest which resulted in massive unemployment and soup kitchens in Lancashire, the English manufacturers began to appraise India with new eyes. The Manchester Chamber of Commerce – a powerful body, because Lancashire cotton spinning and weaving was Britain's biggest industry by far at the time – started to lobby the Government to increase by all possible means the supply of raw cotton from India; a lobby which became more frantic, though no more fierce, when civil war broke out across the Atlantic and cut off American supplies for several years.

In 1861 the Chamber of Commerce demanded that the Government of India should raise (out of its own resources) a loan of between £30 million and £40 million to encourage widespread cotton planting and create better communications to aid transhipment to England; and one eventual result of the demand was the introduction of income tax to India. The Government, however, couldn't raise anything like that sum. Nor was the Secretary of State for India, Charles Wood, inclined to lend himself to what he perceived as a scheme to exploit labour on the sub-continent. 'I consider it my duty,' he told the Viceroy, 'to protect the native.' So infuriated by his attitude were the Mancunians that the president of the Chamber of Commerce (who was also Mayor of Ashton-under-Lyne) called for Wood's impeachment by the Crown. This was ignored, but Government did what it could to solve Lancashire's problem and in the process it wasted a lot of money. Some £750,000 was spent in unavailing efforts to make the River Godavari navigable in Central India. A Manchester Cotton Company was formed to buy newly-planted cotton in the Dharwar district of the Bombay presidency, and after the authorities had put in a road and wharf costing

£250,000 the company went bankrupt and the facilities were never used again. Lancashire did, nevertheless, obtain the sustenance it needed from India. Planting was increased on a gigantic scale and in the years from 1863 to 1865 raw cotton worth £36.5 million was exported to England, with the happiest result for Indians – an uncommon experience in such transactions. Even the peasant cultivators made so much cash that in many districts, for once in their lives, they were able to wriggle free from the tentacles of the moneylenders. More importantly for the future, Indians themselves began to build and run cotton mills with the funds and coal supplies newly at their disposal. The first one had been erected by a Parsi family in Bombay in 1854, and that area became the centre of a new industry based on machinery and remaining almost wholly in native hands. By 1874 there were 19 mills at work and four years later there were 42; by 1914 there were 264 and in 1935 the number had swollen to 365. A rivalry with Lancashire had started on terms that had not existed before and in the long run, after Independence was achieved, it was Lancashire and not the Indians who came off worst.

The tension between Government and private interests at home, which arose over cotton in the 1860s, occurred more often in the twentieth century when a variety of measures were taken to protect native industries from the effects of home-based competition. It was perpetually in evidence between the official administrators and the British business community in India itself. To some extent the box wallahs were regarded with loftiness close to contempt by the ICS men because they were almost incapable of contemplating anything but their own selfish ends, whereas officialdom at least as often as not tried to serve Indian interests as well as British. Throughout the 1860s one piece of legislation after another was passed to improve the condition of workers on the tea estates, involving recruiting controls and health safeguards at the gardens themselves. The Tea Planters Association found loopholes wherever it could, and many abuses continued for a long time because of enforcement difficulties in what were necessarily remote areas. Factory legislation also came down from Government House in a spate, regulating working hours and prescribing minimum safety rules, but it was not until after 1891 that controls were tightened enough to make the laws effective. The Bombay mills were the worst transgressors of all (one official report described many of them as utterly unfit for human beings to work in) but it was the Bengal Chamber of Commerce, dominated by British owners and managers, which was always most strongly opposed to any official interference in the practices of industry. The Government, in fact, was trying to keep pace with its counterpart at home, which in the last quarter of the nineteenth century passed a great deal of the social legislation affecting work, housing and health that considerably improved the lot of the general population in Great Britain. That Calcutta failed in its efforts to imitate Westminster more often than it succeeded was largely because the British non-official members of the Legislative Council, who represented bodies like the Planters Association and the Chambers of Commerce, deliberately put the brake on executive efforts. Though the non-officials sat in no more than an advisory capacity, rebellion by the entire white business community was more than a Viceroy could risk.

Government, however, did make its own tremendous contribution to the industrial transformation and economic improvement of India. The earliest public works, and the most protracted, were designed to reduce the likelihood of famine. This was endemic in a populous land where the rainfall varied from 460 inches a year up in the hills of Assam to a bare 3 inches in upper Sind, and was uncertain everywhere because of the vagaries of the monsoon, which sometimes failed to produce any rain at all. Warren Hastings had ordered the strange shape of the Gola to be built at Patna, so that 137,000 tons of grain could be stored under the enormous dome after a good harvest as an insurance against a bad one.[2] But irrigation was the obvious long-term solution to potential famine, as the Mughals had decided when they dug some canals soon after their arrival. These had fallen into disuse with the slow collapse of Mughal power until the British started to restore them in 1820. Twenty years later they began to channel much of the River Ganges into a canal which, by 1890, irrigated a wide area 400 miles long between Hardwar and Allahabad that had resembled desert except just after the monsoon floods. In the fifty years after the Mutiny, similar waterways were excavated all over India, especially in the more barren north, one of the most ambitious being started up in the Punjab just as the Ganges Canal was being finished. This was the Lower Chenab Canal, cut out of desolate ground visited only by nomads, where water was to be

[2] The Gola was only a strange shape for such a purpose. The dome whose base is flush with the ground had been seen in India since the time of the early Buddhists, who often built Stupas like that to commemorate the founder of their religion and to represent the circularity of the universe.

123

found deep below the surface. Three million acres were irrigated here, and the Government carefully chose the spot in order to siphon off people from far too densely populated parts of the Punjab. Various inducements were offered to settle them as cultivators in new canal colonies, including peppercorn rents for land, hereditary occupation if they proved satisfactory landholders for three years, and crafty devices to prevent the activities of moneylenders. Other colonies along other canals were set up when the Lower Chenab scheme was demonstrably successful, and although the major proportion of waterways had been cut before the First World War began, the work continued as long as the British were in India. By 1947, one fifth of the cultivable land on the sub-continent was irrigated by artificial means.

The most dramatic thrust by Government in matters of this kind came in the sphere of communications and in the person of Lord Dalhousie, who sailed in as Governor-General of India in 1848. It was he who introduced the civil engineer to the country, all previous heavy work having been attended to by the military, and one of his first acts was to create a Public Works Department. In the six years he spent in India, he saw 4,000 miles of telegraph wires strung up at his instigation and a great advance in road-building, beginning with the completion of Bentinck's Grand Trunk Road from Calcutta, which had only reached Benares when Dalhousie arrived but had been pushed beyond Delhi as far as Peshawar by the time he left. Nothing that he did, though, was comparable to his inspiration that the country must have railways. They were a speciality of his, for he had been President of the Board of Trade before coming to India and in that capacity he had been closely involved in the start of railways at home. There had been talk of them a few years before he arrived but nothing had been done because the difficulties of such major engineering in a land of hurricane and flood, to say nothing of mountains and rivers, were all too obvious; and the large matter of investment alone was enough to halt enthusiasts in their tracks. Dalhousie's predecessor, the soldier Lord Hardinge, had thought of the military advantages that might be provided by trains and these were quickly proven when the railways were installed. A regiment that had taken six months to march from Calcutta to Peshawar was able to make the journey in as many days; and a report on the Afghan campaign in 1878 pointed out that one train working a 16-hour day shifted as much as 2,500 camels might move in a fortnight. Dalhousie was not oblivious of strategic considerations but he advocated railways on civil grounds alone. 'The commercial and social advantages which India would derive from their establishment are, I truly believe,' he wrote in his minute which gave the go-ahead, 'beyond all present calculation.' One of the early committees set up to advance the great project gave the following reasons why it should be pursued as vigorously as possible: i famine prevention; ii development of internal and external trade; iii the growth of more remunerative crops in tracts reached by railways; iv the opening up of coalfields; v an improvement of the economic condition of the people.

The first cautious agreement the East India Company allowed Dalhousie to make was for a couple of short experimental lines, to be run by companies called the East Indian Railways and the Great Indian Peninsula Railway. Both were floated by investors at home under company guarantee, the GIPR including the redoubtable George Stephenson among its directors. The arrangement was short-lived, due to the sudden disappearance of the East India Company. In 1869 the Government of India took all responsibility for running the railways, which it did at a deficit until 1900, and simply hired private companies to manage them. But Dalhousie and his assortment of interests had made the breakthrough when, on 16 April 1853, the GIPR's first train of fourteen carriages, with 400 guests aboard, set off from Bombay to loud applause and a field-gun salute for a twenty-one-mile trundle down the line to Thana. Sixteen months later the EIR (which had been having a lot of trouble on the ground, as well as with the diversion of its locomotives from England by way of Australia because of bad weather at sea) got going from Calcutta along a line that had been extended as far as the Raniganj coalfield by February 1855. The Mutiny disrupted further progress, many lines being damaged at the surveying or track-laying stage. But when peace came in 1858, the advance of the railways across India was the most spectacular event the country had ever seen.

The engineering required was sometimes stupendous. The relatively short run from Bombay to Surat required bridges to be built across eighteen rivers, and some foundations had to be driven 140 feet deep to withstand the torrents of floodwater. When the railway was finally pushed up to Simla, the last 60 miles of track were laid along 103 tunnels blasted through the mountainsides. In Bihar, the Ganges flowed so widely during the monsoon near Patna that the engineers had to fling 93 spans nearly two miles long across it, one of the biggest bridges in the world at the time. Confronted with the huge geological fault of the Chappar Rift up in Sind, they delicately placed a filigree of girders across the sky, 233 feet above the gorge. The Western Ghats produced the biggest difficulties of all. This is a long ridge of volcanic rock running, sometimes 2,500 feet high, from north to south just inland of the coastal strip near Bombay. Any train approaching it from the city has to climb what is effectively a precipice broken along its front by deep ravines, and it needed the construction of 22 bridges and 25 tunnels to overcome that problem, with a gradient of 1 in 37 over much of the ascent. A work force of up to 40,000 men navvied their way across the Ghats and nearly a third of them died from accident or disease. One was Solomon Tredwell, the contractor hired to build that section of line, who lasted for only a couple of weeks after arriving from England; whereupon his widow carried on where he had barely started, and completed the contract herself.

Such was the amount of labour needed to build the railways that for the first time in its history India produced the mobile casual labourer; stone-masons from Rajasthan, especially, were on the move to wherever bridges and abutments had to be constructed. Ironwork for the civil engineering was almost all made in Britain, dismantled for shipment and put together again on the site; but only the earliest locomotives and rolling stock came out from Europe and were then used as models for Indian workshops to imitate. By 1906, the loco works at Jamalpur in Bihar were employing 10,000 men to make everything but the wheels of the engine, and there was similar plant in other parts of the country. Another by-product was the beginnings of forest conservation on the sub-continent, because so many millions of trees were felled to provide sleepers for the railway tracks. Well over 10,000 miles had been laid by the end of the nineteenth century (there would be four times as much by Independence) as India's steam trains puffed along in the various liveries of the different companies – the Great Eastern, the Bombay and Baroda, the East Bengal, the Madras, Sind, Punjab and Delhi, as well as the dear old GIPR and EIR. Their individual characters were tiresomely emphasized by the four different gauges extant up and down the country in defiance of Dalhousie's original advice. He had come out to India just as conflicting arguments about the width of railway tracks were reaching a ferocious height in England, and wanted none of the same complications on the sub-continent. It was Lord Lytton, with his zeal for bringing the metric system to India, who started the rot when he was Viceroy 30 years after Dalhousie left.

The trains steamed into stations that were sometimes as breathtaking in appearance as any architecture the Chalukyas or the Mughals had left behind; and, indeed, some of them were quite remarkable combinations of both ancient Hindu and Islamic forms. Others looked like fortresses, and were meant to serve as such in the event of another emergency like you-know-when. Most glorious of all was Bombay Victoria Terminus, opened during the Queen's Golden Jubilee year, which managed to blend Venetian, Gothic and Indo-Islamic styles all in one, with columns of granite from Aberdeen just to give the whole confection a touch of sternness as well. 'Much too magnificent for a bustling crowd of railway passengers,' declared Lady Dufferin, who was Vicereine when the building was finished. She was right about the bustling passengers, though. Never before had Indians moved about their land as they did after the railway age began. One instant effect was a great increase in the numbers going on pilgrimage to the famous holy places, and the British built extremely long platforms at the nearby stations to cope with the masses of people who might be expected to arrive during festivals. A concession they refused to make, although at one time there were four different classes of railway carriage, was the provision of separate compartments for different castes. When challenged about this, the Chief Engineer of the Madras Railway said the only distinction he recommended was that which could be purchased by money.

The advantages of the new transport system were so obvious once demonstrated, that the Indian princes were soon asking the Government to build railways across their states, too. The Gaekwar of Baroda, as befitted one of the senior native rulers, was the first recipient of his own train, and he travelled in a special carriage with a throne installed, one of his court officials riding the engine as a precaution against accidents. The hopes entertained for the new system were set out most lyrically by an English journalist, Sir Edwin Arnold, only a few years after those first experimental journeys had been made under Dalhousie's supervision. 'Railways,' he wrote, 'may do for India what dynasties have never done – what the genius of Akbar the Magnificent could not effect by government, nor the cruelty of Tippoo Sahib by violence. They may make India a nation.' In many ways, Arnold's expectations were not far short of the mark. Though regional and religious consciousness would scarcely be affected by the permanent way, and have remained divisive forces to this day, a certain unification did take place as the wheeze and thud of pistons began to mount, and the long smoke trails began to drift across the great variety of Indian landscapes. The railways were only responsible for this in so far as they represented and literally conveyed the evenness of the British presence throughout the country, and its relationship to the native population as a whole. But if the making of a nation also means its accession of material benefits that had seemed beyond its reach before, then there is no question that the railways contributed more to this achievement than any other single factor; as they did in other lands.

They did prove their value in famine relief very early on, when disaster struck South India in 1877 and four lines every day carried enough food into the area to keep seven million people alive – ten times the amount that could have been distributed with previous forms of transport. It was in the haulage of freight generally that the most impressive effects were seen in a country where, except during military campaigns, the bullock cart didn't have much more than a fifty-mile range along roads that were often impassable because of bad weather. The total value of imports and exports rose from £39.75 million in 1856 to £155 million in 1887 – an increase that could never have happened without the railways, abetted by the introduction of the steamship and the opening of the Suez Canal in 1869. Nor could there have been the great surge forward in industry, from the production of steel to lighter manufacturing, that began at the turn of the century and placed India, by the 1920s, among the eight leading industrial nations of the world. The railways even affected agriculture, by encouraging the concentration of big cash crops like cotton in the areas most suitable to their growth. The only casualty was long-distance steam navigation along the Ganges, which Bentinck had developed. The faster and more capacious railways quickly killed this off. The social effects were striking, quite apart from the unprecedented mobility of people. The railways not only provided a new and direct source of work (a staff of 700,000 by the 1920s) but caused other fresh employment to be available in the industries they stimulated and wage levels generally rose for those who were not still locked in the age-old and primitive subsistence on the land. Bandits found travellers harder to prey on, though many adapted quickly to the new era, and unfortunate passengers were liable to find themselves relieved of valuables as they sat cooling in the air that electric fans blew off ice blocks, when dacoits methodically worked their way down the train.

The railways thus added a new dimension to the national lore, with the romantic symbolism of the Down 42 Express and its peers, bearing as many passengers on the carriage roofs as were packed together inside. And they were incorporated into the work of the biggest romancer ever associated with British India. When Rudyard Kipling was born in Bombay, where his father was Professor of Architectural Sculpture in the School of Art, he had only missed that first run of the GIPR by a dozen years, and his infancy therefore coincided with the moment when the full power of the Victorian Raj was beginning to assert itself. At the age of five and a half, like most British children, he was withdrawn from the care of his ayah and dismissed to England, where he spent one of the most miserable periods of his life; and he didn't see his parents again until he returned to India when he was almost 17. He had side whiskers and bad eyesight, and when he reached Lahore, where his father had become Principal of the Mayo School of Art, and curator of the local museum – the Wonder House, as local Indians called it – he obtained a post in journalism, as much because it was thought that his myopia would handicap him in any of the public services as because he had already shown a talent for writing. He became Assistant Editor of the *Civil and Military Gazette*, a grand title for an all-round job which required him to do everything but set the type and print it. Kipling, in fact, was half the editorial staff of a very provincial newspaper, covering as many garden parties and sub-editing as many columns of district reports as if he had been based in a market town of the English shires.

In Lahore, it was a boon to him. As well as the humdrum work, there were also opportunities to report on Viceregal visits, to attend murder trials, to take notes at an official enquiry into the number of lepers who supplied beef and mutton to the European community. He went to the Khyber Pass in pursuit of a military story and came under fire from tribesmen near Fort Jamrud; and he ranged as far as Calcutta to see the seamy side of the city's life with policemen and log the work of the elite corps of river pilots on the Hooghly there. Invaluably armed with fragments of vernacular he still remembered from his ayah, he would wander round the bazaar in Lahore at night instead of lying sleepless under his mosquito net in the hot weather, making the acquaintance of those who frequented illicit liquor shops and opium dens, watching native dancers, increasing his knowledge of the real India all the time. And with a British infantry battalion and a battery of artillery always stationed near his office, he associated a great deal with the despised other ranks of the Raj. 'My first and best-loved Battalion,' he was to write much later, 'was the 2nd Fifth Fusiliers . . .' On behalf of the *Gazette*, he investigated brothels in the city and reported the failure of the authorities to have prostitutes examined for disease, which meant that 9,000 soldiers a year spent a lot of time in military hospitals all over India. Kipling was himself, for a while, a private in the 1st Punjab Volunteers, part of the civilian auxiliary force, but he consistently failed to turn up on parade and so was drummed out with no sense of loss.

He was not very popular with the British of his own middling level and the most attentive members of the Punjab Club especially thought him a very bouncy young man. It was there, after Kipling had made some cutting remarks about the ICS, that he was only just prevented from fighting a junior civil servant named Michael O'Dwyer, who was later – when he had risen to become Lieutenant-Governor of the Punjab – at the centre of the most disreputable incident ever to stain the British record in India; the Amritsar massacre in 1919. The trouble with young Kipling, according to his British contemporaries, was that he spent far too much time with the lower orders, brown or white (it didn't seem to matter which) and thought he knew it all. He himself was writing to a friend at home that

I'm in love with the country, and would sooner write about her than anything else . . . I shall find heat and smells and oils and spices, and puffs of temple incense, and sweat and darkness, and dirt and lust and cruelty, and above all, things wonderful and fascinating innumerable.

He did find enough of these things to feed on professionally for the rest of his life, in only four years with the *Gazette* and another two with the slightly larger *Pioneer* in Allahabad. He started publishing his stories and his verses while he was still in Lahore, on the newspaper's presses. Instantly he was transformed from an obscure young hack with thick glasses to a name that British India began to talk about as much as it delighted in his tales and his thumping way with metrical lines. So popular had he become shortly after reaching

Allahabad, that his collection of yarns entitled *Soldiers Three* was chosen to launch Wheeler's Railway Library, whose paperbacks could ever afterwards be purchased at station bookstalls (price 1 rupee) for the amusement of passengers with long journeys ahead, the distinctive green covers being designed for many years by Rudyard's father Lockwood.

Kipling left the *Pioneer* early in 1889 because, it is thought, the proprietors wanted him out of the way when a libel case, involving a Captain Hearsay the young author had offended, came to court. He was barely 24 and the plan was for him to take some extended leave out of the country. So he sailed for England by way of the Far East and America, and when he reached London he found book contracts awaiting him that meant he need never again turn to journalism for his chief financial support. He saw India only once more, three years later, when he was an international figure, visiting his parents briefly on the way home from a trip to Australia and New Zealand. But his effect on her was already incalculable. Several more generations of the British would go out there to take part in the ruling processes, and many of them did so because Rudyard Kipling had triggered a fancy. He had caused some to follow where Colonel Creighton had been, he had incited others with his steaming tale of Daniel Dravot and Peachey Carnehan, and some he had enraptured at Nanny's knee, where they first heard the doings of Mowgli, Rikki-tikki-tavi, and the great grey wolf Akela leading his pack to the Council Rock.

SEVEN

CALL US
WHAT YOU WILL

An indisputable truth about Kipling is that he was, in George Orwell's phrase, 'a jingo imperialist,' though most of the evidence comes from the period of his life after he had left India. He is far harder to pin down and label so simply when seen in the exclusively Indian setting of his late adolescence, where his responses were strikingly those of a capable journalist, detached enough to be critical of or sympathetic to rulers and ruled alike, but far less concerned with motive than with symptoms and activity. The difficulty in coming to a neat conclusion is nowhere greater than in Kipling's attitude to race on the sub-continent, which defies facile generalization. It is not easy to reconcile the affectionate portraits he drew of the Lama, Mahbub Ali and Hurry Chunder Mookerjee in *Kim* (published in 1901), with the bleak view expressed thirteen years earlier in *Plain Tales from the Hills* that 'A man should, whatever happens, keep to his own caste, race and breed. Let the White go to the White and the Black to the Black.' Here is ambivalence, with warmth and rejection issuing from the same source. In this, if not always in other respects, Rudyard Kipling typified a common British feeling about the non-white people who inhabited the sub-continent.

There are ample grounds for suggesting that often far too many of them were guilty of, in today's jargon, straightforward racism. During the retribution that immediately followed the Mutiny, the epithet 'nigger' crossed many British lips. At about the same time, educated Hindu Bengalis had become so aware that the British sneered at them as an 'effete' people, that they self-consciously began to practise gymnastics, wrestling and other old athletic skills in an effort to dispel this image, raising such activities into a local cult which persisted well into the twentieth century. For decades after the Mutiny, all manner of racial prejudice was aired wherever in the world the Union Jack flew; and justification was frequently sought in reference to the theories of Charles Darwin, whose *Origin of Species* had come out the year after the Mutiny was finally quashed. It was under the influence of Darwin that a Fellow of the London Anthropological Society argued in 1864 that the Chinese and Indians were superior to the Africans, being more notable for docility, intelligence and industry.

Government did not always distance itself as much as it might have done from such sentiments, but its failings were at least balanced by its attempts to achieve equity, which led to constant friction between officialdom and the British civilian population in India, dramatically so when the Ilbert Bill was published in 1883. This was the inspiration of Lord Ripon, a Viceroy with advanced views about Indian self-government, though it took its name from the law member of his Executive Council who drafted it. It was designed to let Indian judges try Europeans in courts outside the three Presidency towns, as they often had done within them for several years by then. All unofficial British organizations were so incensed by this notion that they boycotted Government House and there was even a plan to kidnap the Viceroy. As a result Ripon had the bill watered down to stipulate that juries – at least half of whom must be European in each instance – must sit on any case in a district court where an Indian judge faced a European in the dock. The division among the British on this topic was reflected by one couple in Bengal. Henry Beveridge, a District Judge there, supported the original provisions of the bill. His wife Annette (well-known for equally progressive views as a rule) vehemently opposed them on the grounds that the bill would 'subject civilized women to the jurisdiction of men who have done little or nothing to redeem the women of their own races, and whose social ideas are still on the outer verge of civilization.' The mass of white opponents drew much less delicate distinctions to justify their antipathy.

The prejudices of the British were always most powerfully exercised in the composition of their clubs, whose committees were so intransigent about who they would and would not admit to membership, that as late as the 1930s an exasperated Viceroy (Lord Willingdon) deliberately founded new clubs in Bombay and Delhi to provide common ground for people of both races. In the same period, a young British ICS official was noting that 'Most of the people here have an anti-Indian prejudice, which is unfortunately so common among the British in India, and particularly among the military.' He was writing when Indian nationalism was approaching its most aggressive height, and British hostility was, most of all, specifically against insurrection. But there were other elements in the prejudice, and to understand what these consisted of it is instructive to read a handbook published in 1915 by a former professor of English at the Presidency College in Calcutta.

This was addressed to Indians who might expect to have dealings with the British somewhere above the menial level, and it is entirely concerned with behaviour. 'To chew anything (such as pan or betel),' it begins, 'in English society is not considered polite. Learn, therefore, to abstain from the practice when you are in the company of European gentlemen and ladies . . .' There are other injunctions against patting or stroking 'any part of your person', against biting nails, against scratching. There is a section which advises reticence both in speech and writing. 'Never use "stomach" or "bowels" ("belly" is worse still). If necessity arises, use "abdomen".' Table manners get careful attention, for 'There is a great art in eating properly. Transact all the business of the table quietly and gently. Do not eat quickly or ravenously and never smack your lips.' If the Indian should be so lucky as to receive an invitation to a party, he should 'Remember that a presentation to a lady in a ball-room for the purpose of dancing does not entitle you to claim her acquaintance afterwards.' And, buried among the 130 pages somewhere between the bowels and the waltz, there is this.

Do not be over-sensitive to criticism. Learn to tolerate criticism . . . Englishmen are apt on occasion to be somewhat rough-and-ready in what they say and do but remember that such downright conduct is not necessarily overbearing, and do not convert a hasty word or what is intended only for jest into a deadly insult.

It is relevant to note that within a few years another handbook appeared, this one advising British newcomers about their behaviour to Indians. They were told to remember that 'if an Indian imperfectly acquainted with English addresses you in English, it is obviously bad form to make sport of the Indian's halting English.' Furthermore,

It cannot be too strongly emphasized that rude and offensive behaviour by Europeans towards Indian fellow passengers in public conveyances is one of the things that causes the greatest resentment and most seriously injures European prestige and influence.

Somewhere near the heart of the matter, in the author's view, was this inspiration.

The Indian attaches great importance to his prestige, 'izzat'. This may be translated as self-respect . . . While it is a cardinal virtue in handling men, whether in the East or in the West, not to reprove them in the presence of others who are subordinates, it is particularly the case in India.

All this is exactly the condescending advice that an English gentlewoman at home might have given to a new butler she was about to employ; or what a Victorian parent might have said to a child just out of infancy. Comparable instructions were probably being offered at about the same time in Great Britain in those institutions which trained English girls to become nannies or paid companions well above their natural station in life. In short, the prejudice against Indians, by early in the twentieth century at least, was more closely related to station and class than it was to race as such. It was not the same prejudice the British had against other coloured peoples in their Empire, who were dismissed as 'savages' and kept totally at arm's length. Where antipathy followed colour patterns on the sub-continent, it was almost always paralleled by similar prejudices among Indians themselves. On the evidence of the first handbook, the British variant allowed for the possibility of dark Indians dancing with lilywhite Englishwomen; and it is assumed in the second handbook that Indians and Britons might occupy the same railway carriage. There is plenty of other evidence that the upper echelons of British and Indian society rarely kept a distance from each other on racial grounds. They played polo and cricket together at every available opportunity, often in mixed teams. One Indian, K. S. Ranjitsinhji, played for an otherwise English cricket team in England in 1893, captaining another one in 1899, almost half a century before a colour bar ended in American baseball and the first black man competed with white men in the major leagues. While Ranji was in England a Parsi from Bombay, Dadabhai Naorowji, was actually sitting in the House of Commons as MP for the London constituency of Central Finsbury, with Bethnal Green represented by Sir M. M. Bhownagree, another Parsi, on behalf of the Tories from 1895 to 1906. The rich and the powerful of both races in India entered each other's homes from the earliest days, forming friendships and occasionally unions that proceeded through generations; and where barriers existed between the upper classes and castes, they were as much due to Indian inhibitions as to British reluctance. That daunting word miscegenation certainly never deterred as many people in India as it did in other parts of the Empire. There was a great deal of mixed blood circulating round the sub-continent by the end of the nineteenth century.

It had started to flow over two hundred years earlier when the East India Company, like the Portuguese before it, had found the cost of shipping out European women to India exorbitant, and began to encourage its servants there to take native wives and mistresses. This they did so eagerly that by the second half of the eighteenth century the offspring of such unions far outnumbered the wholly British there. They were variously known throughout this period and for a long time afterwards as half-castes, as Country-born people, as Indo-Britons, as East Indians and as Eurasians; not until the census of 1911 would they officially be recognized as Anglo-Indians, a title that had previously been adopted by those members of the British community who had been born in India or had spent most of their lives there. To have been the Hindu mother of an Anglo-Indian (as we shall now refer to them here, irrespective of dates) was to have paid a heavy price, for the first and last act of her family on hearing that she had formed a liaison with a European was to 'put her out of caste' and have nothing whatsoever to do with her again. The early British on the sub-continent treated her, as well as any children she bore, much more kindly than that. Many of these children, and their own offspring in turn, rose to the highest levels in the making of British India and founded dynasties whose names still rang round the sub-continent when Independence came. They included a lot of soldiers. Sir Eyre Coote, who fought at Plassey and later became commander-in-chief after Clive, was one. James Skinner, founder of the most famous Indian cavalry regiment, was another, the son of a Scotsman and a Rajput woman. General Sir John Hearsey, who showed much more sense than most British commanders on the eve of the Mutiny (he advised the authorities to let the sepoys provide their own grease for the cartridges), was descended from a marriage between a Jat and an English army captain. Lord Roberts, hero of the 1879 campaign from Kabul to Kandahar and supreme commander in the Boer War, was the grandson of a Rajput princess. He was not quite the most illustrious product of mixed blood. That distinction goes to Lord Liverpool, Tory Prime Minister for fifteen years when the Industrial

Revolution was getting into its stride, whose maternal grandparents were a Calcutta woman and the Mr Watts who profited so much from the extortion following Plassey. Anglo-Indian connections were liable to crop up even farther afield than London. Elihu Yale, Governor of Madras before becoming benefactor of the American college which bears his name, was married to a woman of mixed blood and had three children with her.

Things began to go ill for the Anglo-Indians in the last years of the eighteenth century, when the Company became uneasy at their numerical superiority over the British. There had lately been a number of uprisings in the Caribbean against Spanish and French rule, with black slaves and mulattos of mixed blood combining against European masters, and the Directors were worried lest the same thing should happen in India. This was a crass misjudgement when the local equivalent of mulattos had already demonstrated their loyalty many times and could not, because of Indian caste rules, become serious allies of the Hindu population in any case. If anything, they were even more at odds with the Indian Muslims, who took the severest view of racial and religious purity. Yet steps were taken between 1786 and 1795 to bar Anglo-Indians from the covenanted ranks of the civil service and from all military rank, except in the capacity of bandsmen and farriers. Some were already too far launched on their careers to be retrieved, others put themselves at the disposal of the Indian princes to whom mercenaries were generally welcome, but no new mixed blood was to be admitted to the restricted services of the Company henceforth. The shabbiness of this treatment was emphasized within a few years when, needing all the manpower it could muster to fight the Marathas and Hyder Ali in Mysore, the Company drummed up every Anglo-Indian it could lay hands on to fight alongside full-blooded Britons and Indian sepoys; then disbanded them the moment the last shot had been fired – a process that was repeated regularly up to the Mutiny, whenever battle had to be done.

A much bigger blow than any landed by Company policy, however, fell on the hybrid community when British women began to sail East in quantity in the nineteenth century. Earlier, most Company servants had either openly married native women or had maintained mistresses in a discreet extension to their dwellings, the annexe known as the bibi-khana. Such ménages were sometimes blithely polygamous on an exhausting scale. Sir David Ochterlony, the general who first fought and then befriended the Gurkhas, provided one of the sights of Calcutta around 1820 when he and his thirteen wives made their daily progresses across the maidan, mounted on the backs of one elephant after another. William Fraser, one of Bentinck's commissioners in Delhi, was known far and wide for having killed eighty-four lions – and for keeping six or seven 'legitimate wives' who lived together and regularly bore him children, these being reared as Hindus or Muslims according to their maternity. As late as the 1840s, the fat and benign Meadows Taylor administered the small state of Shorapore with the domestic support of a large and varied female household. This was, chronologically, about the limit of widespread Anglo-Indian propinquity. The white memsahibs by then had settled in some force, the bibi-khana was thought disreputable, and mixed marriages were regarded with distaste. Unions between 'pure' Britons and 'pure' Indians thereafter became very uncommon indeed. At the same time, existing Anglo-Indians found themselves in a social no man's land between the rulers and the ruled, a sort of outcast society by superior and inferior decree.

But they still rallied ardently to the British flag, partly because ostracism by Indians was more fiercely durable than that by Europeans, partly because they were as conscious of position and status as anyone and preferred to think of themselves as junior partners of the British rather than conquered subjects. Given this self-image, it would have been unnatural had they not formed up with the beleaguered whites in Cawnpore, Lucknow and elsewhere when the Mutiny came; and, as in the case of earlier Company crises, they were very welcome then. They produced their own quota of heroes, like George Brendish, an eighteen-year-old telegraphist who stuck to his post in Delhi as the mutineers advanced and tapped out the message that warned the Punjab of the catastrophe that might be coming its way. The British did not overlook such loyalty when peace had been restored this time. As a matter of the deepest self-interest as well as gratitude, they made it a policy to employ people of mixed blood from 1858 onwards in almost all the vital working positions throughout the communications network. The Posts and Telegraphs Department, below managerial level, became a near monopoly of the Anglo-Indians. The Customs and Excise services also recruited them in large numbers. Most famously of all, they were the people who actually *ran* the railways as these expanded across the country. It was they who supplied nearly every engine driver, every guard, every stationmaster, every permanent way inspector. The Railway Institute, an increasingly familiar landmark as communities grew around the new railway junctions and railway workshops, became the great focal point of Anglo-Indian social life.

Like untainted Indians, they developed a great appetite for education when they observed that the British really did allow (sometimes even encouraged) a certain amount of upward social and economic movement, irrespective of colour, caste or creed, provided you had the brains and used them to obtain a qualification. They started some famous schools, such as Doveton College in Calcutta and La Martinière in Lucknow, and they admitted to these institutions a number of equally ambitious Indians of what they regarded as the better class. And, again like pure natives, some people of mixed blood did begin to rise to fairly commanding positions in the British order of things from the last quarter of the nineteenth century onwards. Of those who always recognized India as their home, Henry Gidney's was probably their greatest individual success. He was born in a small town near Bombay in 1873 and brought up as a Methodist, a bright boy who in time was admitted to the Indian Medical Department. This was attached to the Army in India, subordinate to the Indian Medical Service, and open only to Anglo-Indians. But after going to England and passing the requisite examinations, Gidney was admitted to the IMS, then went on to specialize in ophthalmic surgery. After that, his career was indistinguishable from a brilliant Englishman's. He was able to tack some mighty impressive letters after his name, including FRS – and he was the youngest Fellow in the Royal Society's history. He became a lecturer in his subject at Oxford and senior surgeon in a military hospital during the First World War. Then he went home and opened a large private eye hospital in Bombay. Within a few years he was elected to the Imperial Legislative Assembly, the embryonic parliament that India had recently, as last, acquired. By 1931 he was Sir Henry Gidney, a flamboyant man who was hardly ever seen in public without his monocle and button-hole; who collected women as energetically as he bought paintings; and who liked to tell how, when he served with the IMS in Assam, he had bagged fifty-two tigers, four elephants and two rhinos with his own gun. He had also become the leading spokesman of the Anglo-Indian community, whom he once severely advised that 'if there is one thing which you must completely eradicate from yourselves, it is the retention of superiority and inferiority complexes; and you should bring about their replacement with a complex of equality.'

This was asking rather a lot of them when, as Gidney himself had pointed out in the Assembly, an Anglo-Indian ticket collector working his way up through the railway system earned only 32 rupees a month, whereas an English ex-soldier started his second career as a guard at a wage of 125 rupees a month. The former Tommy had doubtless decided to settle down in India after his time in the Army expired because he had married an Anglo-Indian girl and had been advised – or, following his instinct, had realized – that life with a coloured wife in England might not be easy for either of them. The British on the sub-continent were hard enough to bear, with their unpleasant little words for Anglo-Indians, like chee-chee (which mocked their accents) or blackie-white; and in the twentieth century there were patronizing remarks about 'twelve annas to the rupee'. Indians sneered at them just as much, with references to kutcha butcha (half-baked bread) or teen pao (if they were on the dark side) or adha seer (for those almost as pale as their British ancestors). One result of such humiliation was to make the Anglo-Indians excessively conscious of their own physical characteristics. They worried a great deal about the shade of colour they had inherited, and they pursued little snobberies within their own community, cultivating the aquiline, snubbing the broad-nosed. Any family whose daughter began to go out with a British soldier would thrill at the prospect of romance being consummated in wedlock, so that the breeding strain would be somewhat improved. The other ranks of the British Army in India were practically the only white men the average Anglo-Indian girl had a hope of marrying, both partners being at approximately the same level somewhere towards the base of this class-conscious, caste-ridden society. The girls were much in demand by the Tommies, for most of them were very good-looking indeed; as though the chemical processes of assorted generations had compensated the outcast by gradually purging her line of all coarseness until total refinement was reached. Unlike full-blooded Indian women, they cut their hair short and had a taste for artificial curling, and rarely wore flowers or other ornaments on their heads. A single coloured glass bangle on the wrist was about as far as they would go towards conforming to the norm of female decoration in India. And they wore Western dresses, almost never the native

140

sari. They shunned such Indian men as desired them as much as they welcomed the attentions of British troops. Intermarriage with other native communities had never happened much and practically ceased after the Mutiny was put down.

As time passed, the Anglo-Indians became concentrated in certain parts of the country like Calcutta and its hinterland, the area around Madras, and in Bangalore. Comparatively few settled in Delhi and they were almost unknown in the Punjab and Rajasthan – though groups were always to be found in the railway towns anywhere. Almost all of them were Christian; their houses invariably had a gimcrack print of Jesus or some biblical scene hanging on one of the walls; and they spoke patronizingly of wholly Indian converts to their faith. A number of other characteristics became typical as their community developed the laager mentality that history had bequeathed. Parents would prefer to run into debt in order to send their children to fee-paying convent or mission schools, rather than have them associate with Indians in the vernacular schools that the Government provided free. They were desperately afraid that otherwise they might lose their own culture, what they regarded as their mother tongue and their heritage. One domestic aspect of this was maintained in the kitchen, where Anglo-Indian women preferred to cook standing up, instead of squatting on the floor in the custom of other native housewives; and the family would eat from a table, instead of reclining against cushions on a rug. Neither men nor women had much liking for beer, but both sexes were addicted to a milk punch – made with rum, sugar and milk – and to wine, which they called grog. In their gatherings at the Railway Institute the favourite activity apart from dancing or table tennis was housie-housie, progenitor of our Bingo and probably picked up from the British troops. The Institute was generally referred to as the 'Inster', for the Anglo-Indians had a weakness for English colloquialisms rarely used by whites above the level of the sergeants' mess. They tended to bid each other farewell with 'Cheerio' or 'chin-chin', and instead of greeting someone with 'How do you do?' they were more likely to say 'Pleased to meet you'; and in doing so positioned themselves precisely, to within a millimetre, on the scale that Englishmen had evolved to equate speech patterns with social worth. The Institute became an important feature of Anglo-Indian social life because there alone they could gather without having to worry whether they were going to be insulted by the pure British or polluted by the pure Indians. It was where families exhibited their sense of solidarity; where boy met girl and maybe went on to an unarranged marriage; where all forms of social life took place, with a strong emphasis on sports and games. The young men became proverbially fine hockey players, seriously damaging the general impression that to be of mixed blood was to be physically inadequate and rather shifty as likely as not – a fiction that Edgar Wallace perpetrated more than anyone else.

If they had possessed a keener sense of history, if they had attended more carefully to the political winds that were beginning to stir towards the end of the nineteenth century, the Anglo-Indians might have served their own future better than they did. The last years of that era saw the beginnings of Indian nationalism rather than regionalism, of the movement that would ultimately persuade the British to leave the sub-continent and go home. There is little doubt that if the Anglo-Indian leaders had thrown in their lot with the first Indian National Congress in 1885, they would have been welcomed, for it was a movement broad enough to have accommodated them in spite of suspicions and hostilities on either side. They dithered a great deal for a while until their attachment to the existing rulers, that side of them which was the source of all their pride, persuaded them to stand fast yet again by the Union Jack. This was an emotional response which, they soon recognized as the twentieth century advanced, might be costly when Indians at last ruled their own land.

The dilemma of their position was poignantly expressed by one of their number in the 1920s when the ultimate political outcome was too obvious to ignore. 'If England is the land of our fathers,' wrote H. A. Stark,

India is the land of our mothers. If to us England is a hallowed memory, India is a living verity . . . If England is dear as a land of inspiring traditions, India is loved for all that she means to us in our daily life . . . If we lean so heavily to our fathers' side, it is because the creeds and customs of our mothers' people so ordained it. Themselves the victims of a tyrannical caste system and religious orthodoxy, as they have in the present so had they in the past, no option but to repudiate our consanguinity . . . We naturally identify ourselves with the social, economic and political development and aspirations of our mother country. We would live amicably and on terms of mutual trust and respect with our Indian fellow-countrymen, and would have them reciprocate our sentiment . . . In truth we are England's hostage to India, and they who give and they who receive hostages are bound to regard them in trust. If Indians only realized this, our economic and political positions would not seem to us so desperate as it now appears.

The alarm implicit in that appeal was felt strongly enough by Stark's community as a whole for them to lobby Government shortly afterwards for the creation of a separate state within India, to be inhabited by Anglo-Indians alone. The petition was rejected, but the authorities did establish the colony of McCluskieganj in the industrial area of Bihar, and settled 300 families there on 7,000 acres which left ample room for expansion. This never happened, largely because of factionalism among the Anglo-Indians, which was part of their Indian birthright. As the prospect of national Independence loomed nearer, frantic efforts were made to produce a cohesive sense of community, with the formation of bodies like the Anglo-Indian Study Circle and Book Centre in Calcutta. Whatever such groups managed to achieve in promoting a common purpose was invariably offset by the bickering that went on elsewhere, based on regionalism and – inevitably – racial rather than social composition. The Anglo-Indians of the north looked down on those from the south, whose European ancestry was more likely to be Portuguese or Dutch than British. These were scathingly referred to as Feringhis by the northerners, and in their turn they disdained the northerners as uncouth 'Tommy stock'. The only national associations that had a hope of uniting the people of mixed blood regularly split up on such quibbles as these, and sometimes seemed to agree only in their joint antagonism towards poor Christianized Indians, who wished to improve their own security by identifying themselves with the one comparable community that had a certain amount of political strength.

Just before Independence became a fact, thousands of Anglo-Indians left the country, assuming that full-blooded Indians running their own nation would take some form of reprisal for the long decades of small privilege enjoyed by the underlings of the British. About 25,000 made new lives for themselves in Australia, Canada and the United States. Even more made for the hallowed memory of England, where some had a trying time of it, what with the weather and the fact that they no longer had at least one Indian servant at their beck and call. Occasionally they failed tragically to adjust to new ways. Stanley Prater, who had represented the Anglo-Indians for seventeen years in the legislature of Bombay State and was curator of the Bombay Museum, went to London but could only find work there as a clerk and died just over a year later from, it was said, acute melancholia. He had fled from something that never material-ized on the scale that Anglo-Indians had feared. To be sure, those that took their chance and stayed behind lost their privileged role on the railways and in Posts and Telegraphs; but the British had been gradually adjusting that imbalance for half a generation before Independence came. The new Indian Constitution safeguarded their position to a certain extent by recognizing the Anglo-Indians as one of six official minority groups for whom there would be special provisions codified by law – though in practice this left them as much exposed to social prejudice as Indians of the lowest castes, whose position was also nominally protected by the rhetoric of constitutional intent. Their leaders in the new all-Indian parliament were soon fighting real or imaginary battles against those they described as 'Hindu imperialists', especially when moves were made to have English abandoned and replaced by Hindi as the language of officialdom in the republic.

Increasingly towards the end of the Raj, and in the years that followed it, they comforted themselves with nostalgia for times past when their own kind had produced great heroes in this land. They recalled especially James Skinner, a commander of such proportions that the troops who fought under him hailed him as Sikander Sahib, which was a way of comparing him to Alexander the Great. With the nostalgia there was also, as time went on, a certain wistfulness with tart undertones, as they pointed out to strangers various celebrities in a much wider world than theirs and said, 'D'ye know that he's really one of us?': claiming the writer John Masters (in spite of the fact that his novel *Bhowani Junction* irritated them no end), and the entertainers Engelbert Humperdinck (born Gerald Dorsey in Madras) and Cliff Richard (formerly Harry Webb of Lucknow). These were the residual reflexes of a people who felt that history in some puzzling way delivered to them far less than it had promised; that the patrons in whom they had placed such trust had sold them short in the end. The Anglo-Indians were quite the saddest result of British imperialism.

The poster advertising the film *Gunga Din* just before the Second World War. The inspiration was Rudyard Kipling's poem, but the execution was pure Hollywood. The Americans made no fewer than 35 films between the *Hindoo Fakir* in 1902 and *Gunga Din* in 1939, with a common theme of the British putting down their rebellious Indian subjects.

The Remnants of an Army; oil by Lady Elizabeth Butler 1879. The man on horseback is Surgeon William Brydon, of the Indian Army Medical Corps, shown reaching the British fort at Jalalabad in 1842. He was the sole survivor of over 16000 men, women and children who had begun the retreat from Kabul 10 days before. The painting typifies a prevailing British sentiment about imperialism which lasted well into the twentieth century.

Colvin's Ghat and Strand; watercolour by William Prinsep c. 1800-1825. Ghats
are simply steps down to the rivers in India. Colvin's Ghat was one of many along
the Hooghly in Calcutta from which merchandise was carried in and out of the
ships anchored in midstream. The Strand is the riverside road running just

upstream of Fort William, which the East India Company had built soon after establishing a settlement there. By the time the picture was painted, Calcutta had become a community of substance, emphatically designed on European lines, on its way to becoming the second city in the British Empire.

Colonel James Todd travelling upcountry c. 1800. A stylized Indian view of the British Raj moving about its lawful business. Colonel Todd was in the process of rising steadily in the East India Company's scheme of things. Within a few years he had become Resident in the native state of Gwalior, subsequently took charge of Intelligence during the Pindari campaign and finished up as Political Agent in the Western Rajput states.

James Skinner with his troops; from the *Book of Rules for Manoeuvres of the Hindustan Musket Cavalry.* Skinner (on the dias, centre, with his son to the right) was one of the most famous commanders of British India in the early nineteenth century. Skinner's Horse, often known as the Yellowboys, were the senior regiment of Indian cavalry up to Independence, though at one stage they were renamed the Bengal Lancers.

New Delhi completed; watercolour by Marjorie Shoosmith 1931. Mrs Shoosmith was the wife of one of the junior architects of New Delhi, and her picture in the old Indian miniature style shows many of the chief characters in the great imperial enterprise. Lord Irwin, the Viceroy, is seated and the three men approaching him are Sir Edwin Lutyens and Sir Herbert Baker, chief architects, and Sir Alexander Rouse, chief engineer. Top left is Lady Irwin in purdah.

Lady Impey with servants; gouache by a Bengali artist c. 1782. She was the wife of Sir Elijah Impey, Chief Justice of Bengal in the heyday of the Nabobs, who once grumbled during that age of plunder that he had not been able to save more than £3000 a year since coming to Calcutta. The painting is a fine example of what has become known as the East India School of Indian miniature art, so called because its distinctive style developed along lines acceptable to and encouraged by the Company officials who commissioned or simply collected the pieces.

Victoria Railway Terminus, Bombay; watercolour by Axel Herman Haig, 1888. Possibly the most crazily grandiose building the British put up in India. It mixed a number of styles from Europe and India (not all of which are visible here) and some of the columns supporting roofs inside were made from granite brought to Bombay from Aberdeen. Lady Dufferin, Vicereine when it was completed, thought it 'Much too magnificent for a bustling crowd of railway passengers.'

Youngsters playing cricket on the maidan in Bombay c. 1978. The British took their national game to India, and India now has the biggest cricket-watching crowds in the world. The buildings in the background are another memorial to the Raj, the Victoria Railway Terminus, a preposterous medley of shapes and designs.

EIGHT

THE WRITING ON
THE WALL

As the Raj cruised confidently towards the twentieth century, no-one could say that it was quite indifferent to the best interests of its Indian subjects. One of its biggest preoccupations at this time was with curbing the excesses of native moneylenders, whose powers had reached such heights that there were serious riots against their extortions in Maharashtra in 1875. This led to the Deccan Agriculturalists Relief Act, which imposed a more stringent judicial scrutiny of moneylending bonds than India had known before. Some years later a Punjab Land Alienation Act followed it, designed to hamper the predatory acquisition of property from the peasant cultivators by the non-agricultural castes, a practice made possible by ridiculously high interest rates and the foreclosing of mortgages so that the land inevitably changed hands. A Co-operative Societies Act attempted to undermine the moneylenders even further by arranging controlled credit throughout India. Excesses were curbed by such legislation, though they were not stamped out either then or by succeeding measures taken by the British, and they continue to bedevil the country to this day.

It was domestic problems such as these, and the intractable nature of many of them, that proverbially emptied the House of Commons in London whenever most Indian topics were tabled for debate. The British Parliament still had a commanding voice in the affairs of the country, authorizing the near autonomy of the Government of India in Calcutta. The Secretary of State for India, who worked hand in glove with the Viceroy at long distance, was ultimately answerable to Parliament and he also had to pay attention to the views of his advisory India Council. This had taken over the role of the old Company Court of Directors and it consisted of senior men, ex-Viceroys and ex-provincial Governors for the most part, who had actually lived and worked on the sub-continent. They had an emotional rather than a vested interest in what went on there; but it was an interest. Seen from the Members' Lobby in Westminster, however, the profitability of India sometimes seemed to be outweighed by the sheer nuisance of having to govern the place. 'Cabinet,' Mr Gladstone disclosed, 'dreads nothing so much as the mention of an Indian question at its meetings.'

The people whose lives were spent in governing showed much more willingness to take the rough with the smooth, far less boredom with the droning repetition of many problems year after year. Now that the Suez Canal had accelerated the passage to India from about three months to less than three weeks, they could refresh themselves with occasional leaves at home, creating in transit one of the small imperial legends of the British, by courtesy of the Peninsula and Oriental Steam Navigation Co. They avoided the worst of the Red Sea's heat if they booked cabins on the port side going out to India, on the starboard side homeward-bound, thus producing the abbreviation 'Posh' in the P & O booking offices alongside those names that could afford to pick and choose their berths. Armed with Heath's Successful Tasteless Remedy for sea sickness, the governors plied to and fro, though not by P & O if they insisted on taking their family pets with them, for the company would never allow animals on board. On returning from home leave, these people received the warm welcome their servants never failed to give them, caught up with the local gossip that had been amusing the British community in their absence, and settled back into their familiar routines. They tackled the old problems anew, often with quite a fond eye, whether these concerned irrigation, the land revenue, justice or military requirements. They pushed ahead with fresh vigour on those schemes which were dearest to them, and the education of Indians continued to be among these, as the experience of the Kheda district in Gujarat suggests: the seven primary schools the district had known in 1855 had grown to 283 by 1893 and would have reached 597 by the 1920s, which meant that by then almost every village had one. British rule continued to be balanced between the selfish and the disinterested, as it had been in varying proportions from the time of Warren Hastings. The imperial equation is symbolized by two events that took place in Calcutta simultaneously in 1898. At one end of the city, in the small arms factory at Dum Dum, Captain Bertie Clay was producing one of the most wicked implements ever thought up, a soft-nosed bullet which expanded on impact with a man and punched a hole through him the size of a fist (it was the result of much experiment to deter

Afridi tribesmen up on the North West Frontier, who charged British soldiers regardless of what conventional ammunition could do). A few miles away, in the Presidency General Hospital, Surgeon-Major Ronald Ross was at last proving – after even longer experiment – that malaria happened not because there were sickening fumes in the air, but because the victim had been bitten by a mosquito: a gigantic step forward for medicine throughout the world, though medical theories were still so primitive in other respects that, in India, troops continued to march at right angles to the prevailing wind whenever possible, in the belief that this was a useful precaution against cholera.

The governing attitude was summarized in a letter to *The Times* in 1878 by Fitzjames Stephen, who had been the Law Member of Lord Mayo's Executive Council. 'The British Power in India', he wrote,

is like a vast bridge over which an enormous multitude of human beings are passing and will (I trust) for ages to come continue to pass, from a dreary land, in which brute violence in its roughest form has worked its way for centuries . . . on their way to a country . . . which is at least orderly, peaceful and industrious . . . The Bridge was not built without a desperate struggle. A mere handful of our countrymen guard its entrance . . . Strike away its piers and it will fall . . . One of its piers is military power; the other justice . . . So long as the masterful wills which make up military force are directed to the object I have defined as constituting justice, I should have no fear, for even if we fail . . . we fail with honour, and if we succeed we shall have performed the greatest feat of strength, skill and courage in the whole history of the world.

This acknowledgement that the British might fail to hold their imperial bridge in India, was something more than a humbugging gesture of the sort beloved by genteel Victorian society. It was a genuine admission of what anyone with experience of India recognized as a possibility, even when it was conceded with great reluctance. Stephen's humbug lay in his pretence that India had been transformed into a totally peaceful land under British supervision. It was probably more peaceful than it had ever been, but only the senseless in 1878 could have ignored a certain restlessness or have assumed that the relative tranquillity would continue unabated with things as they were.

The intellectual energy that Lord Wellesley had unwittingly stimulated several generations earlier had not only multiplied, but had led to greater expectations than the rulers wished to contemplate and to greater demands than they were ready to allow. The Bengalis, in particular, had learned well the radical philosophies of Europe that Fort William College and other institutions had introduced, and they wished to see these practised in their own land. Their educated elite, the bhadralok (literally the respectable people, the gentlemen) could quote any number of sources – in various European languages as well as English – which argued the immorality of imperial rule, and they had started to work for the subversion of imperialism in India. They were the spiritual successors of Rammohan Roy, and the Bengal Renaissance that had begun in his time now embodied political aims as well as cultural pride. In 1861 a Society for the Promotion of National Feeling among the Educated Natives of Bengal had been launched, inviting everyone to speak and write Bengali, not English, to wear dhoti and chadar instead of coats and hats, to abandon British foods and hotels, to practise all forms of indigenous culture and to take up Hindu medicine again. This was less of a popular success than it was a sign of the times. Another sign was that Indians who felt like that found British allies ready and willing to assist them in their ultimate aims.

The most dedicated of these sympathizers was Allan Octavian Hume, son of the Joseph Hume who had moved the repeal of the Corn Laws and instigated a great deal of social progress in Great Britain. The younger man had made his career in India and during the Mutiny he was the District Magistrate at Etawah, between Delhi and Cawnpore. He was decorated for his bravery there but was made even more conspicuous by his behaviour after the fighting had stopped. The trials he conducted were noted for scrupulous fairness and for a reluctance to impose the death penalty. Only seven mutineers were hanged on Hume's judgements, and he contrived a new form of gallows which made their deaths as quick and painless as possible. Like his superior Lord Canning, he was abused by the majority of Britons for what some called 'an excess of leniency', but he carried on in the civil service until, after thirty-three years of it, he retired to Simla in 1882. There he might have lived undramatically for the rest of his days, inconspicuous to everyone but ornithologists, with whom he had an international reputation, not only for collecting a vast quantity of specimens and organizing observation all over the country, but also for publishing the first book written on Indian birds. Instead, Hume's sympathies for native aspirations plunged him into the forefront of political life at the age of fifty-four and kept him there for more than two decades. He had become convinced that the only way to improve the condition of the Indian masses was through parliamentary government, and decided that Indians must organize themselves to pursue this objective without delay. He therefore wrote to every living graduate of Calcutta University, asking for fifty volunteers to begin a movement for the regeneration of their country. 'There are aliens like myself,' he wrote,

who love India and her children . . . but the real work must be done by the people of the country themselves . . . If fifty men cannot be found with sufficient power of self-sacrifice, sufficient love for and pride in their country, sufficient genuine and unselfish patriotism to take the initiative and if needs be devote the rest of their lives to the Cause – then there is no hope for India. Her sons must and will remain mere humble and helpless instruments of foreign rulers . . .

No clarion call in any land has had a greater consequence without widespread and bloody revolution. Hume's letter was the first act in a sequence of events that saw the last imperial soldier leaving the sub-continent and Indians ruling themselves again within sixty-five years – a timespan any Briton would have ridiculed when the letter was composed. Its initial result was the meeting in Bombay, just after Christmas Day 1885, of the first Indian National Congress, when seventy-two delegates from different parts of the country sat under the presidency of a Bengali lawyer. Someone had proposed that the Governor of Bombay, Lord Reay, should preside over that first session but both he and the Viceroy, Lord Dufferin, advised that an Indian should occupy the chair. There was a notable friendliness between the Government and the Indian Congressmen during those first proceedings; and the Viceroy had been in close consultation with Hume beforehand on the priorities that should be pursued, agreeing that political reforms must come before social betterment could be achieved. For their own part, the Congressmen swore unswerving loyalty to the Crown and declared 'the continual affiliation of India to Great Britain, at any rate for a period far exceeding the range of any practical political forecast, to be absolutely essential to the interests of our own National Development.' They asked for a Royal Commission on the workings of the administration and for military expenditure to be reduced. They deplored the recent annexation of Upper Burma, a British reflex against the growth of French power in Indo-China, and they

149

criticized the policy that so far had allowed only a token number of Indians into the civil service. They let it be known that they wanted elected provincial legislatures as a preliminary to establishing a national parliament. Have temperately run through this agenda, the delegates then elected Allan Hume the first Secretary of Congress, a position he was to hold until the 23rd session in 1908.

The expressions of loyalty by Congress were a recurring feature of its sessions until the end of the century, and the delegates proposing them more than once paid their compliments explicitly to 'the Empire on which the sun never sets.' They were almost entirely professional or business men, with a few representatives of the old Bengali zamindari class, and all had been thoroughly educated in Macaulay's westernizing mould. The Muslims, though they formed nearly a quarter of India's population, would have nothing to do with the movement, having gradually settled into isolation from Hindus after the collapse of Mughal power. Christian Congressmen were rare, though many others – like Mahatma Gandhi later on – admired the Christian ethic and were much influenced by it, while remaining fundamentally Hindu in their own habits and beliefs. They were sophisticated urban people, who conspicuously failed to attract much support for Congress from the rural areas until after the First World War. To some extent this followed from their obsession with liberal reform and purely secular ideals, which had a limited appeal for people in the countryside whose lives were regulated by the rigidities of caste, based on profound religious conviction. Hindu fundamentalism was championed by the likes of Bal Gangadhar Tilak outside Congress at first, though the two strains of Indian nationalism were soon to unite against British rule. Tilak was a Marathi traditionalist who took up active politics hostile to the Raj when the 1891 Age of Consent Act – brought in after an almost infant child wife had died of sexual injuries – raised the age for consummation of marriage to twelve years old, a measure which the majority of Congressmen applauded. Their own differences with the British began to grow after an Indian Councils Act of the following year seemed to them a totally inadequate response to their appeal for elected provincial assemblies. As a gesture towards parity it clearly was. The Bengal Legislative Council, for example, emerged from the new act with twenty-one members instead of the thirteen who had sat for the previous thirty years. Whereas before, the council had consisted of the Lieutenant-Governor of Bengal and a dozen nominated members, now it was formed out of the Lieutenant-Governor, thirteen nominated members, and seven members who were variously elected by Calcutta Corporation (one representative), the other municipalities of the province (2), the district boards (2), the Bengal Chamber of Commerce (1) and Calcutta University (1). The Chamber of Commerce representative was almost certain to be British and, overall, there was no possibility of Indians having an equal voice in that assembly. Bitterness was still some distance away and Congress still set its hopes within the framework of British rule, but nationalist sentiment was distinctly in the air throughout the country when Lord Curzon arrived as the new Viceroy at the start of 1899.

He came, as Macaulay had come, with a reputation for brilliance unequalled in his own generation. Son of that quaintest of all British species, a Lord who was also a country parson, he had glittered academically at both Eton and Balliol, and Oxford had acknowledged his calibre with a dose of under-graduate mockery that was to haunt him all his life:

> My name is George Nathaniel Curzon,
> I am a most superior person.
> My cheeks are pink, my hair is sleek,
> I dine at Blenheim twice a week.

There was a great deal more to Curzon than scholarship and aristocratic connections, though. In spite of a painful back complaint that before long put him permanently into a steel corset, he was a young man of much physical energy who had travelled throughout Europe and the Middle East before he was twenty, had extended his range with five great journeys across Asia within a few more years, and had been awarded the rare Gold Medal of the Royal Geographical Society for tracing the Oxus River to its source in Russian Turkistan. His considerable wandering inspired a number of articles and books that were highly regarded by specialists in their subjects, but the greatest effect of globe-trotting on Curzon himself was to reinforce a belief he had expressed when he was a student that 'There has never been anything so great in the world's history as the British Empire, so great an instrument for the good of humanity. We must devote all our energies and our lives to maintaining it.' He applied himself to this prospectus in the House of Commons at first but, as he later confessed, for a dozen years before he became the youngest ruler of India apart from Dalhousie, he had been carefully preparing himself for the position of Viceroy, governor of one-fifth of the entire human race. He was thirty-nine years old when appointed, he already knew India fairly well from his travels, and even the India Office in London regarded him as 'a regular Jingo, with Russia on the brain.'

This is not to say that Curzon was smugly content with the existing British order of things on the sub-continent. He was obsessive about efficiency and appalled by what he deemed the mediocrity of several highly-placed people in the ICS. He described the Military Member of his Executive Council as 'an obsolete amiable old footler, the concentrated quintessence of a quarter of a century of official life.' His own normal working day was anything between twelve and fourteen hours, and a lot of that time was often spent in redrafting memoranda from officials who, in Curzon's view, lacked both clarity of thought and ability to use the English language precisely. He also battled fiercely with the Army in India on the grounds of incompetence and, much worse, indiscipline. He had less contempt for the Tommy than had the American Jewish Lady Curzon, who once remarked that the ugliest things she had seen in India were the water buffalo and the British solider, but he was outraged by the occasional behaviour of white troops towards Indians when off duty. Almost as soon as Curzon arrived in Calcutta, he heard that infantrymen of the West Kent Regiment had raped an old woman near Rangoon and, when the military authorities began to close ranks around the offenders, he had the regiment posted to the most unpleasant station he could think of, which was Aden at the entrance to the Red Sea. A little later some drunks from a crack cavalry unit, the 9th Lancers, beat an Indian to death and again the officers of the regiment tried to whitewash the affair. These were men of Curzon's own class, sons of the peerage with powerful influence at home, and they let it be known that they were prepared to use all their connections to stifle his interference. Regardless of what back-stabbing might follow from London, Curzon had every Lancer recalled from leave whether the man was in India or not, every officer's leave stopped for the next six months, and the regiment reprimanded in the strongest terms – a disgrace that was soon the talk of the whole Army, as it was meant to be. 'The argument seems to be,' he wrote to Field-Marshal Lord Roberts, 'that a native's life does not count; and that any crime ought to be concealed and almost even condoned sooner than bring discredit upon the Army . . . I have set my face like flint against such iniquity.' Within a few years of Curzon's stand, such assaults were almost unheard of.

By his own lights, he was at pains to safeguard Indian interests. When London asked him to recruit 20,000 coolies to labour on the construction of railways in South Africa, Curzon declined and pointed out the unfairness of such a demand. The notion of British Empire, he said, was disreputable to some Indians because 'in practice it means to India a full share of the battles and burdens of Empire but uncommon little of the privileges and rights.' He set himself energetically to improve the Indian economy by attracting more investment from Britain, and all the relevant statistics rose sharply during his six years in Government House. He extended the irrigation of the land even more enthusiastically than his predecessors had done, and most of the major works in the twentieth century were either started or authorized in Curzon's time. He galvanized the educationists into paying more attention to primary and secondary schooling on the grounds that there was little point in filling universities 'unless we attack, permeate and elevate the vast amorphous, unlettered substratum of the population'; and he did so, in the first place, by summoning a conference of university Vice-Chancellors and other experts who passed 150 resolutions, each of which had been drafted by the Viceroy himself. More than any other ruler of India, Curzon cared for the visible reminders of her history and under him the conservation of ancient buildings and monuments became a high priority. He had the Taj Mahal restored to the glory Shah Jehan conceived, when it had lately been in danger of crumbling into a ruin; and he set trained archaeologists and architects to supervising the preservation of Fatehpur Sikri, the Pearl Mosque in Lahore, the Palace at Mandalay, the temples at Khajuraho, and other neglected treasures. Curzon adhered strictly to his own ideal of British rule and he summarized its principles in one of the last speeches he made before leaving for home in 1905. To be an Englishman in India, he declared, must be 'To fight for the right, to abhor the imperfect, the unjust or the mean, to swerve neither to the right hand nor to the left, to care nothing for flattery, odium or abuse . . . never to let your enthusiasm be soured or your courage grow dim.'

He was as convinced of Britain's imperial destiny as he had been when a student, and if one thing symbolized Lord Curzon's time in

India more than any other, it was the Durbar he organized to celebrate Edward VII's Coronation. The origin of such an event lay distantly in India's native past, when a new ruler would mark his accession with lavish ceremony which was intended to express the raja's sovereignty over his people and their affectionate obedience towards him.[1] The British had memorably followed this usage once before, to signal the proclamation of Queen Victoria as Kaisar-i-Hind, Empress of India, in 1877 and to emphasize the distinguished position of the Viceroy, who attended the ceremonies in her place. The monarch was missing from the 1902 Durbar, too, although on this occasion royalty did come out from England in the person of Edward's brother, the Duke of Connaught. But it was the King Emperor's Viceroy who, having masterminded the whole gorgeous occasion, occupied the centre of the stage from beginning to end. At every point in the pageantry, the king's brother and sister-in-law arrived on the scene and took their places alongside other dignitaries some time before the Viceregal party hove into view, so that they, like all the other imperial subjects present, could pay proper respect to the supreme authority in India. The offical manual for proceedings ordained that Lord Curzon was to make his state entry to the Durbar arena on the back of an elephant, surrounded by horsemen. Then

All present will rise as the Viceroy enters the arena, and will remain standing until he has taken his seat. As HE approaches the Dais, the Guard of Honour in front of the Dais will present arms, the Massed Bands in the centre of the arena will play the National Anthem, the Viceregal Standard will be hoisted, and the Royal Salute of thirty-one guns will be fired. On alighting, HE, preceded by his Staff, will ascend the steps and take his seat on the Throne.

After that, the other dignitaries were allowed to sit down, too.

Curzon's Durbar, as it was subsequently known, was held in Delhi rather than Calcutta, both because that made it more accessible to people travelling from all over the country, and because Delhi had more striking associations with India's own past, which Curzon was happy to enlist in his vision of a contented land at last unified under British rule. He intended it to be an unforgettable occasion, and it was. The Durbar area was so large that a special railway, five miles

---

[1] The word Durbar, however, is Persian in origin and was imported by the Mughals, whose ancestors held celebrations of the same kind.

long, was built to convey people around its various parts on a plain above the city; and with visitors estimated at 173,000 this transport was much needed. The central amphitheatre was merely the focal point of the Durbar. There were also encampments spread out neatly at intervals around the railway circuit – the Viceroy's Camp, the Commander-in-Chief's Camp, the Assam Camp, the Camp of Bombay, Baroda and Central India Railway, and so forth – where officials could entertain guests, change clothes between one event and another, have a snack, or simply take the weight off their poor feet from time to time. There was a huge marquee containing the biggest display of Indian art and craftsmanship ever assembled in one place; carpets and silks, pottery and enamels, work in precious metals, carvings and paintings, priceless antiquities and all; some for exhibition only, but others for sale by arrangement with Messrs Thomas Cook. There was a market where provisions could be obtained for the animals taking part in the various ceremonies and parades, and for the human beings who never left their side. The complexity of the Durbar site was bewildering, but every detail had been meticulously planned beforehand, down to a special Police Act which threatened fines of up to fifty rupees or eight days in prison for a variety of infringements which included soliciting for prostitution and committing a nuisance 'by performing the offices of nature in other than the appointed places.'

The programme of events started on 29 December 1902 and ran right through ten days of the New Year. There were games of football and hockey, a polo tournament, cricket matches, tent-pegging competitions, bouts of native wrestling, a firework display, musical rides by cavalry, club-swinging and running drill by the 15th Sikhs, and other side shows. The massed military bands – and they numbered 2,000 men – provided background music when nothing important was happening, and though Gilbert and Sullivan reappeared frequently in the repertoire, bits and pieces of 'Tann-häuser' easily led the way. All such events, however, were nothing more than intermissions between the great set pieces of the Durbar Curzon had devised. Among these were a review of troops when, for nearly three hours, 67 squadrons of cavalry and 35 battalions of infantry, artillery and engineers – 34,000 British and Indian soldiers in all – trotted and marched past the Viceroy, while he took their salute at a safe distance from the dusty haze they kicked up. There was a similar review of Indian retainers from the princely states, when fifty rulers provided contingents of warriors, camel corps, palki-bearers, banner-bearers, elephants, caparisoned horses, dancers, falconers, bandsmen and the like. There was an investiture, at which Britons and Indians were decorated for their loyalty to the Raj. There was a state ball. There was a special Viceregal reception for all the native rulers of India. There was an open-air service, with prayers for all the people of India offered up just before the congregation sang 'Fight the good fight with all thy might.'

Above all, there was that grand state entry to the Durbar arena on New Year's Day, preceded by a long procession through the streets of Delhi which more than a million people watched as it passed by. India had always known the gaudy spectacle that power could provide, better than any country on earth, but even India had never seen anything so startling to the eye as this. Here were ambassadors from all over the world in their frocked coats and cocked hats, and sheikhs robed in white from Arab lands where the Government of India held them in fee. Here were their own Maharajas and lesser chieftains, brilliant with colour and sparkling with jewels, borne by elephants or horses whose accoutrements alone were each worth a prince's ransom in precious metals and stones. Here were soldiers vividly uniformed in scarlet, gold, green and blue, the sun twinkling merrily on their polished buckles and leather, on the sharpness of lance and sword. And here were all the upright senior men of Government with their ladies, looking stern, or pleased, or gracious as their open carriages wheeled by. Slowly this tremendous column of dignity, extravagance and military swank made its way to the appointed place, where it became a carefully designed setting for the exquisite presence of the Viceroy himself. Trumpeters sounded flourishes after Curzon had ascended the throne. Then a mounted herald rode up to the dais and, after more flourishes, proclaimed the new King Emperor's Coronation (which had actually taken place some six months before). Yet more flourishes and the ultimate in ceremonial bombardment, a full Imperial Salute of 101 guns, before Curzon arose and addressed the throng around him. His speech was of the kind that monarchs make at Westminster before a new session of the British Parliament begins, looking forward to the legislation that might be enacted, setting the scene for what government intends. This homily entertained the most liberal feelings for India and hoped that the sub-continent would enjoy an improving future with more widely distributed comfort and wealth. The final words, however, left no-one with any illusions about Curzon's own view of how this bounty would occur. 'Under no other conditions,' he declared, 'can this future be realized than the unchallenged supremacy of the paramount power, and under no other controlling authority is this capable of being maintained than that of the British Crown.'

That very week, while the Durbar celebrations were in full swing, Curzon was composing a minute for the India Office. It reviewed India's relations with Tibet and proposed a plan of campaign for which even a Viceroy required the approval of the Cabinet in London. As officials there had observed when Curzon was appointed, he had Russia on the brain, seeing the Czar as a perpetual threat to the British paramountcy in India. This was not by any means a figment of his imagination. Since Curzon's arrival, the Russian War Minister himself, General Kuropatkin, had spoken of a coming war with India; and a Russian gunboat had made an ominous visit to the Persian Gulf. A new Amir had become ruler of Afghanistan, and Russian troops were reported to be concentrating on his northern borders. Two Russian newspapers had written of a diplomatic initiative by the Czar towards Tibet, which could be seen in a most sinister light. Tibet was nominally a Chinese protectorate, but China was weakened by internal problems and the protectorate might well fall prey to a powerful neighbour. The difficulty was to know exactly what was going on there in the Forbidden Land, the isolated theocracy run by Buddhist monks. A treaty had allowed only Chinese representation in Lhasa and British intelligence about events in the Tibetan capital, in common with that of all other foreigners, was non-existent. Curzon took the view that if the Dalai Lama and the Czar made any sort of alliance, then India's northern frontier would be dreadfully exposed to the hazard he had been warning London about for years. At first London had scoffed, on the assumption that Russia was far too concerned about her fortunes in the Far East (where she would shortly be at war with Japan) to commit herself to military adventures in the wastes of Central Asia. But when Curzon reminded the Government at home that Tibetan troops had lately violated the border with Sikkim, a princely state under British protection, London was persuaded to allow a mission to set out for Lhasa and try to establish diplomatic relations there – only no-one must know about this purpose. Ostensibly, the mission must be bent on purely commercial aims. Six months after Curzon's

157

Durbar finished, a British party crossed the Tibetan frontier. Thus began the last dramatic episode in the Great Game, the final expansive thrust of the Raj.

Leading the mission was Francis Younghusband, an ambitious army officer who had been seconded years before into the Political Department of the Indian Government. Even earlier he had made a name for himself as an explorer, a great man for the Himalaya and the first European to cross the Gobi Desert. Curzon had become a friend during the future Viceroy's own journeys into Asia, and one result was Younghusband's appointment as Resident in Indore when Curzon sat in Government House. They shared a number of attitudes, especially the imperial dream, but their first excursion into Tibetan territory was a bit of a flop. The British party reached Khambajong, fifteen miles inside the border, and were required to wait there for five months while the local officials contacted Lhasa with news of their presence. In due course word came back from the Potala Palace that the Dalai Lama and his National Assembly of senior monks had no wish to see them. Younghusband retreated to confer again with Curzon, the Viceroy once more queried London, and received in return authorization for a second attempt to be made, this time with enough troops 'to maintain communications'. Curzon was not the man to let ambiguities slip by without taking every advantage of them. In December 1903 Younghusband marched north again, this time with an 'escort' of 8,000 soldiers and camp-followers, and an even larger assortment of pack animals.

Slowly they wound their way up through the pine forests and over the snow-bound mountains on to the plateau beyond, passing through one small village after another, where monks protested indignantly but naturally enough didn't try to stop them. By March, this so-called commercial mission was one hundred miles inside Tibet and there, near the village of Guru, it encountered an obstacle. A crude barricade of boulders had been placed across the track, and milling around it were what appeared to be several thousand people. Horsemen who rode out to meet the British were told to take the damn thing down in fifteen minutes flat or the soldiers would march through it. The Tibetans did nothing. The soldiers began to march, with orders not to fire unless fired on. When they reached the barricade, they started to disarm the waiting multitude. Then the leader of the Tibetans, a monk with a sword in his hand and a pistol at his belt, suddenly shot an Indian trooper through the jaw. It was the signal for frightful retribution. The soldiers quickly withdrew. Then the mission's Maxim gun opened up at once, its four pieces of artillery began to shell the barricade with shrapnel, its riflemen knelt in drill formation and loosed off one volley after another. A few antique muskets banged off in reply. The order to cease fire came very quickly, with between six and seven hundred Tibetans lying dead, their kinsmen standing bewildered in silence at what had come upon them like a thunderclap. A young British officer wrote home that he was so sickened by the slaughter that he had stopped firing before the order was given; and he was probably sincere. Francis Younghusband's remorse was more spurious; he told his own father that at the end of the shooting he felt 'quite out of sorts'.

He pressed on with his mission, of course, and when it was subsequently attacked, Tibetan troops were beaten off after suffering heavy casualties. At which Younghusband wrote to his superior in Calcutta, 'Now that the Tibetans have . . . thrown down the gauntlet, I trust the Government will take such action as will prevent the Tibetans ever again treating British representatives as I have been treated.' Curzon sympathized, but London was aghast at what had been happening and seriously thought of recalling the mission. Instead it imposed a time limit of one more month for negotiations, if these were now possible, and was adamant that no Tibetan territory should be occupied. With this authority, Younghusband carried on to the conclusion of what he called 'the magnificent business'. It was total anti-climax when it came. The mission plodded on to Lhasa with little more interference, and found the legendary place an unlovely slum of open sewers, rotting rubbish and pools of mud, populated by monks in dirty and tattered robes. Only the Potala Palace, with its white stonework, its golden roofs and its tapestried walls came up to the expectations of a numinous place far from the trodden paths of mankind. Worse, the Dalai Lama had fled, so that there was nobody with whom to negotiate as a properly commissioned British representative should. What was quite obvious immediately was that there was not a Russian in sight. There was, though, a rump of the National Assembly that had not taken off with the divine leader, and with these lamas Younghusband concluded a treaty – or, rather, a convention, which didn't carry as much diplomatic weight. The document extracted an indemnity of £50,000 from the Tibetans, to be paid in seventy-five annual instalments, for the trouble to which the British had been put, in return for which the British offered nothing at all. The mission then marched back whence it had come, to face the displeasure of the London Government, which reduced the indemnity by two-thirds and kept Younghusband waiting several years for the knighthood he had craved from the affair. Eventually decorated, he became President of the Royal Geographical Society and devoted the rest of his life to the encouragement of Himalayan mountaineering and a posturing kind of mysticism.

For Lord Curzon, the unsatisfactory end of the mission was something to brood on, but was put behind him for the time being because more pressing matters needed his attention within his own domain. At the very moment that Younghusband was stepping out for Lhasa on his second attempt to get there, Bengal had erupted in anger against a decision by the Viceroy which affected the future of seventy-eight million people there. Curzon was dedicated to efficient government machinery, and the provincial apparatus of Bengal which he had inherited was notoriously the one more likely than any other in India to get itself into a confused mess. The root of the problem had been recognized for decades; the fact that the province named Bengal was just too big and unwieldy to manage competently. It had become an administrative parcel of ancient states, each with distinctive historical, sub-racial and cultural characteristics. Besides the historic Bengal, the parcel included Bihar, Chota Nagpur and Orissa, and the civil servants had long talked of dismantling this cumbersome unit to make its parts more manageable in purely administrative terms. Where others had simply talked, Curzon had decided to act. He proposed to partition the province with a line drawn roughly down the middle of Bengal proper. To a new province of Eastern Bengal would be added Assam; to western Bengal the people of Bihar, Chota Nagpur and Orissa would remain attached. This was all very neat and geometrical and if the area hadn't teemed with conflicting human beings it would doubtless have worked very well. British India had rarely seen such a capable administrator as Curzon, but very few of its rulers had been quite so politically dense. A result of his partition was that Eastern Bengal became overwhelmingly Muslim in character, while in the other new province the predominantly Hindu Bengalis of Calcutta and its immediate surroundings were dominated by Oriyas, Biharis and others with whom almost the only thing they shared was a religion.

Their educated elite in particular, the upper-caste bhadralok, felt isolated from most fellow Bengalis and assumed that this was a deliberate move by Curzon – divide and rule – to hamstring their growing political effectiveness. In the course of his recent educational reforms he had, after all, remarked that the administration of Calcutta University had 'fallen into the hands of a coterie of obscure native layers who regard educational questions from a political point of view.' Before that he had tampered with the composition of Calcutta Corporation, reducing its elected element and putting executive functions in the hands of a committee dominated by Britons. At the time he had defended this change on the grounds of efficient local government; but the bhadralok were inclined to think otherwise.

Partition was not to be effected until October 1905, but its outlines were announced nearly two years before. At once there were public meetings of protest, deputations bearing petitions to Government House, denunciations in the Bengali newspapers – all under the leadership of Surendranath Banerjea, the most distinguished local member of the National Congress. He was a gentle man, well disposed towards the British, though they had blocked careers that might have been open to him at the Bar and in the ICS on grounds that reeked of prejudice. He held a chair in English literature at a Calcutta college and edited *The Bengalee*, whose circulation rose from 3,000 to 11,000 between the announcement and the fact of partition because of the fervour Banerjea stimulated among his English-speaking compatriots. By the middle of 1905 it became clear that partition was going through in spite of the growing protest movement, so the protesters enlarged their activities, calling for a boycott of all British goods and the purchase only of things that were swadeshi – Indian-made. They also demanded that every Bengali holding any kind of office under Government auspices should resign it at once. Indirectly they showed Lord Curzon the door, and he went through it never to return. Things had become too turbulent by far for London's taste since the heady moment of the Durbar. Lhasa had embarrassed the men in the India Office, the partition plan had them very worried indeed, and on top of everything else Curzon had locked himself into a struggle with the Army about the Viceroy's role in its chain of command. It was on this last issue that London forced him into a corner and accepted his resignation with relief. He went home embittered, though in time and after governments had changed, he became a Foreign Secretary just as trenchant as ever he had been Viceroy.

It was therefore his successor Lord Minto, sometime Grand National jockey but lately Governor-General of Canada, who had to deal with the increasing tensions as partition was put into practice. The moderation of Banerjea and his associates (who included Rabindranath Tagore, later to win the first Nobel Prize awarded to an Indian) had proved ineffective in stopping the detested plan; therefore violence began to spread around the reconstituted western Bengal. As in the days of Thugee, Kali was invoked by the most determined campaigners, and before long there were backyard bomb factories from one end of Calcutta to the other. Young men organized themselves into small and well disciplined groups, none of them sanctioned by Banerjea's group, and began to use explosives to kill Britons indiscriminately. Sometimes they would aim for a District Judge, but blow up a couple of English memsahibs instead. Foreign newspapers such as *L'Humanité* applauded the bearing of these bully boys when they were caught and stood their trials with composure. The British, inevitably, turned very tough indeed in the face of such defiance. Newspapers were suppressed, editors were clapped into gaol, hundreds of Bengalis at a time were rounded up and interrogated. Something had started that was to be an intermittent feature of the landscape in that part of India up to the 1930s. The biggest casualty of partition was the unity of the Indian National Congress, which split into two parts on the morality of violence at its 1907 session, with Bengalis forming up in both camps, intransigently opposed to any form of British rule on one side, increasingly distrustful of liberal intentions expressed by the British on the other. A further important consequence was the foundation in 1906 of the Muslim League, to safeguard its community interests in the face of mounting Hindu political pressure through Congress.

Lord Minto pursued a liberal policy soon after taking office. While his police officers were meeting violence with violence, he was urgently addressing himself to the need for political reform. He had a ready ally in the India Office, where a new Secretary of State was John Morley, previously well known as an advocate of Home Rule for the Irish. Together the two men worked out a scheme which would both decentralize government in India and allow more room for Indian opinion to shape events. Morley appointed two Indians to his India Council in London, while Minto recruited a Bengali on to his own Executive Council in the influential position of Law Member; and provincial governments everywhere were told to make similar adjustments without delay. In 1909 the full range of the Morley–Minto reforms were revealed in a revised Indian Councils Act, which made some crucial changes in the existing pattern of rule. From now on, the Imperial Legislative Council was to have sixty members, twenty-seven of them elected, instead of the twenty-five who had sat since the reorganization after the Mutiny. This mixture of British and Indians was to pass resolutions on Government policy instead of acting as a non-voting advisory body to the Viceroy. The provincial legislatures were also to be changed, with a much greater voice for elected Indians. The Bengal Legislative Council (supervising partitioned western Bengal, that is) was enlarged from twenty-one to fifty-three members, with a majority elected instead of nominated; which meant that, provided the Indian members acted together, they could outvote the British representatives. The first practical step had been taken towards the government of India by Indians and, although terrorism still went on, the moderates in Congress acknowledged the significance of the reforms and agreed to co-operate with the British in making them work.

The following year Minto yielded his Viceroyalty to Lord Hardinge, whose grandfather had been a Governor-General before the Mutiny. Indians who quite reasonably complained that the British were slow to concede change, and seemed reluctant when they did so, could scarcely have been prepared for what came next. Hardinge was a career diplomat, reared in the craft of compromise which he had exercised in half the chanceries of Europe before coming East, and he was in full agreement with what his predecessor had done. So was someone else, and he was King George V, who had just succeeded his father on the imperial throne. As Prince of Wales he had visited India at the time of partition, thought little of Curzon's reckless surgery and not much of the general British attitude towards Indians. 'Evidently,' he had written in his diary then, 'we are too much inclined to look upon them as a conquered and down-trodden race and the Native, who is becoming more and more educated, realizes this.' With Bengal still in turmoil, and restlessness beginning to spread elsewhere on the sub-continent, the new King resolved to make a second visit as Emperor, and to reunite Bengal as a gesture of goodwill. Hardinge himself was of the view that 'a grave injustice has been done to the Bengalis, seeing that they are in a minority in both provinces, and this injustice should certainly be rectified.' Then the Home Member of his Executive Council, John Jenkins, made another suggestion. How would it be, he asked, if the rest of India were given a tonic, too – like shifting the Viceroy and his Government from the British creation of Calcutta, to the old chief city of Delhi? This was an idea that had been toyed with since Bentinck's time, on the grounds of climate and geographical convenience. It now became even more attractive to officials who were beginning to wilt in the violent atmosphere of Bengal, and would also be very happy to put themselves beyond the immediate reach of the aggressive British business community there.

Both reunification and the switch of capital were agreed upon within the transmission of a few telegrams between Calcutta and London. But a remarkable secrecy was maintained about these plans, code-named Sesame, while preparations were made for the King Emperor's visit. Fewer than twenty people knew what the monarch would announce when he arrived, and even Queen Mary was ignorant until the royal couple reached India and the Viceroy brought the matter up at his first audience with them. Yet another Durbar, as magnificent as Curzon's, was held in Delhi and it was there, in December 1911, that King George broke the news as he stood under the golden dome of the Royal Pavilion in the centre of the main amphitheatre. 'We are pleased to announce to Our People that . . . We have decided upon the transfer of the seat of the Government of India from Calcutta to the ancient Capital of Delhi . . .' He paused, in the stunned silence of a hundred thousand people; then there was wild and incredulous cheering all around. And when the momentous day was over, when the pageantry had ended till the morrow, when the last of the soldiers had marched briskly away to the thump and pomp of 'The British Grenadier', something happened that spoke of the deepest instincts in this enigmatic land. It was quite unrehearsed, utterly spontaneous. Crowds of spectators, almost all of them unlettered folk, rushed forward across the otherwise deserted arena to where the King Emperor and the Queen Empress had been a little while before. These they had at last seen with their own eyes, beings from another dimension if not another world. Following an impulse bred in India's venerable past, the crowds moved as close as they dared to the Royal

Pavilion; then prostrated themselves before the empty thrones, and pressed their brows against the marble steps.

The transfer of the capital was to take place on 1 April 1912 but any blow that Bengali pride suffered at the reduced status of Calcutta was assuaged by the impending reunification of the province. There was much rejoicing at this news and even the bomb-slingers briefly held their fire in gratification. Surendranath Banerjea said that a new epoch had opened in Bengali history, and suggested that the reversal of partition represented 'the triumph of British justice and the vindication of constitutional methods in our political controversies.' Only the British in Calcutta were enraged for the moment, as were Curzon and his cronies at home. Bengal had received the news during a mini-Durbar on the Calcutta maidan, simultaneously with the announcement in Delhi, and the British there seem to have been totally crushed at first. Their newspapers next day merely recorded events in Delhi, the bare facts of the proclamation in Calcutta, and added that 'Durbar day passed off quietly' there. Then the civilians let their feelings go, and these were infinitely more bitter and angry than the 'chagrin and disappointment' that the Secretary of State for India had foreseen in one of his secret memoranda to Hardinge some months before. One by one, in the next few days, the newspaper reporters picked up the grudges and the smarting calculations of the white man in the street. They were going to lose a lot of money over this, as business flowed out of Calcutta. They had spent a lot of money on developments necessary to the Government machine, and now it was all down the drain. They would no longer be able to exercise their rightful influence on Government, now that it was taking itself beyond their reach. Lord Hardinge must bear the responsibility for this, as he had clearly misled the King . . . and so on, in interviews and protracted correspondence to the editors which went on for several weeks, usually under pseudonyms like Civis, A Liberal Disgusted, Ichabod, Patria Cara, and Cricket. The Secretary of State in London, briefing the first Governor of the reunited Bengal, characterized these people well: 'The Calcutta English . . . community includes, I am sure, a number of honest, capable and likeable people; but I am not less sure that they are spoilt children in many respects, full of their own historical and social importance, anti-Indian *au fond*, and keen to scent out "disloyalty" in any independent expression of opinion, hidebound too in class prejudice.' Of them all, only the Turf correspondent of their leading newspaper *The Statesman* appears to have accepted matters philosophically. 'Would a change of capital from London to the ancient capital, Winchester,' he asked his readers one morning, 'have any effect upon racing at Epsom, Newmarket, Ascot or Doncaster?'

Perhaps he didn't appreciate that what had lately happened in India, what was rather more than symbolic in the devaluation of Calcutta, was the beginning of the imperial retreat.

NINE

BEATING A RETREAT

Just as the British had never ruled India in a vacuum, sealed from what went on in the rest of the world, so outside events contributed to the withdrawal of imperialism there. Indians were encouraged to press their nationalist claims after watching little Japan topple one of the two superpowers, Russia, which made them wonder whether it was within their own competence to do likewise to the other. The difficulty the British had experienced in subduing the South African Boers was another incentive to rebellion. Most powerfully of all, the First World War undermined any lingering mystique Europeans might have enjoyed in the eyes of extremists and moderates alike. India had been bundled into the conflict willy nilly, as an imperial retainer, supplying 800,000 troops to fight for the British in a number of theatres overseas. Over 50,000 of them served on the European battlefields and thus set eyes on the land that had produced the British Raj: the Brighton Pavilion was turned into a hospital for wounded Indians and may have been a small comfort to them, with its familiar domes and ogees derived from the native building shapes. There wasn't much other inspiration obvious 7,000 miles from home. When the survivors returned to India, they were able to spread eye-witness accounts of what by then all Indians knew; that Europeans had fought each other with a savagery quite as great as that which all white men had long condemned on the sub-continent. They could also report that the homeland of the British was not nearly as impressive as might have been supposed from the lustre of imperial Durbars, or even from the behaviour of box wallahs strolling down their Indian Malls and civil servants climbing into gharries outside their clubs. A few hundred Indians had discovered this already, when education or eminence had taken them abroad. But now the word began to pass round the villages and the bazaars as well, and helped to sharpen an appetite for freedom. In the aftermath of war, one more thing enlarged this taste. President

Wilson of the United States had come up with his Fourteen Points for lasting peace, which made an oblique genuflection to the idea of self-determination for all people. Well?

The British, in fact, had set in motion machinery that would result in this very end for India a few months before the American leader seized the opportunity to put his country in the centre of the international stage at last. In August 1917 the Secretary of State for India, Edwin Montagu, had told the House of Commons that it was proposed to take 'substantial steps as soon as possible' to realize responsible self-government in India 'as an integral part of the British Empire'. Quibblers might murmur that this was not the same thing as self-determination, and the British version certainly went no further than an India run by Indians, as Canada was by Canadians and Australia by Australians, in a federation linked by allegiance to the Crown with a number of economic and other material arrangements making this more than a simply emotional loyalty. In November, Montagu went out to India and toured the country for five months with a new Viceroy, Lord Chelmsford, to test opinion there for himself. By the following July, the British Parliament had received a report prepared by the two men and the outcome was a Government of India Act at the end of 1919, which embodied proposals that became known as the Montford reforms. The substance of these was self-government by stages, with a review of how things had gone ten years after the act had been put into effect. Immediately, there were to be changes at all levels of government in India. The Viceroy's Executive Council was to have six members apart from the Viceroy himself and his Commander-in-chief, and three of them were to be Indians. In each province there was to be dyarchy, double government, with an executive council appointed by the provincial Governor and ministers answerable to a legislative council that would be elected by popular vote. All legislative councils were to be enlarged; that of Bengal rose from 54 seats under the arrangement of 1912 to 139 seats in 1919 – with an electorate of over one million to choose the members.

Most importantly of all, the biggest check on Viceregal authority was to be given much greater power. The Imperial Legislative body was to be known henceforth as an Assembly instead of a Council. In place of the 60 members the Morley–Minto reforms had authorized, the Montford plan reckoned on 146, and 106 of them were to be elected. In addition, there was to be a Council of State of 61 members, an upper chamber to review legislation passed by the Assembly. In other words, India at last had something resembling a genuine parliament, and like the model at Westminster it had two houses – one in which the people's vote could be exercised, the other representing the big landed interests of the country. About one sixth of the elected seats in both houses were earmarked for Europeans, but the rest were in the gift of Indians. The franchise was considerably extended to everyone in the country with a property qualification based on the payment of income, house or land tax, together with those holding a degree or membership of a chamber of commerce. This meant that there were over five million voters for the provincial councils, a million or so for the Legislative Assembly, and 17,000 for the Council of State. In a country of 150 million adults it was a long way from one man, one vote. But the Montford reforms didn't pretend to be more than a start on something which had an inescapable logic of development and growth.

The reforms came just a bit too late to mollify the extremists in the nationalist movement, and the men who sought to change things violently. Terrorism had started again as soon as the euphoria over the reunification of Bengal had petered out; most dramatically when a bomb was thrown into the howdah on top of the elephant bearing Lord Hardinge on his state entry to the new imperial capital of Delhi at the end of 1912. It blew to pieces the servant holding the State Umbrella over the howdah and seriously injured the Viceroy. Agitation generally was growing, especially after Tilak and his supporters became the major faction in Congress and in 1914 made a pact with the Muslims, the one native group that had been crestfallen at the reversal of partition. Under Curzon's plan the Muslims had been given ascendancy in Eastern Bengal, and they were resentful when this was so swiftly removed by Hardinge and the King, very ready to do a deal with Congress and get their own back. They agreed to support the Hindu demands for self-government and in return Tilak's men promised to recognize separate Muslim constituencies when self-government was gained. Another pressure point came with the formation of a Home Rule League at the instigation of that strange Englishwoman, Mrs Annie Besant. She had come to India in 1893 some years after she had left her husband, a Lincolnshire vicar, in favour of Charles Bradlaugh's National Secular Society and the Fabians. In England she had organized a matchworkers' strike and she had become enamoured of Madame

Blavatsky's new doctrine of theosophy. In India she decided at once that she had been reincarnated there many times before, adopted a young Madrassi named Krishnamurti as her son and pronounced him Messiah, was instrumental in the founding of a Hindu college in Benares, and became extremely active in Congress, which made her its President in 1918. In her more elliptical moments she claimed to be 'an Indian tom-tom waking all the sleepers so that they may work for their motherland'. But Mrs Besant also had a practical streak which had led to the organization of the matchworkers' trade union in England. It made her Home Rule League yet another force the Government had to reckon with seriously.

So perturbed was it by the spreading unrest that while Edwin Montagu was on his fact-finding tour of India, Mr Justice Rowlatt was starting work with a committee to investigate the extent of revolutionary conspiracy and to suggest some remedies. The result was two Rowlatt bills which would authorize judges to try political cases without juries and allow provincial governments, as well as the Government of India, to intern people without trial. These powers were never, in fact, used; but they didn't need to be to inflame public opinion even further. One of the bills was dropped at an early stage of legislation, and that didn't matter either. It was enough that the other was enacted within a matter of weeks – when the Montford proposals were taking months to become law – and that this was accomplished by the Government's use of its official representation in the Imperial Legislative Council to secure a majority, when every elected Indian had voted against. Had the Rowlatt bills been presented after the reconstitution of the Council into an Assembly, the outcome would almost certainly have been different. As it was, disturbances were immediately reported from all over the country, and for once Bengal was not in the eye of the storm. That position was occupied by the Punjab, which had been strained more than any other area by the economic drain of the war as well as by the call on its manpower; the province had contributed 60 per cent of the troops India had supplied for Britain's needs, from one sixteenth of India's population.

Its Lieutenant-Governor was Sir Michael O'Dwyer, who years before had nearly come to blows with Rudyard Kipling in Lahore. He now decided to use what he called 'fist force' to repulse the 'soul force' invoked by the nationalists for the end of March 1919, when a hartal was to be declared all over the country, a traditional form of protest like a 24-hour general strike. This was observed in most cities, including Amritsar, one of the chief trading centres of the Punjab and the holiest place known to the Sikhs, whose Golden Temple there sheltered the Granth Sahib, the religion's most sacred book. All shops and businesses in the city closed on the appointed day and 45,000 people attended an open-air meeting at which the Rowlatt bills were condemned. There was no trouble during the hartal, but over the next few days there were various demonstrations, and a poster appeared on the civic clock tower exhorting all-comers to 'Prepare yourselves to die and kill others.' On 10 April riots broke out, in which several buildings were set on fire and banks looted. A number of people were killed, including three Britons; and Miss Marcia Sherwood was assaulted by a mob. She was a doctor who had worked for fifteen years in Amritsar for the Zenana Missionary Society, and she had been riding her bicycle down a street when a gang of youths shouting nationalist slogans knocked her to the ground and beat her there until they thought she was dead. She survived because a Hindu family dragged her into their home, treated her injuries and then smuggled her at night into British hands. By then, Sir Michael O'Dwyer had summoned reinforcements for the local garrison. They came by train from Jullundur, fifty miles away, and Brigadier-General Reginald Dyer came with them to take up the Amritsar military command.

Dyer was an ailing old sweat, suffering from arteriosclerosis and the bronchial effects of chain-smoking. Ill health had kept him out of the First World War, but he had distinguished himself as a young officer up on the Frontier, though even then he had been known as a man with a short temper who was likely to over-react under pressure. He was to do so again in Amritsar with the most dreadful consequences. His first act was to proclaim that all further meetings were prohibited, but in spite of this announcement hordes of people were reported to be gathering on Sunday, 13 April, as pilgrims poured into Amritsar for Baisakhi Day, one of the most important festivals in the Sikh calendar. That afternoon, thousands were crammed into the Jallianwala Bagh, a piece of waste ground popular among travellers as a rendezvous and resting place, virtually surrounded by high walls, with access through a narrow alley. Many of the people there that Sunday were pilgrims from the countryside, probably unaware that Dyer's proclamation had been made; but political agitators were certainly among them, exhorting the crowd and displaying pictures of a local leader who had been detained three days before. Dyer personally led some troops to this place – all Indians apart from one other British officer and an NCO – with a couple of armoured cars bringing up the rear. The cars were too wide to be driven through the alley into the Bagh and remained outside, while fifty riflemen and forty Gurkhas armed only with kukris entered at the double, their commander marching purposefully behind. He gave the crowd no warning. He simply ordered his riflemen to open fire. And when precisely 1,650 rounds of .303 ammunition had been expended, he ordered them to stop; then to about-turn and withdraw; which they did, marching with their rifles at the slope. They left behind panic, an uncounted number of wounded, and a death toll which was officially put at 379 later on, but which Indian sources reckoned at anything between 500 and 1,000.

Six days later, as Amritsar struggled to come to terms with grief and shock, Dyer visited Miss Sherwood in hospital, where her life was still in the balance. Then he ordered that every Indian who wished or needed to go down the street where she had been assaulted must do so by crawling on all fours. He also had a whipping frame erected there, for the punishment of those who had beaten the missionary; and on this six youths were flogged purely on suspicion, without any trial. Word of these events was not allowed to get out for some time, because Sir Michael O'Dwyer imposed press censorship at once. It was October before even London was properly informed of what had happened in Amritsar six months before, and the Hunter Committee of inquiry was set up to establish facts and apportion blame. It did not accept Dyer's excuse for the massacre; that he acted as he did because he feared another insurrection throughout India on the scale of the Mutiny and wished to nip it in the bud. Nor was it content with his posting out of Amritsar shortly after the shooting, to take command of a brigade in the third Afghan War. When the Committee had condemned his behaviour he was asked to resign his command and return to England, where he died in 1927. But his disgrace was not acknowledged by all his fellow-countrymen. A debate in the House of Lords produced a majority of 121 to 86 in Dyer's favour. Prompted by Sir Michael O'Dwyer and Sir Edward Carson, leader of the Ulster Protestants, the *Morning Post* launched a fund for 'The Man who saved India' which raised £26,317 4s 10d to comfort the dying brigadier . . . and £10 of that sum was subscribed by Rudyard Kipling. Even after Dyer was buried, the repercussions of that week in Amritsar rumbled on in British public life for many years. The last was not heard of them until O'Dwyer was shot dead at a meeting in Caxton Hall, London, in 1940, by a survivor of the Jallianwala Bagh, who was hanged for the offence.

Indians were so outraged by everything Dyer had done that for some time it seemed as if he might have opened a breach between them and the British that nothing could ever heal. Rabindranath Tagore, who had lately been knighted for his services to literature, flung the honour back at the Raj with the contempt he felt for the crawling order in particular, telling the Viceroy that 'I wish to stand shorn of all special distinctions by the side of those of my countrymen who, for their so-called insignificance, are liable to suffer a degradation not fit for human beings.' Someone else, the man who had called for the hartal in March, declared that henceforth 'co-operation in any shape or form with this satanic government is sinful', abandoned hopes he had held of Indian self-government under allegiance to the Crown, and repeated Tagore's gesture with decorations of his own – the Zulu War Medal and the Kaisar-i-Hind Medal, which he had been awarded for serving as a stretcher bearer to the British in South Africa and in Europe. He was Mohandas Karamchand Gandhi, whose presence from now on would dominate everything that happened in India until the British left.

Gandhi had been born into the merchant caste in the tiny princedom of Porbandar on the coast of the Arabian Sea, where his father was the hereditary chief minister of the local ruler. Married as a child to a child-wife, he had gone alone to England at the age of nineteen to study law and in time was called to the Bar. His family had been divided about this venture, and its stricter members had insisted that he was outcast for making a journey overseas. He lived frugally in England as he tried to adopt local ways but in the end he fell back on his own culture, although he became inspired by the New Testament, especially by the Sermon on the Mount. He went home to practise law without success before accepting the invitation of a Muslim with business interests in South Africa, to act as his legal adviser there. As a result he became the leader of the growing Indian community at the Cape over the next twenty years, and it was there that he developed passive resistance to legislation requiring Indians to carry identity cards. He called this form of defiance satyagraha, literally 'truth force'. Half way through the First World War, after visiting England again and raising an Indian ambulance unit there, he sensed that his talents were needed more by his own people in his own land, returned to India and began to preach his doctrine in the nationalist cause. Tagore dubbed him Mahatma (great soul) for this, and the title stuck as Gandhi gradually ousted Tilak from the leadership of the Congress.

He did this – and everything else he accomplished – by a combination of moral force and extreme shrewdness about people and their political moods. India had never known the time when power did not mean, ultimately, the rule of the sword and the violent suppression of the weak by the strong. Gandhi genuinely believed in the rejection of violence in all its forms, including the non-physical violence that Brahmins and those of the caste into which he himself had been born had always offered those below them in the Hindu social scale. That was the basis of his moral force. His shrewdness included the recognition that numerically the weak in India were far greater than the strong, and that if they could somehow be enlisted and unified in a cause they might very well prevail in the end. This was a prescription he was prepared to advocate both to cure the native ills of his country and to rid it of its foreign overlords. It included Gandhi's elevation of the lowest caste, the untouchables, to Harijans, the Children of God; and embraced the symbolism of that humblest implement, the spinning-wheel. Nobody had ever identified with the masses of India so brazenly or so gently. Nor had anyone proclaiming lowliness in himself shown such deft ability to play the political game, whether among his own people in Congress or when treating with the British. There was revelation for all Indians in the preposterous anomaly of Mahatma Gandhi, in the spectacle of power exerted by someone of feeble appearance; bandy-legged, toothless before his time, short-sighted, stooping and bald. It mattered not that his shrewdness sometimes took him close to hypocrisy. He carefully cultivated the legend that he always travelled third class by train (even when, at the height of his power, this meant that he and a handful of acolytes always had an otherwise empty third-class carriage reserved for them), and he once let it be known that he was settling down in Calcutta's foulest bustee to pray for an end to inter-communal strife (when, in fact, he took up his abode in a large mansion set in the middle of the slum). Such inconsistencies were ignored by his devotees. Nor were they nonplussed when Gandhi sometimes took his philosophy to ridiculous lengths; as when he seriously urged the British, as late as 1940, to meet the threat from Hitler non-violently. It was enough for his followers that although he opposed the British at almost every turn in India, he appeared to gain their grudging respect. More than this; he made the British feel, as Percival Spear has said, 'uncomfortable in their cherished field of moral rectitude'. Gandhi represented the attainment of something that most Indians thought beyond their reach.

He rose to full power on the debris of bitterness and disillusionment that Amritsar left behind. What that had obscured was the fact that the British were already beginning to let go of the sub-continent. What it convinced Indians of was that no such thing could be taken for granted, that they needed greater determination than ever if they were to come into their own at last. After denouncing the government as 'satanic', Gandhi called for general non co-operation with the British, persuading the Muslim League to stand alongside Congress in boycotting all institutions associated with the Raj. The boycott met with only limited success but it contributed to a general feeling of insurrection, in which demonstrations and riots regularly occurred, while the British showed that they had at least learned something from General Dyer's calamitous performance. After Amritsar they were loath to use the military in civil disorders again, leaving mobs to be dealt with by policemen armed with lathis – bamboo staves often tipped with iron. The most defiant demonstration was mounted under the nose of royalty, when the Prince of Wales visited India in the autumn of 1921, to find Gandhi addressing 60,000 people only a few hundred yards from where he landed in Bombay. His speech finished, the Mahatma set fire to a pile of foreign clothes before the crowd began to disperse, as he had intended it should. What he had not intended was the simultaneous movement of extremists in other parts of Bombay, who began to beat up Europeans, or any Indian who looked like a Christian or a Parsi; the Parsis, being pale complexioned, could be mistaken for people of mixed blood, and as a community they had invariably allied themselves with the British almost as much as the Anglo-Indians had. Twenty-four hours after the demonstration, what had started as a peaceful protest against British rule had deteriorated into sectarian violence, with a score of corpses on the streets.

The Bombay riot brought Gandhi up against two enduring facts of Indian life; not only that cohesion is the most elusive goal for any leader there to achieve, but that violence is liable to break out in the most peaceful circumstances. It is significant of the first that when, a few months later, the British sentenced Gandhi to six years in prison (though they released him after two) there were no more than minor disorders in protest, while in any other volatile land the whole country would have been in uproar at the incarceration of such a leader. By the time he emerged the alliance between Congress and the Muslim League was in shreds, and Muslims and Hindus were killing each other everywhere. The British, meanwhile, had repealed the unused Rowlatt Act, they had at last begun to make some headway with the Indianization of the ICS, and they had fostered India's entry to the League of Nations. They had also been keeping their guard up against Russia, which was still regarded as a threat even after the Czar had been displaced by a revolutionary committee. Lenin had pointedly written a letter of sympathy to all Indians in the nationalist newspaper *Amrita Bazar Patrika* as soon as he heard about the massacre in Amritsar. Rebellious souls like Muzzafar Ahmed had slogged their way north over the Hindu Kush to Termez in Soviet Tadzhikistan, where a Red Army band had played them aboard a train for Tashkent and its new Indian Military School, which taught political philosophy and the mechanics of the machine gun. There the Indian Communist Party had been born in 1920, and within a few years its members would have organized an eight-month strike in the Bombay cotton mills, hand-in-hand with the All India Trade Union Congress. At the same time, the Russians were known to be encouraging disaffection among the tribesmen of the North West, who were always spoiling for a fight anyway; which is why the British now had anything up to 50,000 troops at a time manning the Frontier.

They tried, none the less, to carry on as though nothing untoward was happening on or adjacent to the sub-continent. Most conspicuously, they got on with the construction of their new imperial capital as though they expected to be around for another thousand years at least. The planning of New Delhi had begun the moment the 1911 Durbar was over, and it had been entrusted to Edwin Lutyens, who had just finished designing an exhibition of 'Shakespeare's England' at Earl's Court when the King was announcing his surprising news. Lutyens's reputation as an architect was already well founded on grandiose domestic buildings at home like Castle Drago and Nashdom, and he had been a consultant in the making of

Hampstead Garden Suburb. In India he was being asked to supervise the most ambitious project that could come the way of a man in his profession; an adjunct to the old city of Delhi which would cover ten square miles and be topped by an awe-inspiring sequence of buildings from which the Government of India would function in future. He wouldn't design every single thing in New Delhi; many parts of it came off other men's drawing boards. But Lutyens was in charge of the whole concept and divided the architecture of the plum feature, the Government buildings, between himself and his chief collaborator, Herbert Baker. The two were old friends, and Baker had made his name on public buildings in South Africa. In India, Lutyens decided that he would create the palatial Viceroy's House and its surroundings, while Baker would design the nearby Government Secretariat and the building for the Imperial Legislative Assembly. Between them, they would style the approaches to the entire imperial edifice, an arrangement that was to result in a planning disaster and a broken friendship.

The King Emperor would have liked his Indian capital to repeat the form and flavour of the Mughals 'if it was not so dreadfully expensive', while Lord Hardinge favoured 'Western architecture with an Oriental motif'. Lutyens, who could be anything from withering to patronizing about all forms of Indian building he had seen, settled for the latter as something approximating to his own inclinations. A hastily-cut foundation stone had been laid by King George after the Durbar, but work on the ground didn't really start for over two more years, and four Viceroys had ruled India before the palace intended for men in their position was finished in 1931. The war impeded progress at first, committees wrangled lengthily over every stage, and construction was held up when quarries were worked out and fresh sources of material had to be found. The complex of Government buildings was made from the same red and buff sandstone that Akbar and Shah Jehan had used in their own extravaganzas centuries before, the interiors lavishly covered with a variety of marbles the Mughal Emperors had also employed – white from Jodhpur, green from Baroda, black from Gaya, pink from Alwar, yellow from Jaisalmer. Some 2,500 masons fashioned the blocks and slabs, and in the busiest year there were 29,000 men working on the slopes of Raisina Hill, where the headquarters of British India were going up. Gradually the Viceroy's House took shape as a long vision of colonnaded splendour with a colossal dome above and, in the foreground, a monumental column of stone the like of which had not been seen since Trajan pulled off the same braggart stroke in ancient Rome. When finished, the palace was fit for an Emperor, let alone his Viceroy. It was two-thirds of a mile round the foundations, which made it bigger than Louis XIV's palace at Versailles, and it had 340 rooms, in each of which Edwin Lutyens had left his distinctive mark – down to the design of the lamp fittings in the nursery, playfully arranged to depict two hens above broken eggshells which were, in practice, the lampshades.

But somehow the entire creation had become irrevocably flawed. The grand design was for an approach to all the Government buildings along the King's Way, a wide thoroughfare one and a half miles long which came first to the Great Place – an enormous open expanse where ceremonial parades could be held – and then passed up Raisina Hill between the Secretariat buildings to the wrought-iron gates which announced the Viceroy's House standing in its own grounds beyond. The idea was that the vision of the palace constantly in sight would draw all comers like an imperial magnet as they proceeded along the King's Way. At the planning stage there was a great deal of argument about the gradient that could be allowed on the hill, which horse-drawn carriages would have to ascend. A ratio of 1 in 22 was fixed and construction went ahead with that in mind. Building was well advanced when the awful truth dawned; that the gradient caused the Viceroy's House to perform a disappearing act for anyone coming from the bottom of the King's Way to the foot of Raisina Hill. This was not a symbol the British in India wanted at that time, especially at an overall cost of £10 million. Lutyens blamed Baker for the gaffe, and Baker reckoned that Lutyens was at fault. At planning conferences thereafter, each sat at opposite ends of a long table, their personal assistants ferrying messages back and forth between the two disgruntled architects, who didn't exchange a word for the next five years.

A number of minor palaces went up in the vicinity of the King's Way, town houses for the more important native rulers of India, who fulfilled an important role in the British scheme of things. They were an extraordinary bunch, already an anachronism with varying local powers maintained only by kind permission of the Raj, and some of them had been oddly stranded by history as lords of what they could survey. The Nizam of Hyderabad, a miser reputed to be the richest man in the world, was a Muslim ruling a Hindu population in an area equal to the British Isles; while the Hindu Maharaja of Kashmir exercised his limited sovereignty in a predominantly Muslim state. Many were noted for their ostentation, like the Gaekwar of Baroda, who had one Rolls-Royce upholstered in tiger skin and another reconstructed to act as a shooting brake. Some were plain eccentric, like the ruler of a small state in Rajputana, who was so suspicious of everyone that he devised a secret language known only to himself and his right-hand man, and had it stamped on his local currency. One prince, the Maharaja of Dewas State, did English literature a good turn by employing E. M. Forster as his secretary, with *A Passage to India* as one result. What all the rulers had in common by the twentieth century, however, was more or less steady devotion to the Crown. The Nizam actually styled himself, among many rhapsodic titles, Faithful Ally of the British Government. Like many of his colleagues he had been nothing less than that in the war, raising troops out of his own pocket and adding them to what the official Indian Army sent overseas. The cricketer Ranjitsinhji, properly known as the Maharaja Jam Saheb of Nawanagar, had served as a staff officer on the Western Front. At home, such men were equally reliable in the struggle the British were having with the nationalists. Seen from the Viceregal throne, they were partners who would dampen insurrection in their own domains and make appropriate sounds nationally when gathered in the Chamber of Princes, the consultative assembly created for them in 1921. In return, provided they didn't overstep certain implicit limits of civilized behaviour towards their subjects, they were allowed to run their own shows throughout the country. When the Government heard that the Nawab of Bahawalpur State was grazing a herd of racing camels on the fields of his subject peasants, it protested to His Highness and remitted the cultivators' taxes to compensate them for the damage done. But there was no time after 1902 when the Maharaja of Mysore, among others, was bound by treaty to accept any advice his British Resident offered him.

The princes certainly didn't figure in Mahatma Gandhi's plans for self-government, though he cheerfully accepted the financial backing of the rich industrialist G. D. Birla, who saw in Gandhi's movement the best insurance policy possible against communism and any of its left-wing sympathizers. This was but another curious interlocking in the jigsaw of Indian politics, which became progressively more complicated as the last years of British rule rolled by. When Gandhi emerged from prison in 1924 the provincial governments as reconstituted under the Montford reforms had discovered that, given the will and agreement among themselves, Indian ministers could get things they wanted done in matters like education and local economy without interference by the superior British authority. There were factions within Congress which regarded such ministers as traitors to the ultimate cause and in Gandhi's absence a breakaway Swaraj Party was formed to contest provincial elections and render the provincial governments unworkable. The Mahatma, calculating that the British would provide a much better excuse for his further intervention before long, withdrew to his ashram near Ahmedabad and bided his time after staging the first of his many fasts, which he was to use time and time again to make his political points. He spent the next three years in spinning and weaving khadi cloth, and writing hundreds of articles to broadcast his casteless outlook around the land. There was much need of them. In Travancore, a low caste Pulaya was estimated to pollute a Nambudiri Brahmin at ninety-six paces. There were many parts of the country where religious law still excluded the low castes from roads, schools, office buildings, government service and even temples; and most of those bans were not lifted until the British enacted a Temple Entry Proclamation in 1936.

Gandhi's moment came in 1927 when the Simon Commission was appointed, a little earlier than promised, to review the workings of the Montford reforms. All well and good – except that every member of the commission was British. Again there was the noise of outrage from Congress, which refused to have anything to do with the commission, and more demonstrations followed across India. Two of the young Congress leaders wished to make the occasion an outright test of strength between nationalism and the Government. They were Subhas Chandra Bose, a Bengali who had once written home from Cambridge University that 'what gives me the greatest joy is to watch the whiteskins serving me and cleaning my shoes'; and Jawaharlal Nehru, a Kashmiri who had also been to Cambridge (and Harrow before it) before being pointed in the direction of politics by Annie Besant; an elegantly passionate man but more temperate than Bose. They were carefully headed away from a course that might well have ended in general bloodshed by a characteristically astute Gandhi ploy. He made his own peaceful protest – and made sure that the authorities were informed of it before he began – by walking sixty miles from his ashram to the coast at Dandi, where he proceeded to condense a small amount of salt from the sea; an illegal act, when the manufacture of salt was liable to tax. The Government tried not to notice, but this was impossible when Gandhi was accompanied on his march by hundreds, and when sympathetic processions and hartals were happening all over India, with riots breaking out in some places. In the disorders that spread and grew, only the Muslims refused to associate themselves with the protest. Once again Gandhi saw the inside of a British prison, as he was to do several more times before Independence was reached. On this occasion he spent only a few months there. The Viceroy Lord Irwin not only ordered his release, but invited him to come and talk in Lutyens's almost brand-new masterpiece.

Irwin was one of the gentler Viceroys, who genuinely tried to put into practice his Anglo-Catholic faith (a virtue that was to be quite lost on Adolf Hitler, with whom he would be negotiating a few years later, when he had become Lord Halifax and Neville Chamberlain's Foreign Secretary). He and Gandhi took to each other at once. The Englishman thought the Indian had 'a very good mind; logical, forceful, courageous, with an odd streak of subtlety'; while the Mahatma said later that 'I succumbed not to Lord Irwin but to the honesty in him.' Both laughed at Winston Churchill's comment in the House of Commons about their meeting;

It is alarming and also nauseating to see Mr Gandhi, a seditious Middle Temple lawyer, now posing as a fakir of the type well-known in the East, striding half-naked up the steps of the Viceregal palace, while he is still organizing and conducting a defiant campaign of civil disobedience, to parley on equal terms with the representative of the King Emperor.

The two men talked together, on and off, for a couple of weeks and by the end they had made a pact. The Government would release all political detainees except those convicted of violence, and Congress would call off its civil disobedience movement. Gandhi also agreed to attend a round-table conference in London, which had already had one session boycotted by Congress and was due to start another one shortly. The most important outcome of the talks, however, was intangible. Irwin had convinced Gandhi, who was nobody's fool, that the British genuinely did mean to grant self-government to India. The only thing to be settled was the rate of progress.

Yet this new amity collapsed almost at once. Gandhi made a

larger impression on the British public in 1931 than on the London politicians. The end of that year brought a new Viceroy, Lord Willingdon, who disliked him, and a new British Government at home, which believed in ruling rather than compromising with the Indian nationalists. Civil disobedience began again, on a bigger scale than ever before, and by May 1932 there were 36,000 Congressmen in gaol with Gandhi, inevitably, among them. For the next two years, indeed, his life settled into a spectacular rhythm of arrest, release, rearrest, release, with fasts 'unto death' at moments when he decided they would convey the impression that imperial rule had reduced India to helpless despair. But in 1934 he made the gesture of calling off civil disobedience, though it had practically worked itself to a standstill anyway, and turned his attention to the growing factionalism within the nationalist movement. The extremists had been gaining the upper hand in Congress and Gandhi wanted none of them, if only because they might provoke the British into even more uncompromising measures. Skilfully he isolated Subhas Chandra Bose and drove him into a political wilderness, promoting the more biddable and balanced Nehru to a position as heir apparent just below the pedestal on which he himself sat with his spinning wheel. At the same time, in spite of his own rough treatment by the British, he clung to his belief in the integrity that he had felt in Irwin.

His trust in that was not misplaced. Though they had lately been offering Indians a mailed fist in India, the British in London had been preparing a new Government of India Act; not without difficulty, because every step towards it had been doggedly opposed by Churchill and others of the old imperial guard. But in 1935 it became law. In one respect the Act could be mistaken for a suspiciously conservative document. It proposed an Assembly in Delhi enlarged to 250 seats representing constituencies in British India, and 125 occupied by members from the princely states, though the latter provision was not one that could be forced upon the native rulers, as a multitude of treaties with them ensured. They had to agree voluntarily to the plan and, in fact, took so long to make up their minds about it that events overtook them and they never did participate in the reform, to the consternation of those Britons like Churchill who had hoped they might obstruct any tendencies towards socialism in India. The offer to the princes, however, was not a cynical one; it was consistent with the policy behind the Act of safeguarding a land containing profound native rivalries from being dominated by any one group. Congress and the Muslim League, Hindus outside Congress, Muslims within it, Sikhs and other minorities, would have to make majority agreements and compromises in order to get any legislation passed. The same principle was to be applied in provincial government, where dyarchy was abandoned, so that whichever native administration was formed after election would not be even partly answerable to a British Governor. Not only that, but the provinces were now given autonomy from the central Government, which would only be allowed to interfere with their running after extraordinary emergency powers had been assumed. The provincial franchise was increased once more to include one sixth of India's population, and for the first time women were given the vote on the same terms as men. There were many other complexities in the Act, but the most important changes were these, adding up to a federation which might soon choose to sever its connection with Britain. They meant that India was bound to become independent within a generation at the most. The Viceroy would have to follow the advice of Executive Councillors, who would be members of an elected Assembly overwhelmingly Indian in composition. Some Indians looked sideways at the 1935 Act; but paid testimony to it fifteen years later, when large sections of it were incorporated into the Constitution of their independent nation.

With the princes still dithering and the British unwilling to bully them into a decision, only provincial elections were held early in 1937. Congress took all but three of the eleven polls, formed provincial governments, and to all intents and purposes became the Indian Raj for the next two and a half years. Arrogantly, the majority of Hindu leaders pushed aside claims to form coalition governments, reasonable in some cases, made by Muhammed Ali Jinnah, the Bombay lawyer who led the Muslim League; and Mahatma Gandhi, withdrawn once more into the problems of caste, preferred not to intervene. It was from this moment that the partition of an independent India, on a religious basis, began to be considered by the Muslims. The idea was scarcely forming in their minds when the Second World War broke out and the latest of the Viceroys, Lord Linlithgow, did something even more crass than the Congressmen. On behalf of India he declared war on Britain's enemies without consulting a single Indian, an old imperial reflex of the Raj. The military machine rumbled into gear again, as in 1914, and Indian soldiers were once more posted overseas. There were 189,000 native troops in 1939, two and a half million by the end of the war, and whether or not they saw the Germans, the Italians and later the Japanese as their own foes, that made them the biggest volunteer army the world has ever known; not one of them was a conscripted man.

Insulted by the Viceroy, and seizing an opportunity presented by the British suddenly having more urgent matters than Indian independence to attend to, the eight Congress governments promptly resigned and refused to co-operate in the war effort. Muslim League administrations in Bengal and Sind backed the British, as did the mixture of Hindus, Muslims and Sikhs governing the Punjab. One effect of these manoeuvres was to strengthen Jinnah's political standing; another was to persuade Muslims throughout the land – 90 million now in a total population of 400 million – that no longer need they submit to the inevitability of being dominated by a Hindu majority. When the Congressmen resigned, Jinnah tauntingly ordered his people to observe a Thanksgiving Day. By 1940 he had become bold enough to state publicly that Pakistan was his League's objective after the war. The word was contrived from an amalgamation of initials – Punjab, Afghans, Kashmir and Sind, with the affix of Baluchistan tacked on behind. It had been coined a decade earlier in Cambridge, when some Muslim undergraduates were dreaming of a homeland in the north-west of the sub-continent.

At first the country was fairly cool in the wake of the resignations and Gandhi announced that he did not seek independence out of Britain's ruin. He did, nevertheless, encourage civil disobedience again in 1940 and the British responded by arresting people in droves. One of them was Subhas Chandra Bose, but before his trial he fled the country and made his way to Berlin, where Hitler welcomed him without being quite sure what use to make of him. Eventually he was sent by submarine to solicit the Japanese, who had an excellent idea, which Bose accepted at once. Many Indian prisoners had by then been taken at the fall of Singapore, in Malaya and in Burma. Bose was to persuade as many as possible to form up into an Indian National Army against the British and recapture their country from the imperialists. Some 20,000 accepted this option in the Japanese prison camps, but 45,000 did not, and suffered greatly from disease, deprivation and brutality as a result. Bose never lived to see his fantasy of ruling India under Japanese patronage vanish in their defeat. He died when his plane crashed on Formosa in 1945.

Meanwhile, the Americans had started to lean heavily on the British in India. The days were long past when a President of the United States would speak fulsomely of British rule, as Theodore Roosevelt had in 1909, comparing their 'admirable achievements' to those of the Roman Empire and declaring that 'The mass of the people have been, and are, far better off than they would be now if the English control was overthrown and withdrawn.' Not all Americans had shared his sentiments even in those days; on at least two occasions during the troubled period leading up to Amritsar, well-wishers of the nationalist extremists in the States had raised the money to provide thousands of revolvers which were intercepted before the ships carrying them reached the Indian coast. Nationalism had always appealed to the idealistic streak in the American character and the Indian variety had been extensively propagated by Hollywood, which had made 35 movies between the *Hindoo Fakir* in 1902 and *Gunga Din* in 1939, with a recurring theme of the British putting down rebellion on the sub-continent. There was also a frustrated commercial interest in the country. Yankee merchantmen had traded freely and profitably with India between 1784 and 1815, but thereafter the connection had declined as the British progressively shouldered all competitors out of the way, leaving American business brooding in envy of the greatest market in the East. There were several factors behind the United States Government's actions at the beginning of 1941. The chief one may have been its self-image as a bastion of freedom.

America was still the best part of a year away from entering the war itself, but President Franklin Roosevelt was ready to help keep Britain afloat with a Lend-Lease programme, in spite of public and political hostility to the idea in the States. While the necessary bill was still being blocked in the US Congress, and while the *New York Times* was running a campaign in support of Indian nationalism, he sent his special envoy Averell Harriman to see Winston Churchill in London with a clear message: get out of India soon, or you may not get what you need now. Two weeks later the Lend-Lease Bill was signed. Two months after America at last committed itself fully to the war, members of the Senate Foreign Relations Committee were arguing that 'extensive assistance to Britain justified participation in imperial decisions,' and at about the same time Roosevelt was writing to Churchill that American public opinion couldn't understand why the Indians shouldn't have self-government straightaway.

It was a topic which produced more friction than any other between the two leaders. And it was a subject which caused British cynics to wonder whether altruism was really what had motivated the Americans – the more so in 1945 when Britain secured from Washington a loan of $3.75 billion for post-war reconstruction, partly in exchange for ending imperial trade preferences in the not yet independent India.

The British were not disposed to tackle independence at once in 1941, when they had their backs to the wall in Europe and the Middle East. But in March, 1942, Stafford Cripps, a socialist member of Churchill's War Cabinet, flew to New Delhi with a fresh offer to the Congress leaders. It included an invitation for them to join the Viceroy's Council at once, where they would act as the Cabinet of the Indian Government, and it promised India complete freedom when the war was over, inside or outside the British Empire, whichever she wished. Cripps also offered the Muslims the prospect of their Pakistan. With the Japanese advancing rapidly through Burma at that moment, there may have been something of desperation in the British offer; but even so, it would scarcely have been possible to go back on it later on. Most of the Congress leaders, including Nehru, were in favour of accepting on the spot. Mahatma Gandhi, however, talked them out of it. Cripps, he said, was inviting them to receive a 'post-dated cheque on a failing bank'. Nehru rearranged himself alongside his master who, a few weeks later, declared that the British in India were a provocation to the Japanese. He demanded that they withdraw at once. They said nothing. So he produced a slogan – Quit India – and with it incited the biggest wave of civil disobedience the country had known.

Gandhi and the rest of the Congress leadership were at once interned, with a nice sense of irony, in the Muslim Agha Khan's palace at Poona; and there they remained until the end of the war in Europe. Lesser rebels didn't fare nearly as well when the British turned savagely on those who were disrupting communications throughout the country and doing over a million pounds-worth of damage on the side. For the first time since Amritsar, soldiers were used to quell civil disorder, and over 1,000 people were killed, another 60,000 arrested and put into gaols much less salubrious than the palace where Gandhi and his associates were confined. A much bigger horror came round the corner in 1943, when famine devastated Bengal. Several things compounded the catastrophe, apart from weather that had produced poor rice harvests for several years. One was certainly British failure to recognize the danger early enough and to organize adequate relief; another was Indian profiteering on the black market, where plaster of paris was added to flour, making it inedible as well as expensive. No-one ever got round to counting all those who starved to death, but the figure was probably somewhere between 1.5 and 3 million. Fatalities did not slacken off until a new Viceroy took over in October that year. He was Lord Wavell, and the first thing he did was to go to Calcutta and see things for himself. Then he ordered the Army to drop whatever it was doing and get food supplies into Bengal. Suddenly, British soldiers were popular.

Wavell was a soldier himself, but an unusually sensitive one; a shy man with a dry sense of humour (he found it easier to remember that the senior Indian princes were those of Hyderabad, Kashmir, Mysore, Gwalior and Baroda by bearing in mind that Hot Kippers Make Good Breakfast). He was a capable administrator but he was more at ease with the Muslims than the Congressmen who, in his view, had behaved indefensibly in fomenting civil disobedience when he and his troops already had their hands full preparing to repulse the Japanese. That apart, he had neither the temperament nor the experience necessary to prevent the political rough-house that began with the end of the European war in 1945. The Congress leaders were at once released but refused to countenance a coalition government with the now powerful Muslim League, to finish off the war against Japan. They wanted a test of strength and when elections were held the result was a kind of stalemate; Congress held the whip hand over Hindu India, the League was impregnable wherever Muslims were concentrated. By the late summer of 1945 both had been left in no doubt that the British were, indeed, on their way out of the sub-continent. Just before the atom bomb was dropped on Hiroshima, the British at home had thrown Churchill out of office and elected a Labour Government with a massive majority. The Labour Party had long been dedicated to the principle and was now sworn to the achievement of Indian independence without delay, which made for one of history's perfect circles. The Prime Minister who was about to sign away British rule in India, Clement Attlee, was a former pupil at Haileybury, the school which had been invented to nurture the Raj.

Attlee, a tough-minded, underrated man, despatched a mission to

India, whose object was to get the independence preparations going for a united nation if at all possible. Various devices were suggested to accommodate the conflicting Hindu and Muslim demands, but intransigence had set in all round. Nehru, speaking for Congress in his immaculate white cap and tunic coat, was laying down policies as though the British had already left him in control. Jinnah, the image of a statesman in his elegant Bond Street suit, was contemptuous of all he heard, playing for time. Downstage now, Mahatma Gandhi sat wringing his hands in despair; with good reason. After meeting Nehru in Bombay, Jinnah announced that he had nothing more to say to his adversary, and called for a Direct Action day by Muslims. This unleashed a series of dreadful riots in Calcutta, ten days of communal violence that didn't stop until 45,000 troops had been drafted in to enforce a peace, by which time 3,467 bodies had been accounted for, with probably as many more dumped in the Hooghly and swept away. Even the politicians were too stunned by that to continue their wrangling; but only briefly. With the whole country clearly moving towards civil war, the bickering broke out again and Lord Wavell reported that neither side would listen to reason, which meant compromise. Not even Attlee's summoning of the Indian leaders to London for talks in a cooler atmosphere could persuade them to settle their differences. Congress wanted to rule all the land that Britain was handing over; the Muslim League would have none of this.

And so the British decided to propel them all into a solution by making them face up to a time limit. In February 1947, it was announced that power would be relinquished not later than June the following year. In the same statement, Attlee recalled Wavell in favour of someone more robust and much more accustomed to getting his own way. The last Viceroy of India was to be Lord Mountbatten, the brilliant, charming and aggressive sailor who had been Supreme Allied Commander in South-east Asia – and also happened to be cousin of King George VI. His charm worked on Nehru from their first meeting and he also got on well with Gandhi, treating him with a respect that the shrunken old man had received from only one Viceroy before. Nothing, however, would budge Jinnah from his unbending position; not quarter-deck crispness or mess-deck warmth – not even the good nature of Lady Mountbatten, who was captivating all other Indians with a public relations exercise of her own. Eventually it was Nehru who gave up a cherished wish, and conceded that there was nothing for it but a partition of the land. The alternative was something so unspeakable that no sane man could contemplate it. Civil war had broken out by then in the Punjab, where Amritsar and Lahore were smoking wrecks. That was what caused Mountbatten to drop his own bombshell at yet another fruitless meeting with Indian politicians. Not bothering to consult Attlee in London, relying on more personal authority than any Viceroy before him had dared to invoke, he announced that Independence would come at midnight on 14 August 1947 – just over ten weeks away. By his own account, he didn't make up his mind about that date until the last minute before he spoke; he might just as easily have suggested mid-September, but on a sudden thought came down in favour of the second anniversary of the Japanese surrender to the forces under his command.

There has been argument ever since about the wisdom of that hasty ending to British rule. Many have reasoned that it was responsible for the carnage that followed in the north-west within a few days of Independence becoming an accomplished fact. The partition line dividing India from Pakistan ran straight through the Punjab, and there Hindus, Muslims and Sikhs butchered each other without mercy. In addition to the local community, the area was swollen with transitory refugees; Muslims from all over India making for Pakistan, Hindus coming south to start new lives among people of their own faith – something like five and a half million people travelling each way. Many never reached their destinations on either side of the new frontier. Trains were found standing still in the middle of nowhere, their carriages packed with mutilated corpses. Convoys of trucks were ambushed and the men, women and children in them were subjected to every kind of atrocity. A Boundary Force of 50,000 Indian troops had been positioned in the area beforehand, to police the social upheaval expected there, but the terrible conflicting loyalties of the moment made them pretty ineffective. For obvious reasons no British soldiers were employed, apart from a handful of Indian Army officers who remained with their units until their services could be dispensed with by the two new national governments: it would have been insupportable to put the forces of imperialism into action against former subjects who had just been set free. The human cost of that limited civil war was never accurately known; the most informed estimate was half a million or so dead. When challenged about this later, Mountbatten would say that it was appalling enough but that he had decided on the swift withdrawal because he feared something on the same scale not only in the Punjab but all over the sub-continent; and in view of the rapidly collapsing situation he was faced with in June, it would take an over-confident man to insist that his assessment was wrong.

The British left India with sadness and goodwill, and some of their feelings were shown by Indians to them. This was perhaps the most remarkable thing about the Raj. Other European nations abandoned their old colonies later and in great bitterness. The Dutch did not relinquish sovereignty in their old East Indies for another two years, after battling with the Indonesian nationalists all the way. The Belgians were still fighting to hold on to their possession of the Congo in 1960. The French did not get out of Algeria until a terrible war had finished in 1962. It took guerrillas with foreign aid to extract the Portuguese from Angola in 1975, as it had taken the Indian Army to remove them from Goa in 1961. But as midnight and Independence arrived in New Delhi there was nothing but harmony between the last Viceroy and the first Prime Minister of the new nation. Jawaharlal Nehru made a speech to his countrymen, full of hope for the future, from the balcony of the Constituent Assembly, before the Union Jack was hauled down and the Star of India was run up. Then he went with the other leaders to the palace Edwin Lutyens had built, where Mountbatten awaited them with a decanter of port. 'To India,' said the Englishman, as he raised his glass. 'To King George VI,' replied the Indian who had spent so much time in imperial gaols. The chief character in the long struggle that had just ended was missing from the room. Unwilling to face a celebration that had sealed forever the division of his country, Mahatma Gandhi was 800 miles away in Calcutta, sustaining himself with prayer. He would be dead in a few more months, assassinated by a Brahmin who was obsessed with caste. Another crucial figure was absent from the gathering in what had just been translated from the Viceroy's House into Rashtrapati Bhawan, where Presidents of India would reside before long. He was Muhammad Ali Jinnah and, twenty-four hours earlier, Mountbatten had insisted on riding with him in an open car through the streets of Karachi on Pakistan's Inauguration Day. Mountbatten heartily disliked the inflexible Muslim by then, but the security people had got wind of a Sikh plot to murder the creator of Pakistan, and the Viceroy decided that his own presence alongside

Jinnah would lessen the chance of a bomb being thrown into the car, with a consequence for millions if it were.

All over the sub-continent the British were packing up to go home, apart from a few civil servants and scores of box wallahs who would remain to carry on business as usual for many a day. In the ministries in New Delhi and the provincial capitals, in the offices of District Magistrates and Collectors of revenue, most ICS men were squaring off their paperwork and handing over their files to Indian colleagues who knew perfectly well how everything should be run. In Lucknow, some sappers hauled down the Union Jack from the flagstaff on top of the ruined old Residency, where by special decree it had flown day and night ever since the Mutiny; then they demolished the staff itself and filled up its base with cement, so that nobody else's flag should fly over that poignant place. In Pakistan, an official of the Peshawar Vale Hunt went round the stables and the kennels, putting down every horse and hound, unwilling to leave them to whatever fate might spread from the tormented Punjab. Some of the British were carefully scrutinizing their newspapers, where long-distance adver- tisements had been placed by the Dormy House Hotel in Westward Ho, the Montpelier Hotel in Budleigh Salterton and others, coyly asking 'Are you leaving for England?' In the same columns Miss Grove, of the Garden School at Gulmarj in Kashmir, was offering to escort children to their final destinations in England for the part- payment of her own fare home. Upcountry, people closed the shutters on their bungalows, took a last look round the garden, shook hands with all the servants and, sometimes, gave the ayah a bit of a hug. John Rowntree, a Forest Officer in Assam, was one who found it hard to drag himself and his family away: 'We left behind our weeping servants, bundled our weeping children into the car and, near to tears ourselves, set off down the hill road which I had first climbed eighteen years ago.'

The soldiers departed, too. They mounted their last guards, had some splendid farewell parades, and with all the controlled flourish that tradition had bred they handed their responsibilities over with great ceremony to the independent armies. In platoons and companies and battalions they mustered their equipment and loaded it into trucks, and began to roll down from the hills and across the plains towards Bombay or Karachi and their embarkation points. It takes even longer to shift the military in peacetime than it does in war, but presently all had gone except the officers and men of the 1st Battalion, the Somerset Light Infantry. They fell in for the last time on Indian soil on 28 February 1948, not far from the Gateway of India, an enormous triumphal arch the British had erected by the water's edge in Bombay to mark the spot where their King Emperor had made his landfall in 1911. Indian troops were drawn up in formation as the Somersets marched on to the quay, a great phalanx of men from all over the nation standing in impeccable lines, every man at attention with a new kind of pride. An old familiar command; and the Indians presented arms in a Royal Salute, while their band played *God Save the King*. Another command; and this time the Somersets returned the compliment, to the sound of *Bande Mataram*. The Indian commander, a Lieutenant-Colonel of Sikhs, handed over to the Englishmen a parting gift. It was a silver model of the Gateway, and on it were the words; 'To commemorate the comradeship of the soldiers of the British and Indian Armies. 1754–1947.' More commands; and slowly the King's Colour and the Regimental Colour of the Somersets were trooped to the waiting transport ship through the Gateway itself, to the playing of *Auld Lang Syne*. The thing was finished. A promise had been kept.

Disraeli suggested that she ought to be known as Empress as well as Queen, and so a tremendous Durbar was held to announce the fact.

Tea being loaded at one of the Lipton gardens for transport to Calcutta and export to England. Although China tea had been drunk in London for 150 years before planting started at Darjeeling, by 1888 the consumption of Indian tea had overtaken it, a lead that was never to be lost.

The start of railways in 1853 was the beginning of industrial transformation in India, as well as of unheard of social mobility. The engineering required was remarkable and accidents such as this – during track-laying about 1880 – were commonplace. Some 40000 men navvied the track over the Western Ghats and nearly one third died from injury or disease.

Cartoon from *The Indian Punch* 1863. Interesting above all, perhaps, for its self-mockery. Prejudice against Indians, which had been virtually unknown until the nineteenth century was well under way, became highly developed in the years after the Mutiny. The British who practised it took themselves very seriously indeed. The cartoonist evidently wasn't one of them.

Above left: Dadabhai Naorowji MP. Bombay Parsi who sat in the British House of Commons, representing Central Finsbury from 1892 to 1895. The Parsi community was notably Anglophile and prospered in commerce and the professions under British rule.

Above right: James Skinner; oil by William Melville c. 1836. Skinner, the son of a Scottish soldier and a Rajput woman, is one of the great heroes of the Anglo-Indians. He founded India's senior cavalry regiment, Skinner's Horse, and the troops under his command compared him to Alexander the Great by calling him Sikander Sahib.

A Royal Progress during the railway age. The Prince and Princess of Wales (later King George V and Queen Mary) have come to Gwalior in the course of their Indian tour in 1905. Their host there will be one of India's senior princes, the Maharajah Scindia, ruler of his independent state. Beyond the

train his richly decorated elephants are drawn up ready to convey the entourage to the Maharajah's palace. Meanwhile, one of the station platforms has been transformed by tenting into a medieval fantasy.

State Opening of the Delhi Durbar, New Year's Day 1903. This was Curzon's Durbar, arranged to proclaim Edward VII's Coronation, which had taken

place some months before. The proclamation was really an excuse for a display of pageantry such as even India had never seen before.

Lord and Lady Curzon on a tiger shoot. Curzon was one of the most brilliant administrators Britain ever sent to India, and the man who saved many of her ancient monuments – including the Taj Mahal – from ruin. But he was also politically obtuse and his decision to partition Bengal was so disastrous that it had to be revoked under a later Viceroy.

Drawing room tent at the Viceroy's camp, as used by Lord Elgin during a visit to the princely state of Bhopal in 1895. His successor Curzon had something like this erected whenever he and his Government took to their annual summer refuge up at Simla, because Curzon disliked staying in the Viceregal Lodge there.

Brigadier-General Reginald Dyer (1864 – 1927). Born in India, he was responsible for the most infamous act in the last decades of British rule. During political disturbances in the Punjab in 1919, he led troops to the Jallianwala Bagh in Amritsar and ordered them to open fire on an unarmed crowd; an official report estimated that 1500 were killed or wounded. Dyer was relieved of his command and forced into early retirement. But from the bitterness left by the Amritsar massacre and by Dyer's subsequent 'crawling order', Mahatma Gandhi's independence movement gained a momentum it had not known before.

Annie Besant was one of many Britons who flung themselves wholeheartedly into the political struggle for Indian independence. Her Home Rule League exerted much pressure on the Government just after the First World War, and her influence helped to turn young Jawaharlal Nehru towards direct action.

Mahatma Gandhi with cotton millworkers in Lancashire 1931. The Indian leader had just attended the Round Table Conference in London, to discuss his country's progress towards self-government. The British politicians were much less friendly than were factory workers in the North of England, when Gandhi toured some of their towns after the conference.

A corner of Park Street Cemetery, Calcutta. Cows sometimes graze among these crumbling tombstones, and poor people camp on the pavements outside the cemetery walls. Many of the early British in India ended up here,

among them William Makepeace Thackeray's father, Walter Bagehot's father-in-law, and sons of Charles Dickens and Captain Cook.

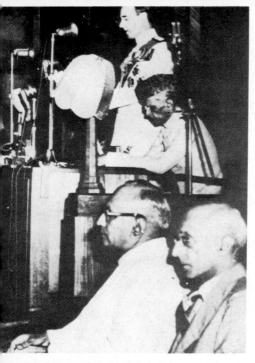

The last Viceroy bows out. Lord Mountbatten is reading the King's message to the Constituent Assembly of the newly-created Pakistan. The following day – 14 August 1947 – a similar ceremony in New Delhi marked the end of British rule in India, too.

Jawaharlal Nehru and Lord Louis Mountbatten. Nehru had been a vigorous fighter for freedom and had often been imprisoned by the British, while Mountbatten's background represented a great deal of the tradition that Nehru and his colleagues had worked to overthrow. But they happened to like each other, and their friendship was largely responsible for the goodwill which infected India's Independence.

TEN

THE LEGACY

A few years after Independence, President Roosevelt's widow visited India in the course of an Asian tour on behalf of a United Nations committee. She later wrote a book about her impressions and in it she rather went out of her way to indicate the defects of the Raj, repeatedly referring to the British 'occupation' of India; an expression which, as she well knew, still had the most terrible connotations with Hitler's brief rule over much of Europe. But she was also honest enough to report something that obviously baffled her:

In India, after the departure of the British, the resentment previously felt towards them was in a large measure transferred to us (the Americans). Never convinced that the British really intended to keep their promise to leave, the Indians were deeply impressed when they actually did, and the disappearance of their hostility was almost an overnight phenomenon. I do not think they have forgotten the long years of inferior status, or the economic damage the English inflicted on India, but even though they recognize that some of their present-day ills stem from British rule, their grievances have been swallowed up in a surge of genuine friendliness. They tend to remember the good things the British did and to ignore the bad; and it is a fact that today the British are remarkably popular there.

Some Americans were much warmer than Eleanor Roosevelt, among them the political commentator Walter Lippmann, who wrote that

with an elegance and style that will compel and receive an instinctive response throughout the civilized world, Attlee and Mountbatten have done a service to all mankind by showing what statesmen can do not with force and money but with lucidity, resolution and sincerity.

Mrs Roosevelt's bewilderment, and that of others who perhaps knew only of the more dramatic episodes in the history of the British on the sub-continent, is understandable enough in view of the relationship Indians chose to maintain with the old imperialists when they were free to do whatever they liked. Here were people who had, in Mrs Roosevelt's terminology, spent nearly two centuries under a foreign yoke. Yet on becoming independent they had accepted a dominion status under the Crown comparable to that of Australia, Canada and New Zealand; and even when, in 1950, they decided to proclaim themselves a republic, they still preferred to remain inside the British Commonwealth – unlike South Africa, which before long cut all its links with the Crown. Not only that, but the Indians invited the last Viceroy to remain in New Delhi as Governor-General of the Dominion, which Lord Mountbatten did for almost a year after Independence. Several other senior British administrators likewise stayed behind for a while at the request of Nehru and his government, and these included the Governors of Bombay and Madras. Such preferences for retaining connections of one sort and another were not those of a people for whom hostility had been the dominant feature of their relationship with their former rulers. And it would be patronizing to assume that some of the things said by prominent Indians at the time of Independence and later on were uttered purely in euphoria or in some clubbable concept of 'good form'. Rajendra Prasad, who became India's first President at the declaration of the Republic in 1950, said the granting of Independence had been the 'consummation and fulfilment of the historic tradition and democratic ideals of British rule.' When George VI died in 1952, Nehru received a private message from the Indian High Commissioner in London, who was that doughty old nationalist Krishna Menon, lamenting the last King Emperor's death; 'He was a really good man and a greater man than usually believed. He was very thoughtful of us and understood and respected us.' Nehru himself often spoke well of his country's former masters. Even when spending one of his periodic stints in their prisons, during the war, he had remarked of the old Orientalists that 'India owes a deep debt of gratitude for the rediscovery of her past literature.' The tributes of Prasad, Menon, Nehru and others may well say more for Indian generosity than for anything the British contributed to the relationship. But they do not square with a conventional view of imperial rule.

The British left India with many problems, almost all of which had existed before their time. The moneylender still flourished and the excesses of caste could still produce misery up to and including bloodshed, in spite of the fact that the Constitution of 1950 refused to recognize caste distinctions and specifically forbade the practice of 'untouchability'. Corruption remained widespread and policemen continued to be regarded as potential brutes. Wealth was still grotesquely uneven, with appalling poverty endured by most people and fantastic luxury enjoyed by relatively few. The economy, as always, was overburdened by a population which increased at astounding rates even after attempts to control it by artificial means of preventing conception. Violence still lurked everywhere and was liable to be let loose whenever there was dispute or grievance, in spite of Mahatma Gandhi's teachings and the veneration in which he had been held. One of the most conspicuous things about India a generation after Gandhi's death was how little he seemed to count in popular esteem. Apart from ritual genuflections by politicians at pregnant moments of state, and away from the dogged devotion of rural eccentrics like Sunderlal Bahaguna, leader of the Chipko movement to preserve trees, Gandhi's name was scarcely ever invoked by his fellow countrymen. Visitors to his old ashram at Wardha were few and far between, though a group of benign ladies tended it carefully in case it should ever again become a place of great pilgrimage. The Gandhi Museum in Delhi was at the same time deserted even on a holiday afternoon, though it contained many relics of the great man, including the garments he was wearing when he was shot. The ultimate rejection occurred in Calcutta in 1970, when left-wing Naxalites smashed Gandhi's statue and flung the pieces into a water-tank.

It may reasonably be asked why the British did not do more to solve the problems they passed on to independent India after taking charge for so long. There is no adequate answer to this except maybe to point out that most of the problems were rooted in human nature itself. Solutions could only have been imposed by rulers who were prepared to be more ruthless than they were; and such ruthlessness rarely appears in the history of any land except from revolutionary native rule. The marks the British did leave on the country were big enough anyway. To examine the imperialists at one of their weakest points, they did approach India from the outset in a spirit of greed, and for a long time they manipulated the economy for their own benefit rather than that of Indians. To a surprising degree, some of them continued to profit from the country even after Independence. Tea planting was still largely in British hands up to the 1960s; and ten years after that, Calcutta's public transport system and its electricity undertaking were still run by private companies with innumerable shareholders in the British Isles. Yet in the last few decades of their rule, the British had encouraged the growth of the native economy to the point that, by 1939, it had last reached a favourable balance of payments in trade with Great Britain. In part this was due to the series of measures taken by the imperial Government to protect rising Indian industry from powerful competition at home, a typical one being the act which enabled the Indian Tin Plate Company to get going in 1922 in a sphere which had hitherto been regarded as the preserve of manufacturers in South Wales. The particular beneficiaries in that case were the energetic Parsi family of Tata. The first Jamsetji Tata had founded the Indian iron and steel industry in 1907, and his son and other relatives expanded it so vigorously, with the help of British legislation, that by 1945 the Tata empire was worth £54 million, employed 120,000 people, and in a multitude of activities gave India a very solid base of heavy industry to start independence with.

The most important after-effect of imperial rule was the institution of elected parliamentary government. It was overlong in coming, but before they properly put it into effect the British paradoxically had fired Indians with a determination to have a democracy like their own. The delay in setting up elected government was mighty unpopular but may unwittingly have been more propitious for the future of the free nation, though it was scarcely so in the case of Pakistan. Whether or not Indians prized parliamentary rule so highly because they were only allowed to try it for themselves in slow stages, discovering its penalties and imperatives without having to bear the full consequences themselves, the truth is that democracy was planted more deeply in the political mind of India than anywhere else in the old colonial world, where dictatorships became the rule rather than the exception, and where elections could be postponed for years on end on any pretext or none at all. In India the electoral processes have been consistently upheld ever since 1947, even at moments when some jeremiahs have forecast that they might be cynically dispensed with at last. The biggest test was passed in 1977 when Nehru's daughter, Indira Gandhi, had become a thoroughly unpopular Prime Minister as a result of draconian regulations which some compared to the worst times of British rule. In such quarters it was announced that Mrs Gandhi had effectively resorted to dictatorship which she would not relinquish except to force. But in

1977 she duly submitted herself to general election and, inevitably, she lost; only to be re-elected with a landslide majority three years later when the populace at large had become disillusioned by the performance of her sternest critics. If Independence had been India's proudest moment, that submission thirty years later should have run it a close second, for it was the assurance that even in the bleakest circumstances India would abide by its independent ideals.

The rule of law, and the nature of that law, was the best of what the British left behind, together with the parliamentary vision. The Constitution that Indians themselves formulated after Independence and decreed in 1950, was derived from several sources. Large stretches, as we have already noticed, were taken from the 1935 Government of India Act. A Bill of Rights was also incorporated, so that fundamental liberties should not be left in the unwritten custody of public opinion as in the United Kingdom, but be spelt out, as in the United States; and some of the phraseology in the Indian version is identical to that in its American model. Underpinning everything in the Constitution, however, was the ultimate authority of the law. It was decided to leave unaltered the entire legal system the British had bequeathed, which was based on what an Indian Attorney-General has since described as 'the towering structure' of Lord Macaulay's penal code. Macaulay had frequently been an object of nationalist anger and nationalist justification ever since the infancy of the Indian Congress, because of the views he promoted at the time of the great education debate in the 1830s. It was left to the historian K. M. Pannikar to put him more clearly in perspective over a century later with the following footnote: 'It is the genius of this man, narrow in his Europeanism, self-satisfied in his sense of English greatness, that gives life to modern India as we know it. He was India's new Manu[1], the spirit of modern law incarnate.'

With a Constitution and a parliamentary system answerable to an initial electorate of 175 million people, India also had an administrative machine in good order to make things work, a benefit no other nation emerging from colonial status in the years after the Second World War would enjoy on anything like the same scale. The structure of the civil service had been one of the sorest points among the nationalists in the early years of the struggle for independence,

[1] The Manu Samhita, written sometime during the first two centuries A.D., was the text which inspired ancient Hindu law.

with its favouritism for Britons in the superior ICS and its relegation of most Indians to the less attractive provincial civil service. In the latter, an Indian could act as a Magistrate or a Collector or in several comparable roles, but unless he was promoted into the ICS he would not have a future in the administration of his country at the highest level. From the time of the Montford reforms the British at last made serious efforts to correct this imbalance, recruiting more Indians directly into the ICS and making promotion easier for those who had entered the provincial service on smaller qualifications. The last intake of Britons into the ICS was in 1939, and when Independence came the composition of this renowned elite (which hardly ever amounted to 1,000 men) was just about half and half; and the infinitely larger provincial service below it was almost wholly Indian. The consequence was that when the British left India there was no chaotic period of adjustment as inexperienced men fumbled their way through the unfamiliar complexities of administering an unusually labyrinthine society. Enough Indians had already been doing the job for years, with as much deftness and assurance and wisdom as the finest civil servants that ever came out of the British Isles – and they were to guard very carefully in the years to come the best reputation the ICS had earned; for incorruptibility. There was hardly anything in the new India that had to start from scratch. All the professions were stocked with competent men, none more than the law, which was possibly over-stocked. There were also 92,000 registered doctors who had been trained in every branch of Western medicine, almost 100,000 university professors and lecturers, with well over half a million teachers lower down the educational scale. There were skilled craftsmen in every trade, who could make motor-cars, build bridges, fly aeroplanes, adjust electrical devices and print scurrilous articles on indigenous subjects now that the most obvious target had removed itself. India, at Independence, was only an undeveloped nation in so far as the majority of her people still lived primitively on the land (as, coincidentally, Mahatma Gandhi had urged), her biggest resources not yet properly tapped, her substance shockingly apportioned. That amounts to a terrible 'only'; but the assets tend to be overlooked in its shadow.

These – together with the extensive public works in railways, roads and irrigation – were the nuts and bolts of the British legacy to India. In modern times it has been suggested that some of the material benefits were more apparent than real. The railways have been criticized on the grounds that they were too expensive for a low-level economy to maintain, and because vast areas of forest were felled to provide fuel for the locomotives, with a serious consequence to the moisture content of the soil. It has also been argued that the irrigation canals were much less marvellous than the Victorians and Edwardians believed, because they upset the delicate hydrological cycle of the earth, damaged wells, made land barren by inducing salinity, caused swamping and an increase in malaria, and promoted corruption among local water board officials. The Public Works Department as a whole has been indicted for commandeering large amounts of dung in the mysterious processes of brick-making, thereby leaving the peasants with insufficient manure for the fruitful cultivation of their lands.

Whether or not, and to what extent, such criticisms are valid, the fact is that there was rather more to the imperial residue than the obvious changes wrought by administrators and engineers. Cultur-ally, the religion introduced by Europeans made relatively little impact on a Hindu society which had powerful protective devices like social ostracism, and a capacity to absorb new flights of fancy and produce yet another mutant without yielding any of its own essentials. Though the six million Christians who remained in India when the British withdrew amounted to more than the Sikh popula-tion, most of them were Anglo-Indians and their expression of faith was part of the ghetto mentality into which they had been forced by everybody else. By contrast the English language flourished every-where except among the peasantry, because it had long been recognized as the indispensable vehicle to success and prosperity under the Raj. Yet it had not flourished at the expense of the local tongues, as Macaulay's greatest critics had feared, and every educated Indian was at least bi-lingual, sometimes more than that, fluent in whichever speech he chose. To some degree, English helped towards the unification of the country after Independence. There remained, as there always had been, strong regional loyalties which expressed themselves vigorously through and in defence of regional languages. A man from the far south of India, whose native language was Tamil or perhaps Malayalam, was no more likely – or even inclined – to understand a man from Delhi, whose upbringing was in Hindi, than a Londoner without French could comprehend what a Parisian without English was saying. In India such difficulties of communication were eased, almost erased, by the widespread use of

199

English. At all-India conferences, speeches were generally translated into that language immediately they had been made in a local tongue, so that every delegate present could take them in. At a more ordinary level, it had become customary to hear two Indians chattering away privately in their local language, with English expressions (like 'typewriter' or 'pianoforte lessons') peppering their conversation every other sentence or so.

Other memorials abounded. The British, enthusiastic patrons of the monumental sculptor at home and abroad in the nineteenth and early twentieth centuries, scattered statues of their heroes and dignitaries across the sub-continent almost as liberally as they erected them in the civic squares of the United Kingdom. Soon after Independence, King George V was removed (discreetly, without popular demonstration) from his pedestal at the foot of the King's Way in New Delhi, and companion pieces up and down India were dismantled, fetching up as often as not in warehouses until a market for them could be discovered among private collectors of imperial bric-a-brac. But a great number were left standing for years after the British left. As late as 1969, it was still possible to count sixteen on the maidan in Calcutta, including the effigy of Lord Mayo, who had been assassinated by an Indian in 1872 and whose inscription still bore the words, 'The People of India, mourning and indignant, raise this statue'.[2] Not far away, in the Park Street Cemetery, a congestion of stone pyramids, crossed swords, gun-barrels, trumpets, banners, scythes, arrows, torches and other funeral symbols marked the place where hundreds of lesser Britons had come to rest 7,000 miles from home. It would be possible to produce a book – and someone has doubtless done so – on such testimonies to the mortality of the Raj. There can be no town between the North West Frontier and Cape Comorin without its quota of British gravestones, all of them sobering, some peculiarly sad, like the one in Bihar (until it mysteriously vanished a few years ago) to 'Thomas Oulam Roberts, formerly of the Victoria Foundry, Foreman Jamalpur Erecting Works. Died 1864 after an untimely encounter with a tiger. Aged 27 years.' Occasionally a monument is guaranteed to set the teeth on edge. There is a church in Kanpur which was built to commemorate

[2] It, with the other 15 statues, was removed shortly afterwards by a Communist Government of West Bengal, exercising its independence from New Delhi's authority under constitutional provisions which originated in the 1935 Government of India Act.

those who died at the hands of Nana Sahib's mutineers. On one wall is a marble slab listing some of their names. Above this is the injunction 'Vengeance is Mine, saith the Lord.' That needs to be read in the knowledge that away to the north-west there is another monument in the gardens that were once the wasteland of Jallianwala Bagh, where an inscription points out that 'This place is saturated with the blood of about two thousand Hindu, Sikh and Muslim patriots who were martyred in a non-violent struggle to free India from British domination.'

There are places in India where you can walk round a corner into a building which you would swear you have already seen in a more frigid climate than this. Railway stations galore, of course, complete with booking offices carpentered in heavy and dark wood just as they used to be in England when the LMS steamed out of Euston and the LNER out of King's Cross. Calcutta is especially rich in the architecture of the British, with its Raj Bhawan still looking like Kedleston Hall, its Marble Palace (still sheltering two statues of Queen Victoria even today) resembling a mini-Chatsworth, its New Market clock tower in the likeness of Victorian Huddersfield or Wigan, and its church of St John the spitting image of St Martins-in-the-Fields; as it ought to be, because Lieutenant Agg of the Bengal Engineers used the plans of the London original when he began to build it in 1784. While Calcutta is a permanent exhibition of decaying English Classical buildings, Bombay still glories in preposterously confident Gothic Revival constructions like the Law Courts and the Posts and Telegraph Offices, as well as the Victoria Terminus which outdoes everything in sight. Elsewhere, such reminders of the past are not so thickly assembled in one place, though a stroll round any Indian city will sooner or later bring an Englishman up against something familiar. In Benares, the Sanskrit University that Jonathan Duncan founded when the Orientalists were redeeming those old Hindu texts, stands quadrangled and Gothic not a mile from the Ganges ghats; and were it not for the heat and the glaring light, the rickshaws and the sacred cows, the Eastern sounds and the overwhelming crowds, it would be possible to believe that it was even closer to the banks of the Cam.

Benares, in fact, is no longer Benares. The word was a British corruption of a Mughal corruption of its old Hindu name, and after Independence the Indians restored Varanasi to its proper place. But Annie Besant Road is there because the eponymous lady did her bit for India's freedom inside and outside the prisons of the Raj. There are even towns still known by the names of Britons who started them, or won battles near them, or died in them – Dalhousie, Herbertpur and Clutterbuckganj in India, Abbotabad and Jacobabad in Pakistan. There are regiments of the Indian Army today where portraits of their former British commanders still hang in the officers' mess, to be toasted on anniversary days. There is a firm of printers in Mount Road, Madras, which still trades under the name of Higginbotham, though it was long ago totally Indianized. There are games of cricket being played on every maidan in this part of the old Empire, with the traditional courtesies still observed, though these are now thought stiflingly old-fashioned everywhere else; and every large city has at least one immense stadium where the biggest cricket-watching crowds in the world gather to follow the progress of a five-day Test. In the lobby of the Great Eastern Hotel in Calcutta, where Kipling used to stay, there is a shop selling Indian textiles; and on its plateglass window, in a low-relief gilt lettering which is carefully polished every day, are the curving words 'By appointment to HM the King Emperor and HM the Queen Empress' – with the imperial coat of arms just above. Where it has survived, Lord William Bentinck's tree planting on either side of the Grand Trunk Road provides blessed shade for travellers now, as it was intended to 150 years ago. But Warren Hastings's Gola, having been taken over by the municipality of Patna, is used for the storage of school text books and other inedible objects, instead of grain. There will not be a corner of India where some memory of the British doesn't wait to be conjured up. Strangest of all is what happens once a year in New Delhi on Republic Day. This has become a tradition of magnificent ceremonial and spectacularly gorgeous parades. At one point the President of the Republic rides with an escort up the old King's Way, sitting in a carriage which was built for the use of Viceroys. In the evening, at the Great Place, thousands of people watch silently as soldiers perform their ritual of Beating the Retreat. Its climax comes movingly, after much marching and counter-marching in quick-time and slow, when at sunset the Star of India is very slowly hauled down from the nearby flagstaff by two troopers wearing spotless white gloves. As the bunting descends, the massed military bands play – as the British instructed them to generations ago – that solemn Christian hymn 'Abide with me'.

It was Bismarck who once said that 'Were the British Empire to disappear, its work in India would remain one of its lasting monuments.' Like most people who peer at the world from the loftiest heights of power, it never occurred to him that those who were ruled might also have a lasting effect on the rulers: as India has had on the British. A superficial view of the exchanges might suggest that what India managed to convey was paltry compared with what she found herself absorbing. Cricket was swapped for polo, which is almost the least popular game played in the British Isles. There may not be half a dozen buildings in the United Kingdom which owe more than the vaguest detail in their design to the inspiration of the sub-continent, though two are certainly outstanding. The strange combination of Mughal and Hindu styles which infectiously make the Brighton Pavilion the jolliest building in England came about because the architects responsible, Porden and Nash, had studied Thomas Daniell's pictures and thought such exotica would charm the Prince Regent. The Prince may have been more inclined to accept this idea after seeing Sezincote House in Gloucestershire, which had already been completed for one of the Nabobs, Sir Charles Cockerell; a full-blooded Mughal country mansion, but with a Hindu temple in its park and two cast-iron Brahmin bulls standing on a bridge which Daniell designed. Indian references in the highways and byways of Britain are almost as rare as suggestive buildings, so that nostalgia is excited by the discovery of a Kidderpore Avenue in London and a suburban dwelling called Ballygunge in Hertfordshire, not far from where Haileybury now provides the comfortable middle classes with an education fit for businessmen. The strictures of Hinduism, if nothing else, ensured that there could never be more than a few posthumous traces in Europe, though Rammohan Roy was buried in Bristol in 1833 and two Tatas came to rest before the Second World War at a necropolis in Surrey. The military have done more than most to keep old memories alive, with innumerable Indian battle honours on all those regimental banners gently decaying in garrison churches – while dear old Johnny Gurkha still supplies a full Brigade of troops to what is left of the British Army. Rather a lot of imperial plunder is dispersed around the land, the monarch setting the pace with Ranjit Singh's famous bauble, the Koh-i-Nor diamond, among the Crown Jewels in the Tower of London. Superb examples of Indian miniature painting have been accumulated at the Victoria and Albert Museum among others, and many a stately home has something in oils (like Alexander Caddy's great Durbar canvas at Knebworth House) celebrating some impressive moment of the Raj. British diplomacy still functions around the Durbar Court of what was once the India Office, and the East India Company's furniture is still used in the room formerly occupied by the Secretary of State for India – though the Minister now working there spends most of his time struggling with the Common Market, and because it is unlikely that two Indian princes will ever again wish to cross his threshold simultaneously, one of his twin doors has been sealed to keep out the draught.

This is comparatively trifling evidence that the British spent two centuries and more living off India, caring for India, behaving in turn abominably and decently towards Indians. But it is not the only evidence we have, and the most subtle and lasting mark that India left on its old rulers has been pressed forever into the English language. Some years ago an Indian academic, casting around for a new subject that might be worthy of his research, decided to work his way through the full extent of the Oxford English Dictionary and note every entry that had an Indian connection. He came to the conclusion that there were something over 900 words authoritatively recognized in English, which were either straight transliterations of words in various Indian languages, corruptions of such words, or words that the British themselves had created out of their Indian experience. An example of the last is civil servant, which originated in the East India Company. One example of a corruption is the slang expression Blighty, which soldiers picked up from the Hindi bilayati, meaning foreign and especially European. Another is juggernaut, which derives from Jagannath, the Hindu god whose greatest festival is held at Puri in Orissa, where an immense wooden carriage on sixteen wheels, each 7ft in diameter, is rolled out of the shrine and down the streets to the seashore, occasionally crushing fanatical pilgrims who throw themselves in its path. One of the straight transliterations is pariah, the Tamil name for one of the lower castes in southern India. Most of this essentially Indian vocabulary in English is not in everyday use, but the words do sprinkle the language across a wide area, as the following small sample shows: bandanna, bangle, bungalow, calico, cheroot, chintz, chit, chukker, chutney, cot, cushy, dinghy, dungaree, gymkhana, gunny, jodhpurs, kedgeree, khaki, lascar, loot, musk, punch (the drink), pundit, puttee, pyjamas, sandal, seersucker, shawl, swastika, syce, thug, tom-tom, tonga, verandah and yoga.

It is not beyond the bounds of possibility that this vocabulary may quietly expand a little under our very noses, though that depends upon our own capacity to assimilate in all sorts of ways. Another lasting link with the sub-continent has been the settling in Great Britain of immigrants from India, Pakistan, Sri Lanka (Ceylon) and Bangladesh, who would not have come here had there never been such a thing as the British Empire. By 1971, there were almost half a million people with their origins in that part of Asia, and while some had lived here for a couple of generations or more, the majority had come over after Independence. They have not by any means transformed the country and they have not even changed it, as the British changed theirs. But they have begun to give parts of it a slightly different and more piquant sensation, with their halal butchers, their curry houses which must now be as numerous as fish and chip shops, and their boutiques which offer as much glitter and brightness as any bazaar in old Delhi; with, in short, the colour they have introduced to many a community which in the post-imperial age was becoming rather drab. This is quite apart from the fact that they have put themselves alongside the native British in factories, transport undertakings and hospitals, as well as on the dole registers, with no complaints about their industry from anyone who employed them. Their troubles have been almost entirely at the seeking of others (with no argument possible here that prejudice was a form of class/caste distinction rather than sheer racial antagonism). They themselves have been among the least offensive people in the land, anxious to adapt publicly to British ways, dutifully queueing for buses or anything else – which is not a habit that comes naturally to anyone reared in the hurly-burly of the East. To the extent that they have held themselves apart, it has usually been to do with purely private things like religion; though the older women, like the British memsahibs before them, have often been reluctant to learn more than smatterings of the local tongue and will probably remain insulated until the day they die. Their children will not, however. In time a new community of Anglo-Indians will take shape and add to the social landscape, able to look back several generations on both sides of the family to antecedents in Birmingham or Bradford or almost anywhere in the urban British Isles.

The memories by then of the British Raj will have jumbled into the distance. They are becoming confused even now, as that period of history slips further behind in our wake. Thirty years ago, one could have said with confidence that most families in this country could recall some connection with India in their past. If they were upper or middle class there would at least be an uncle or a distant cousin who had been a civil servant there, or someone who had done his bit for the family fortunes by his ventures in trade. If they came from the mass of artisans then there was likely to be some rheumy old codger within recollection who had served as a lance-corporal on the Frontier and who (it would be remembered with a chuckle or a sigh) used to say that what with the heat and the dust and the boredom and all, a man could go Doolally if he didn't look out; or maybe that was Uncle Bob, still quite young, who spent a month in Bangalore with the RAF during the war, a great authority ever since on all things Indian, from garam masala to the intricacies of caste. No other part of the old Empire produced such a weight of memories as these. The connection with Africa was shorter, the British neither gave themselves to it so whole-heartedly nor brought so much away; and Africa, in any case, never had an ancient civilization like India's waiting to capture the imagination, or such a rich variety of people and customs that would dazzle and fascinate.

The sharpest memories are starting to fade, as old men and women who can tell of British India die and are succeeded by those who took no part in the ruling process, who care little about that past. The successors are puzzled when they hear of ageing couples like Tusker and Lucy in *Staying On*, eking out their genteel lives on pensions in hill stations, because they couldn't bear to tear themselves away from India when the time came for going home. They are amused when they read an obituary in *The Times* which marks the passing of yet another burra Sahib, because that life now seems ridiculously remote and because the obituaries sometimes read like parodies of material that even the satirists have stopped using. ('He was much liked in Hyderabad society by reason of his quiet efficiency, broad and scholarly outlook, and social gifts,' according to one such notice in 1981.) The old men who remain look forward like billyho to exchanging familiar gossip about those days with others of their kind. There are still annual luncheons for the surviving ex-officers of Skinner's Horse and King George's Own Central India Horse. Once, not so long ago, Claridge's or the Guards Club would have played host to annual *dinners* of these old Indian Army cavalrymen, but now the memories must falter in the middle of the day – either because the chaps are getting on a bit to stay out late at night, or because according to one of those subtle distinctions of precedence, British India has at long last slipped a notch in the natural order of things.

Do you remember, they say to each other, that time we were up at Swat when one of our daffadars carried young Jenkins six miles out of the hills, though he had a broken collar bone himself? Where was it Willy found a first edition of *Gulliver's Travels* underneath all that junk in the bazaar, with Henry Lawrence's book-plate on the cover? D'ye know what I reckon the most marvellous thing about the Taj was? – It was the way those stones retained the heat right into the cool of the evening, so that you could feel it coming off them ten paces away. Frightened as hell, I was, when that mob started coming towards us – wouldn't have minded so much if that beggar Gandhi had been there, taking his chance with everybody else, instead of just inciting 'em from God knows where. When did you last hear from old Gupta; lovely man – Did I ever tell you how he once got me out of the most dreadful mess? Who was that girl Palanpore married not long before we left? Australian girl, became a Muslim . . .? I still miss it, y'know; and the funny thing is that I miss most of all the things I didn't much care for when we were there, like the smells and the noise of all those crowds pushin' and shovin' their way through the bazaar . . .

'Bless 'em,' they muttered to themselves, when they heard that India's parliament had gone into recess to mourn Lord Mountbatten, as soon as the news reached New Delhi that he had been killed by an IRA bomb.

Acknowledgements

The publisher wishes to acknowledge permission to reproduce the illustrations as follows:

Colour Illustrations

p1	(top)	Ronald Grant
p1	(bottom)	Tate Gallery
pp2 & 3		Spinks Auctioneers
p4	(top)	ET Archive
p4	(bottom)	National Army Museum
p5		Lord Halifax
pp6 & 7		ET Archive
p8	(top)	India Office Library
p8	(bottom)	Patrick Eagar

Black and White Illustrations

p1		ET Archive
pp2 & 3		ET Archive
p4	(top left)	India Office Library
p4	(top right)	India Office Library
p4	(bottom)	India Office Library
p5	(top)	India Office Library
p5	(bottom)	Ray Gardner
p6	(top)	Oriental Club
p6	(bottom)	Victoria & Albert Museum
p7	(top)	ET Archive
p7	(bottom)	India Office Library
pp8 & 9		National Army Museum
p10	(top)	ET Archive

Chronology

GOVERNORS-GENERAL	EVENTS	
	1727	Accession of George II
		Rise of Maratha chieftains
	1739	Marathas conquer Malwa. Persians invade and sack Delhi
	1742	Dupleix Governor of Pondicherry
	1744	War of Austrian Succession
	1746	French capture Madras
	1748	Ahmad Shah becomes Emperor
	1749	Madras restored to British by Treaty of Aix-la-Chapelle
	1750	Wars of succession in the Deccan and Carnatic
	1751	Siege of Arcot
	1754	Dupleix recalled to France
		Alamgir II becomes Emperor
	1756	Seven Years War begins
		Siraj-ud-Daula takes Calcutta and his prisoners die in the Black Hole
	1757	Battle of Plassey
	1759	Shah Alam becomes Emperor
	1760	Accession of George III
	1765	Robert Clive Governor of Bengal
	1767	War with Hyder Ali in Mysore
	1772	Warren Hastings Governor of Bengal
	1773	Lord North's Regulating Act, the first Government intrusion into the Company's Indian affairs
Warren Hastings, civil servant	1774	The Rohilla War
	1775	First Maratha War
	1776	American Declaration of Independence
	1779	Second Mysore War
	1784	Pitt's Indian Act
Sir John Macpherson,* civil servant	1785	

GOVERNORS-GENERAL		EVENTS
2nd Earl Cornwallis, soldier	1786	
	1789	French Revolution begins
	1790	Third Mysore War
	1793	Permanent Settlement in Bengal
Sir John Shore, civil servant	1795	Marathas defeat Nizam of Deccan
		Hastings acquitted after impeach-ment
Marquess Wellesley, landowner	1798	
	1799	Fourth Mysore War. Tipu Sultan dies at Seringapatam
	1800	Fort William College opened
	1802	Battle of Poona
	1803	Second Maratha War
	1804	War with Holkar
2nd Earl Cornwallis† Sir George Barlow,* civil servant	1805	Death of Shah Alam. Wellesley recalled after siege of Bharatpur
	1806	Mutiny at Vellore
		Akbar Shah II becomes Emperor
1st Earl of Minto, lawyer	1807	
	1809	Metcalfe's mission to Ranjit Singh
		Haileybury College opened
1st Marquis of Hastings, soldier	1813	
	1814	War with Nepal
	1817	Pindari Campaign
	1819	Pacification of Central India
	1820	Accession of George IV
		First coal mined at Raniganj
John Adam,* civil servant	1823	
Earl Amherst, diplomat		
	1824	War with Burma
Lord William Bentinck, landowner	1828	
	1829	Abolition of suttee in Bengal
		Start of campaign against Thugee

GOVERNORS-GENERAL		EVENTS
	1830	Accession of William IV
		Abolition of suttee in Madras and Bombay
	1831	Raja of Mysore deposed
	1833	Renewal of Company's Charter
Sir Charles Metcalf,* civil servant	1835	Macaulay's education minute
Earl of Auckland, lawyer	1836	
	1837	Accession of Queen Victoria
		Bahadur Shah II, last imperial descendant, becomes King of Delhi
	1839	Death of Ranjit Singh
		Invasion of Afghanistan
	1840	Dost Mohammed deposed
	1841	First tea planted at Darjeeling
Earl of Ellenborough, politician	1842	Retreat from Kabul
	1843	Conquest of Sind
Sir Henry Hardinge, soldier	1844	
	1845	First Sikh War
Marquis of Dalhousie, politician	1848	Second Sikh War
	1849	Annexation of Punjab
	1852	Second Burmese War
	1853	Annexation of Nagpur. Company's charter renewed. Bombay–Thana railway opened
	1854	First jute mill at Serampore
		First cotton mill in Bombay
Earl Canning, politician	1856	Annexation of Oudh

VICEROYS		EVENTS
	1857	Indian Mutiny begins at Meerut
Earl Canning	1858	Peace proclaimed. Government of India transferred from Company to Crown

VICEROYS		EVENTS
	1860	Indian Councils Act. Macaulay's penal code becomes law
8th Earl of Elgin,† politician	1861	American Civil War begins. Indian cotton boom starts
Sir John Lawrence, civil servant	1863	Simla becomes summer seat of Government
	1864	Bhutan War
	1867	British Reform Bill passed
6th Earl of Mayo,† landowner	1869	Suez Canal opened
		Birth of M. K. (Mahatma) Gandhi
1st Earl of Northbrook, politician	1872	
1st Earl of Lytton, diplomat and poet	1876	
	1877	Victoria proclaimed Empress of India. Durbar in Delhi
	1878	Second Afghan War
1st Marquis of Ripon, politician	1880	Major-General Roberts leads forced march from Kabul to Kandahar
	1882	Rudyard Kipling joins *Civil and Military Gazette* in Lahore
	1883	Ilbert Bill
1st Marquis of Dufferin and Ava, landowner and diplomat	1884	
	1885	Third Burmese War
		Inaugural session of Indian National Congress
	1886	Annexation of Upper Burma
		Hindu–Muslim riots in Delhi
5th Marquess of Lansdowne, landowner	1888	
	1891	Age of Consent Act. Bal Gangadhar Tilak begins extremist agitation
	1892	Indian Councils Act
9th Earl of Elgin, landowner	1894	

VICEROYS		EVENTS
	1897	Plague in Bombay
Marquess Curzon of Kedleston, politician	1899	
	1900	North-West Frontier Province formed
	1901	Accession of Edward VII
		Coronation Durbar in Delhi
	1904	Younghusband mission reaches Lhasa
		Co-operative Societies Act
4th Earl of Minto, soldier and diplomat	1905	Partition of Bengal
	1906	Muslim League formed
	1909	Morley–Minto reforms
Baron Hardinge of Penshurst, diplomat	1910	Accession of George V
	1911	King Emperor visits India and holds Durbar in Delhi
		Announces switch of capital from Calcutta to Delhi
		Partition of Bengal revoked
	1914	First World War starts
	1915	Gandhi returns to India after years in South Africa
3rd Baron Chelmsford, lawyer	1916	Mrs Besant's Home Rule League founded
	1918	Montagu–Chelmsford Report
		Rowlatt Committee Report
	1919	Disturbances in Punjab. Amritsar Massacre. Third Afghan War. Death of Tilak
	1920	Hunter Commission reports on General Dyer's actions in Amritsar
		Elections for reformed Imperial Legislature
1st Marquess of Reading, lawyer	1921	Bombay riots during visit by Prince of Wales
	1922	Gandhi imprisoned for civil disobedience

VICEROYS		EVENTS
Lord Irwin, landowner and politician	1926	
	1928	Simon Commission
	1930	Gandhi's salt march to Dandi
		Round-table conference begins in London
Marquess of Willingdon, landowner and politician	1931	Inauguration of New Delhi
		Irwin–Gandhi Pact
		Gandhi attends London conference
	1932	Civil disobedience begins again
	1935	Government of India Act
2nd Marquess of Linlithgow, soldier and politician	1936	Jawaharlal Nehru becomes President of Congress
	1937	Congress wins majority of provincial elections
	1939	Second World War starts. Congress ministries resign. Muhammad Ali Jinnah calls for Thanksgiving Day
	1942	Fall of Singapore. Subhas Chandra Bose arrives in Japan to recruit Indian National Army. Cripps Mission to New Delhi. Gandhi's Quit India demand
Viscount Wavell of Cyrenaica, soldier	1943	Famine in Bengal
	1945	End of Second World War. New British Labour Government prepares for Indian independence
Viscount Mountbatten of Burma, sailor	1947	Inauguration Day in Pakistan
		Independence Day in India
	1948	Gandhi assassinated. Jinnah dies
	1950	India becomes a republic

* acting Governor-General.   † died in office.

Sources

The following titles are those of books I have drawn on repeatedly in sketching this outline of British India. Other sources are listed under the chapters in which they have been mainly used.

Anstey, Vera, *The Economic Development of India* (London 1929)

Gadgil, D. R., *The Industrial Evolution of India in Recent Times 1860–1939* (London 1971)

Knowles, L. C. A., *Economic Development of the British Overseas Empire* (London 1924)

O'Malley, L. S. S., *The Indian Civil Service* (London 1965)

Low, D. A., *Lion Rampant; essays in the study of British imperialism* (London 1973)

Moorhouse, Geoffrey, *Calcutta* (London 1971)

Pannikar, K. M., *A Survey of Indian History* (London 1960)

Roberts, P. E., *History of British India under the Company and the Crown* (London 1952)

Spear, Percival, *A History of India* (London 1970)

Stokes, Eric, *The Peasant and the Raj* (London 1978)

Thompson, Edward and Garratt, G. T., *Rise and Fulfilment of British Rule in India* (London 1934)

Woodruff, Philip, *The Men Who Ruled India* (two vols, London 1953–4)

Prologue – AS THE SUN BEGAN TO SET

The quotation from Herbert Edwardes comes from his *Memorials* Vol. 1 (London 1886).

One A QUIET TRADE – AND A PROFITABLE ONE

Bamber Gascoigne's *The Great Moghuls* (London 1971) is a good and readable account of the Emperors. Angus Calder's *Revolutionary Empire* (London 1981) covers British imperialism generally up to the

1780s with scholarship and flair. Percival Spear's *Master of Bengal* (London 1975) is the best short life of Clive, and the same author's *The Nabobs* (London 1963) is a classic on the subject. *The Nabobs in England* by J. M. Holzman (New York 1926) supplements it. The outstanding and most recent analysis of early Company activities in India is *East India Fortunes* by P. J. Marshall (London 1976).

Two ORDER OUT OF CHAOS

Keith Feiling's *Warren Hastings* (London 1954) is the standard work on this subject. *The Personal Fortune of Warren Hastings* by P. J. Marshall (Economic History Review, Vol. XVII No 2, 1964) is required reading as a codicil to that. Three studies by Bernard S. Cohn shed much light on the effect of Company policy: *From Indian Status to British Contract* (Journal of Economic History, Dec. 1961), *The Initial British Impact on India* (Journal of Asian Studies Vol. XIX, Aug. 1960) and – with M. Singer – *Structure and Change in Indian Society* (Chicago 1968). For the Cornwallis and Wellesley periods, *British Orientalism and the Bengal Renaissance* by David Kopf (Calcutta 1969) is indispensable. A recent book by Mildred Archer, beautifully illustrated, *Early Views of India* (London 1980) is an expert survey of the Daniells. The most comprehensive analysis of caste in India is Louis Dumont's *Homo Hierarchicus* (Chicago rev. edition 1980).

Three A MORAL DUTY TO PERFORM

The English Utilitarians in India by Eric Stokes (London 1959) and *Lord William Bentinck* by John Rosselli (London 1974) are both important works. John Clive's *Thomas Babington Macaulay* (London 1973) is an excellent account of the polymath up to the point of his leaving India. H. T. Bernstein's *Steamboats on the Ganges* (London 1960) fully investigates a topic that historians usually only mention in asides.

Four HIGH NOON

Christopher Hibbert's *The Great Mutiny* (London 1978) has become the classic on the events of 1857-8, drawing on everything that has previously been written, as well as much unpublished material. It should be read in conjunction with *The Other Side of the Medal*, by Edward Thompson (London 1925) and *From Sepoy to Subedar* (the memoirs of Sita Ram Pande), edited by James Lunt (London 1970).

A general survey of Englishwomen in India is Pat Barr's *The Memsahibs* (London 1976); a good biography of one of them is *Flora Annie Steel* by Violet Powell (London 1981). No-one yet appears to have written extensively about Queen Victoria's Indian servant. The fullest accounts of the Munshi appear in *Recollections of Three Reigns* by Sir Frederick Ponsonby (London 1951) and in Elizabeth Longford's biography *Victoria R.I.* (London 1964). My reference to the remarkable Frederic Tudor comes from *The Maritime History of Massachusetts* by Samuel E. Morison (New York 1925). Of many books about Anglo-Russian rivalry in Asia, M. E. Yapp's *Strategies of British India* (London 1980) is an excellent academic study of the period up to 1850. Two popular accounts covering a longer period are *Playing the Great Game* by Michael Edwardes (London 1975) and David Gillard's *The Struggle for Asia 1828–1914* (London 1977).

Five CROWN IMPERIAL

O'Malley and Woodruff (cited above) are the two authorities on the ICS, and they complement each other: you go to O'Malley for information, to Woodruff for feeling. Philip Mason's *A Matter of Honour* (London 1974) is a fine history of the Indian Army, while Roger Beaumont's *Sword of the Raj* (New York 1977) contains much detail of British military organization in India that is omitted by Mason and other writers on the subject. Pat Barr and Ray Desmond, in *Simla, a hill station in British India* (London 1978) have produced a lively account, illustrated with many period photographs, of the summer headquarters of the Raj. The Gambit of the Second Reminder was told by Philip Mason in Charles Allen's splendid collection of anecdotes *Plain Tales from the Raj* (London 1975).

Six A WORKSHOP IN THE EAST

Apart from the works by Gadgil, Anstey and Knowles, there is Sir Percival Griffith's monumental *History of the Indian Tea Industry* (London 1967). On cotton there is *Imperialism and Free Trade: Lancashire and India in the 1860s* by Peter Harnetty (Toronto 1969) and *Manchester Men and Indian Cotton 1847–72* by Arthur W. Silver (Manchester 1966). On jute there is hardly anything outside the three general studies of the Indian economy and industry (if someone is looking for a PhD subject, he could do much worse than to investigate the economic and social relationship between Calcutta and Dundee). The analysis of jute mill dividends is quoted by Anstey, from *Capital*, 12 May 1927. Michael Satow and Ray Desmond have lately produced a fine pictorial account of the railways in *Railways of the Raj* (London 1980). There is also *Indian Railways: One Hundred Years*, published by the Indian Ministry of Railways (New Delhi 1953). Lord Birkenhead's biography of *Rudyard Kipling* (London 1978) is more illuminating than most; the reason why it was suppressed for nearly 30 years. Marx was writing in the *New York Daily Tribune*, 8 August 1853 (cited by Stokes in *The Peasant and the Raj*).

Seven CALL US WHAT YOU WILL

Christine Bolt's *Victorian Attitudes to Race* (London 1971) is a useful introduction to the subject. The two handbooks referred to are *English Etiquette for Indian Gentlemen* by W. T. Webb (Calcutta 1915) and *Hints for Europeans engaged in Commerce and Industry on their first arrival in India regarding Correct Conduct in Relations with Indians*, by an anonymous author (Calcutta 1923). The gymnastic cult of the Bengalis has been studied by John Rosselli in *The Self-Image of Effeteness* (Past & Present No 86, Feb. 1980). The bulk of the chapter draws on *The Anglo-Indians* by V. R. Gaikwad (London 1967), *Britain's Betrayal in India* by Frank Anthony (Bombay 1969) and *Hostages to India* by H. A. Stark (Calcutta 1926). The quote from the young British ICS official comes from *The District Officer in India 1930–1947* by Roland Hunt and John Harrison (London 1980).

Eight THE WRITING ON THE WALL

Congress and the Raj, edited by D. A. Low (London 1977) combines both British and Indian scholarship on the subject. A masterly survey of events in Bengal in the late nineteenth and early twentieth centuries is J. H. Broomfield's *Elite Conflict in a Plural Society* (Los Angeles 1968). David Dilks's *Curzon in India* (2 vols, London 1969–70) is the best account we are likely to have of the Viceroy and his imperial doings, written by an Englishman. My description of his Durbar also draws on *The Coronation Durbar official directory* (Delhi 1903).

Nine BEATING A RETREAT

The most recent account of General Dyer and the Jallianwala Bagh massacre is *Amritsar* by Alfred Draper (London 1981). The fullest biography of Gandhi is D. G. Tendulkar's *Mahatma* in eight volumes (Bombay 1952 et seq.), but a good concise version is *Mahatma Gandhi* by H. S. L. Polak, H. N. Brailsford and Lord Pethick-Lawrence (London 1959). Sarvepalli Gopal has so far produced two of the three volumes he plans for his *Jawaharlal Nehru* (London 1975 and 1979) and the books already available cover the years 1889–1956. On the builder of New Delhi and his work there is the *Life of Sir Edwin Lutyens* by Christopher Hussey (London 1950) and the sumptuous *Indian Summer* by Robert Grant Irving (London 1981). On the relationship between the United States and India there is *America Encounters India* by G. R. Hess (Baltimore 1952) and *American Shadow over India* by L. Natarajan (Bombay 1952). Out of the welter of books written about the approach to Independence and the transfer of power, I have paid most attention to *The Transfer of Power in India* by V. P. Menon (London 1957), *Wavell: the Viceroy's Journal*, edited by Penderel Moon (London 1973), *Reflections on the Transfer of Power and Jawaharlal Nehru* by Lord Mountbatten (London 1968) and *The India We Left* by Humphrey Trevelyan (London 1972). The quotation from John Rowntree comes from his book *A Chota Sahib* (Padstow 1981). The definitive source book on Independence is *The Transfer of Power 1942-47*, edited by Nicholas Mansergh, Penderel Moon and others – of which 10 volumes have so far appeared.

Ten THE LEGACY

Eleanor Roosevelt's book was *India and the Awakening East* (London 1954). Walter Lippmann's article appeared in the *Washington Post* and is quoted by Menon. The Indian Attorney-General is M. C. Setalvad and his reference to Macaulay comes in his book *The Common Law in India* (London 1960). The figures on qualified doctors and teachers come from the 1951 Indian census; the reference to the number of immigrants is taken from the 1971 British census. The academic who investigated the derivation of words in the English language is G. Subba Rao, who published his findings in *Indian Words in English* (London 1954). The criticisms of public works are cogently marshalled by Elizabeth Whitcombe in *Agrarian Conditions in Northern India* (Berkeley 1972).

Index

representation in Indian Government, 169; Belgians, 190; for British *see also* East India Company; Government of India; ICS

Evangelicals, Evangelism: 67, 69, 70, 75; dogma and racialism of, 91; *see also* religion

Executive Council: 101, 133, 147, 152, 163, 164, 168, 183

exports: 120–22, 128

factory legislation: 122

Faizabad: 85

Falkland, Lady: 92

famine: causes and antidotes, 123, 128; devastates Bengal, 187

Faruksiyar, Emperor: 32, 47

Fategarh: 89

Fatehpur Sikri: 23, 153

Fay, Mrs: 91

First World War: 117, 167, 174

football: 155

Formosa: 184

Forster, E. M.: 179

Fort Jamrud: 129

Fort William: 37, 40

Fort William College: 60, 67, 71, 148; founding of, 60; curriculum at, 60; orientalia at, 60

Fountain, James: 67

Francis, Philip: 46

Fraser, William: 138

French: 35, 38, 48, 58, 68, 190

Frere, Sir Bartle: 107

Gandhi, Indira: 196

Gandhi, Mohandas Karamchand 'Mahatma': 61, 150, 195; born a Vaishya in Porbandar, 173; married as child to child-wife, goes to England to study law, advises Muslims in South Africa, leads Indian community at Cape, *satyagraha* pledge, returns to India preaches nationalism, Tagore calls him Mahatma, ousts Tilak from Congress, 173–4; rejects violence in all forms, 174; protests Amritsar Massacre, 175; acknowledges Harijans, 174; spinning wheel symbol, 174; calls for non-cooperation with British, 175; Bombay riots and, 175; organizes

alliance Muslim League and Congress, 176; periods in prison, 176, 181, 182; alliance collapses, 176; released and fasts, 180; defuses anger of Bose and Nehru, 180; and Lord Irwin, 181; visits London, 181; promotes Nehru within Congress, 182; encourages civil disobedience, 184; 'Quit India' campaign, 186; interned until end of War, 186; in despair, 188; and Mountbatten, 188; assassinated by Brahmin, 190

Gandhi Museum: 195

Ganges Canal: 123

Ganges River: 51, 52–3, 87, 89, 125; paintings of, 53; steamboats on, 73, 128; channelling of, 123; ghats on, 201

Garhwalis: 107

Ganjam: 109

'Gateway of India': 192

Gaya: 53, 177

Genghiz Khan: 22

George III, King: 51

George V, King Emperor: 163–4, 169, 192; reunites Bengal, 163–4; moves Government to Delhi, 164–5, 176, 178; 1911 Durbar, 164, 177

George VI, King: 188, 190, 194

Ghosh, Girish Chandra: 89

Gidney, Sir Henry: 189

Gilchrist, John: 61

Gilgit: 105

Gladstone, William Ewart: 146

Goa: 25, 190

Gobi Desert: 158

Godavari, River: 121

Gokul Ghosal: 33

Gola: 123, 202

Goldbourne, Sophia: 92–3

Golden Jubilee: 97

Government House, Calcutta: 60, 98, 101–2, 123, 133, 153, 158, 161; rulers in, 102

Government of India: 101, 111, 112, 132–3, 145; British Crown, 95, 100–2, 168–9; Victoria's wish for Indian involvement, 96–7; Executive Council, 101, 133, 147, 152, 163, 164, 168, 183; Legislative Council, 101, 123, 139, 163, 169; attempts to include Indians in, 101–4, 168–9; Warrant of Precedence, 103–4;

but some support European culture,
77–8

Origin of Species: 132

Orissa: partition and reunification of
Bengal, 160, 163

Oriyas: 160

Orme, Robert: 36

ornithology of India: 148

Orwell, George: 102, 132

Oudh: 47, 48, 51, 53, 73; Indian Mutiny
in, 84; Lord Dalhousie's effect on, 84

Outram, General Sir James: 88

Oxus, River: 151

Paine, Thomas: 61

Pakistan: 196; Jinnah declares objective
of, 184; origins of word, 184; Cripps
offers, 186; Muslims die trying to
reach, 189–90; Inauguration Day,
190

Palmerston, Lord: 81

P&O shipping company: 146

Panipat, battle of: 22

Pannikar, K. M.: 197

Panopticon: 68

Parkes, Fanny: 93

Parsis: start cotton mills, 122; MPs in
House of Commons, 135; attacked by
nationalist extremists, 175; Tata
family of, 196

Partition: Jinnah seeks, 183; Nehru
concedes, 189; violence as result of,
189–90

partition and reunification of Bengal:
160–65

A Passage to India: 179

Pathans: 82, 105, 107

Patna: 123, 125

Pearl Mosque, Lahore: 153

peasant cultivators: 33, 57, 145

Penal Code, Macaulay's: 178–80

Penang: 33

Permanent Settlement: 56, 63

Persian Gulf: 110, 157

Persians: 37

Peshawar: 90, 124; Vale Hunt, 191

pilgrims: 127; at Amritsar, 171

Pindaris: 62

Pioneer: Allahabad, 130, 131

Pitt, William (the elder): 39

Pitt, William (the younger): India Act,
48; selects Cornwallis, 54

Plain Tales from the Hills: 132

Plassey, battle of: 38, 40, 44, 58, 136

policemen: 175, 195

polo: 135, 155, 203

Polo, Marco: 24

Pondicherry: 35

Poona: 64, 68, 186

Porbandar: 173

Portland, Duke of: 71

Portuguese: 24, 25, 58, 136, 143, 190; as
proselytizers, 25; Bombay a possession
of, 34

Potola Palace: 158

Prasad, Rajendra: 194

Prater, Stanley: 143

presidencies: 29, 39, 48, 57

President of Republic of India: 194, 202

press censorship: 76, 172

Prime Minister of India: 190, 196

princely states: 104, 155, 178–9, 182

Princes, Indian: 110, 183; precedence of,
104, 186; request own railways, 127;
and Anglo-Indians, 137; Maharajas,
156; and Delhi, 178; support British,
179; Gandhi indifferent to, 179–80

provincial government: dyarchy
introduced, 168; Indian ministers
partially autonomous, 180; Swaraj
Party contests, 180; become
autonomous, 183; franchise of, 183

Public Works Department: 124, 199

Pulaya: 180

Punjab: 57, 64, 82, 83, 87, 110, 123, 138,
141, 191; Sir Henry Lawrence, 87;
Lieutenant-Governor of, 111, 114;
Lieutenant-Governor Sir Michael
O'Dwyer, 130, 170–72; Education
Board of, 90; irrigation of, 123–4;
hartal and massacre at Amritsar, 171;
government supports British in
Second World War, 183; civil war in
Amritsar and Lahore at
Independence, 189

Punjab Club: 130

Punjab Land Alienation Act: 145

Punjab Railway: 126

'Quit India' campaign: 186

Qutb Minar: 53

racial prejudice: 91, 161, 165; Queen
Victoria on, 98; Kipling and, 132;
British and, 133; ICS and, 133;
British handbook for Indians, 134–5;

History in Paladin Books

Africa in History   £2.95 ☐
Basil Davidson
Revised edition of 'one of the most durable and most literate guides to
contemporary knowledge of Africa' *Tribune*

A Higher Form of Killing   £2.50 ☐
Robert Harris and Jeremy Paxman
The escalating nuclear capabilities of the superpowers have been
extensively publicized. Less well documented has been the revival of
interest in chemical and biological weaponry. Drawing extensively
on international sources, this book chronicles for the first time the
secret history of chemical and germ warfare. Illustrated.

Decisive Battles of the Western World (Vols 1 & 2)   £3.95 ☐
J F C Fuller   each
The most original and influential military thinker Britain has ever
produced: his major work.

The Paladin History of England – the first three titles of the series are

The Formation of England   £2.95 ☐
H P R Finberg
This volume deals with Britain in the Dark Ages between Roman and
Norman conquests.

The Crisis of Imperialism   £3.95 ☐
Richard Shannon
England in the realm of Victoria. A time of development, expansion,
colonisation, enormous social upheavals and reform.

Peace, Print and Protestantism   £3.95 ☐
C S L Davies
C S L Davies' book deals with the period 1450–1558 encompassing
the reign of the Tudors and the breakaway from the Church of Rome.

To order direct from the publisher just tick the titles you want
and fill in the order form.   **PAL7082**

All these books are available at your local bookshop or newsagent, or can be ordered direct from the publisher.

To order direct from the publisher just tick the titles you want and fill in the form below.

Name _____

Address _____

_____

Send to:
Paladin Cash Sales
PO Box 11, Falmouth, Cornwall TR10 9EN.

Please enclose remittance to the value of the cover price plus:

UK 45p for the first book, 20p for the second book plus 14p per copy for each additional book ordered to a maximum charge of £1.63.

BFPO and Eire 45p for the first book, 20p for the second book plus 14p per copy for the next 7 books, thereafter 8p per book.

Overseas 75p for the first book and 21p for each additional book.

Paladin Books reserve the right to show new retail prices on covers, which may differ from those previously advertised in the text or elsewhere.